RELIGION
as a Province of
MEANING

Editors for this volume

Bernadette J. Brooten
and
Francis Schüssler Fiorenza

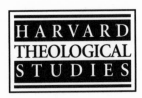

RELIGION
as a Province of
MEANING

The Kantian Foundations
of Modern Theology

Adina Davidovich

Fortress Press
Minneapolis

Religion as a Province of Meaning:
The Kantian Foundations of Modern Theology

Harvard Theological Studies

This volume was prepared for publication by the staff of the *Harvard Theological Review* and appears in substantially the same form in which it was approved as a doctoral dissertation by the Committee on the Study of Religion, Harvard University.

Book design and typesetting at the *Harvard Theological Review*

Managing Editor: Tamar Duke-Cohan

Editorial Assistants: Ellen B. Aitken and Laura Nasrallah

Library of Congress Cataloging-in-Publication Data

Davidovich, Adina, 1954–
    Religion as a province of meaning : the Kantian foundations of
modern theology / Adina Davidovich.
       p.   cm.—(Harvard Theological Studies)
    Includes bibliographical references and index.
    ISBN 0-8006-7090-6 :
    1. Religion—Philosophy—History—19th century. 2. Religion—
Philosophy—History—20th century. 3. Philosophical theology.
4. Kant, Immanuel, 1724–1804—Religion. 5. Otto, Rudolf,
1869–1937. 6. Tillich, Paul, 1886–1965. I. Title.
BL51.D3624   1993
210—dc20
                                        93–28255
                                           CIP

Manufactured in the U.S.A.   AF 1–7090

97   96   95   94   93   1   2   3   4   5   6   7   8   9   10

To Ehud Benor

CONTENTS

Part Two

ACKNOWLEDGMENTS

This book results from a long quest to understand the proper relations between philosophy and religion. Of the many from whose knowledge and wisdom I benefited, some must be singled out for special gratitude. Nathan Rotenstreich alerted me to the open-endedness of critical philosophy and provided for me an enduring example of profound and exacting scholarship. Hilary Putnam impressed upon me the significance of Kant's quest for hope. I am deeply indebted to his passionate involvement in my work. Richard R. Niebuhr inspired my investigation of the interests of reason and the cognitivity of feeling. His continuous encouragement was invaluable. Gordon D. Kaufman reassured me in the quest for the anthropological foundations of religious belief. I benefited greatly from his keen theological insight and from his penetrating criticism. Francis Schüssler Fiorenza persuaded me to bring the book to print; I am grateful for his boundless generosity and unfailing support. The final draft has been much improved by the superb editorial skills of Tamar Duke-Cohan and the staff of the *Harvard Theological Review*.

I wrote this book while residing at Harvard's Center for the Study of World Religions, where I was privileged to discuss my ideas with people of different philosophical and religious persuasions and practicing a wide variety of academic disciplines in the study of religion. I cherish the warm friendship and wise counsel of my neighbors at the Center, Harriet Crabtree, Kenneth Rose, and Miranda Shaw. I am also grateful for the many hours I spent with Ellen Haley discussing the bearing of feeling on our orientation in life.

The book is dedicated to Ehud Benor. His sound advice, insightful comments, and constant reassurance sustained me throughout this project.

—*Adina Davidovich*

PREFACE

In part two of the *Critique of Judgment* Immanuel Kant wrote that teleology leads to theology.[1] This assertion culminates Kant's search for a perspective from which we can judge spatio-temporal events purposeful and can hope that history leads, eventually, to the realization of moral ends. The following chapters interpret this claim and study its implications for our understanding of the concept of religion and of the relation of religion to other realms of culture. My study offers a radical interpretation of Kant's *Third Critique* and demonstrates that the book's central argument, that reflective judgment bridges the gap between nature and freedom, led Kant to a contemplative conception of religion that differs significantly from the conception of

[1]See, for example, Immanuel Kant, *Critique of Judgment* (trans. Werner S. Pluhar; Indianapolis: Hackett, 1987) 281/399, 337/481, 376/481. For the German edition, see idem, *Kritik der Urteilskraft* (1790; reprinted in *Kants Gesammelte Schriften* [Deutschen Akademie der Wissenschaften; 33 vols.; Berlin: de Gruyter, 1902] vol. 5). For all references to Kant, where a page is referenced by two numbers: the first is the page number of the English translation, the second that of the German Academy edition. Translations quoted in the text are taken from the English translations cited.

religion of the first two *Critiques*. I further show that the theories of religion of Rudolf Otto and Paul Tillich are deeply indebted to the *Third Critique* and develop its seminal ideas to characterize two distinct conceptions of the essence of religion and its relation to other realms of culture.[2]

Contrary to prevailing interpretations of the *Critique of Judgment* as a collection of loosely related discussions, I argue that the book is a systematic confrontation of the problem of the unity of Reason that results from Kant's distinction between the theoretical and practical functions of Reason. I argue that the *Third Critique* develops some of Kant's tentative and preliminary ideas, in the Dialectics of the first two *Critiques*, into a comprehensive theory of reflective judgment according to which contemplative thought about a moral designer of the universe is a necessary reflective principle of both science and morality. Kant claims, accordingly, that teleology leads to theology and to religion. I contend that Kant's suspicion of traditional religion prevented him from developing these insights into a systematic critique of religion.

I further argue that Kant's suggestive ideas were taken up by Otto and Tillich, who turned them into the cornerstones of their influential theories of religion. According to all three thinkers, religious consciousness expresses a fundamental requirement of Reason to achieve certainty that the concepts through which it tries to understand the world and to shape it are not merely valid constructs but are indeed

---

[2]The road from Kant to Otto and Tillich passes through the influential works of Friedrich Schleiermacher, who sought to distinguish religion from morality and science by characterizing religious consciousness as the bridge which connects theory and praxis and secures the unity of the personality, and Ernst Troeltsch, who argued that religion, like science and ethics, has its own distinct religious a priori, but never pursued the issue systematically and, eventually, gave the project up. We find a first systematic Kantian development of these ideas in the writings of Otto and Tillich, who developed specific insights of Kant's *Critique of Judgment* further and indicated how they could become the foundations of a philosophy of religion, of theology, and of a normative science of religion. For definitive discussions of Schleiermacher and Troeltsch, see Richard R. Niebuhr, *Schleiermacher on Christ and Religion: A New Introduction* (New York: Scribners, 1964); and H. Richard Niebuhr, "Ernst Troeltsch's Philosophy of Religion" (Ph.D. diss.; Yale University, 1924).

the concepts through which the world is shaped. It follows from their theories that religion must be understood and evaluated in its own terms, that the science of religion must be normative and must synthesize the insights and the findings of the history and the philosophy of religion and of theology.

I ask the reader to become involved with a discussion of difficult questions, many of which may seem at first highly outdated, because I believe they address issues that are crucial to us today. Otto and Tillich, like Kant, understood human thought as constructive and sought to delineate the parameters of the dominant modes in which we construct our universe. In this respect their work is firmly at home in the contemporary intellectual scene in which various modes of Kantian constructivism have great influence in science, moral theory, and theology. In this intellectual milieu, Kant's *Critique of Judgment* raises once again the fundamental question concerning the relations between the various worlds we construct for ourselves—the relations between what the phenomenological school designated "realms of meaning." Kant's challenge to himself to establish the unity of reason beyond its diverse functions may challenge us to bring our modes of construction of the universe into a unified world view. The suggestions of Otto and Tillich and, to a certain extent, also of Kant himself, that the required unity is established by a religious consciousness, is likewise a challenge to contemporary thought about religion.

Philosophy is called upon to address religion as a major mode of cognitive and evaluative construction and to rethink the relations between philosophy and religion as closely related contemplative modes of thought. Religion is marginalized in contemporary discussion because it is thought not to be one of the central modes of our knowledge of the world or of our duties. If, however, religion is contemplative and has its own cognitive function, then, like science and morality, it requires philosophical scrutiny. Furthermore, religion and philosophy will have to address the relations between them as two modes of reflective thought. A theology that accepts the constructive conception of reason must regard itself a cultural creation related to other cultural creations, which it must comprehend and to which it must be accountable. Theology is called upon to rethink its relations to the sciences and to the humanities and to undertake the synthesis of a coherent contemporary world view. If Tillich, Otto, and Kant are right, then theological insights will be expressible primarily in symbolic language, the construction of which is a conscientious task of the theologian. The science of religion must, accordingly, undertake to identify the various modes of symbolic expression through which religious consciousness has manifested itself in history and to present them to critical evaluation.

It is a main goal of my study to put renewed emphasis on the questions that a Kantian philosophy of religion addresses. This, however, is not all that my study does. Throughout we shall encounter various attempts to answer these questions, some of which, I shall argue, manifest profound insights into the nature of religion and of religious thought and deserve serious attention of thinkers who would address these questions today. Among these are Kant's depiction of philosophical thought as ultimately contemplative. Another is Otto's argument that religious feelings are, at the same time, affective and cognitive. Last is Tillich's contention that our spontaneous intellectual constructions require supplementation with a reflective conviction that they are not mere arbitrary impositions through which we create an illusory world. The following chapters will interpret these ideas as they were developed by the different thinkers. In most cases these interpretations will be new departures from standard commentaries.

My project as a whole is built around a radical reinterpretation of Kant's *Third Critique*. This reinterpretation differs from standard interpretations by claiming that the book is one sustained argument intended to solve the problem created by the bifurcation of the functions of reason into the two mutually exclusive perspectives of the theoretical and the practical. I argue that the most studied part of the book, the aesthetic, is but a prolegomenon for the further stages of an argument that proceeds, according to Kant's outline in the introduction of the book, to the conclusion that the unity of reason is established in a moment of contemplative thought about a moral designer of the universe. My interpretation shows that Kant's ideas about religion developed beyond his well-known refutation of the speculative proofs of the existence of God and beyond his equally well known moral argument according to which religion is at best an adjunct to morality and limited in its validity to the practical sphere. I contend that in his last systematic works Kant considered religion an essential bridge between the worlds of theory and praxis and elevated its status as such to that of a necessary principle through which alone the unity of reason is established. According to this conception of religion belief in God is neither theoretical nor practical. I argue that through his discoveries in the *Critique of Judgment* Kant came to consider belief in God as a contemplative belief. This new interpretation enabled Kant to sketch a new understanding of his idea of the Highest Good and to forge a new concept of contemplative hope for a philosophy of history.

Although Kant's theory of judgment promised to be a fertile ground for a philosophy of religion and for an interpretation of religious experience, Kant's subsequent work on religion failed to fulfill this promise. In his *Religion within the Limits of Reason Alone* Kant was concerned primarily with preventing the danger of fanaticism, which he associated with historical religion. Although Kant himself did not continue to expand his suggestive conception of contemplative hope into a comprehensive philosophy of religion, the central elements of Kant's theory of judgment in the *Third Critique* were developed further by Rudolf Otto and Paul Tillich, whose respective theories of religion have had formative impact both on modern science of religion and theology.

My discussion in the following chapters will present the respective theories of Otto and Tillich as two alternative ways of developing Kant's arguments into a systematic theory of religion. My analysis of Kant's *Third Critique* enables us to interpret Otto's theory of the numinous experience, in *The Idea of the Holy*, as an argument for the cognitivity of religious experience. I show that Otto, who returned to Kant through the works of Leonard Nelson and Jakob Fries, drew upon Kant's discussion of aesthetic taste and presented a theory of religious feeling as determined a priori by a distinct religious category of the numinous. Similarly, my understanding of Kant's notion of contemplative thought enables us to interpret Tillich's discussion of the relation between theonomy, autonomy, and heteronomy as an extension and elaboration of Kant's belief that spontaneous reason requires the assurance that its constructions are also discoveries. Reliance on Kant allows Otto and Tillich to present religion as a distinct province of meaning that must be understood and evaluated in its own terms.

I shall explain, as we proceed, that the two theoretical alternatives can also become foundations for distinct types of theology. Otto's theory can become, perhaps against his will, a foundation for a conception of religion according to which religion is not necessarily accountable to morality and to science. Tillich's theory, on the other hand, stresses the essential interdependence of religion and the other realms of culture. It is important to emphasize that in spite of the differences between them, both thinkers share Kant's wariness of fanaticism and turn back to Kantian critical philosophy in order to establish a concept of religion within the limits of reason.

My interpretations of works by Kant, Otto, and Tillich identify a Kantian school in the philosophy of religion and explain some of the problems it faces and the options it has for dealing with them. Yet the argument of my study is primarily philosophical, not historical. I turn to Kant and to his followers not merely because they are there and are misinterpreted, but because I believe they have something to say that is important for us to hear. From Kant we learn to appreciate the quest for the unity of the constructs of reason and to consider the possibility that the solution to the problem is essentially contemplative and religious. The Kantian analysis is important and suggestive because it seems to me to capture something that has always been an essential task of religion, namely, to offer a perspective from which we could unify our diverse concerns in life in a world view that encompasses our understanding of the world we live in, of our duties and aspirations, and of our hopes. From the Kantian analysis, which identifies a central role for religion to play in our cultural life, we can derive a formal concept of religion based on the essential function of religion to bring meaningful unity into an internally diverse intellectual and affective life.

From the works of Otto and Tillich we learn that religion may in fact be able to assume its central role in culture if it would overcome tendencies to defend itself against rational criticism and cultural relativism by fortifying itself behind nonrational appeals to revelation and scriptural authority. We learn from their work that Kant's idea can be brought to fruition when it is boldly developed into a comprehensive approach to religion that involves not only a philosophy of religion, but also a comparative history of religion and a theology. Their work shows that religion does indeed seek to comprehend the meaning of the totality of the experience of a culture and to construct appropriate symbols, in language and in action, to express its reflective comprehensions, and that it is probably the only aspect of culture that can assume this crucial task. We learn from their work that the phenomenon of religion will only be properly understood by a science of religion that studies the various ways in which religious constructions have taken place and the role they have played in their respective cultures. It is the further task of a philosophy of religion to interpret these constructions, to ascertain their guiding principles, and to evaluate their success in a unifying role. If religion is to be able to assume its rightful place in culture, it must develop a theology to reflect on the ever-changing cultural situation and to construct new symbols through which we shall be able to comprehend the totality of our experience.

The Kantian approach to religion, the foundations and the implications of which will be analyzed in the following chapters, presents us with a conception of religion as a quest for an Archimedean point, for a point of reference, which integrates all our concerns into a unified world view. The return to Kant in religious thought is in essence a declaration that religion has a decisive role to play within culture. If theology is to find a place for religion in modern life, it will find this place not outside of reason, as an alternative to culture, but within reason. The surprising message of the Kantian school is that once religion confines itself to the limits of reason, it can establish itself as the supreme rational principle through which all the constructions of reason are brought into unity.

Part One

1

INTRODUCTION

K ant, a true child of the Enlightenment, never considered religion worthy of an independent critique. Religion can only be based, according to his official philosophy of religion, on the postulates of Practical Reason and on the moral need to project an externalized reification of our conscience. In addressing the problems of the relation between the realms of Reason which he critically separated and in attempting to establish the unity of Reason beyond its diverse functions, however, Kant was forced to raise questions of great metaphysical and theological significance. Through analysis of the faculty of reflective judgment, Kant reevaluated the claims of rational hope and sought to establish the idea of a moral designer of the universe as a fundamental belief that necessarily underlies scientific and moral ventures. In the following pages I shall argue that it is possible to extract from these discussions a philosophy of religion more profound than Kant's theory of the postulates of praxis. I shall further argue that thinkers like Rudolf Otto and Paul Tillich recognized the significance of these Kantian discussions and developed them further in their writings.

In the introduction to his critical corpus Kant acknowledges that humans have always entertained certain questions which they cannot disavow because Reason itself, which Kant often likens to a dynamic agent driven by interests and needs, cannot rest until it reaches ultimate answers. These questions deal with God, freedom, and immortality. Traditionally, these questions were the subject of metaphysics. Whereas in the past metaphysics was regarded as the queen of all the sciences, in Kant's time it was mocked and ridiculed. Philosophers who confronted these questions seemed unable to answer them definitively; all they could do was to refute each other's attempts. The result was an attitude of indifference to the subject. Yet, Kant maintains, we cannot truly be indifferent to such questions since they are made necessary by the nature of Reason itself.

Philosophical empiricism frustrated all attempts to establish the validity of metaphysical claims on the basis of empirical experience. Kant concludes that if these notions cannot be derived from experience or proven speculatively, they must arise from Reason itself. Having reached this conclusion Kant directs his investigation to Reason, in order to seek a resolution of the philosophical impasse regarding the central questions of metaphysics. He finds the source of the impasse in the lack of solid method. Kant concludes that before we embark on inquiries about God, freedom, and immortality, we need to establish such a method by way of critical investigation of the very apparatus that deals with these issues. In other words, a Critique of Pure Reason itself is a prerequisite. The first task of the critique is to determine what Reason itself contributes spontaneously to cognition. It is this investigation that the three *Critiques* undertake.

In the *Critique of Pure Reason* Kant argues that we can know the world we inhabit because the human mind legislates to sense perceptions, thereby transforming the "rhapsody of impressions" into an organized and unified world of objects. The fundamental law that governs this phenomenal realm is that of mechanistic causality. The ultimate goal of the Understanding is to find a complete explanation to all phenomena in terms of their causal connections. It cannot interpret phenomenal events in terms of their goals or purposes. Human action is understood in terms of its antecedent determining grounds of which the subject is no longer in control. For the Understanding human action is as determined and as predictable as eclipses of the sun and moon, as high and low tides of seas and rivers. Since knowledge is limited to objects in space and time, humans cannot detect in this world a divine providence that guides the evolution of nature and the progress of history.

In the *Critique of Practical Reason* Kant presents humans as being under absolute obligation to the moral law. Kant argues that the moral law originates, as a "fact of Practical Reason," from the innermost foundation of the human mind and is not imposed upon it either by nature or by God. Human beings are the sole legislators of the moral law, and the will's respectful obedience to it takes place in the noumenal realm of things in themselves, independent of natural incentives. In obeying the decree of the moral law humans transcend the bounds of natural causality and realize their autonomy.

Striving to establish the validity of both scientific and moral judgment, Kant is careful to show that the theoretically necessary principles that apply to phenomena and the practically necessary principles that refer to noumena are not logically incompatible. Yet Kant knew that demonstration of mere logical compatibility cannot suffice. Moral agents who strive to realize their autonomy by obeying the command of Pure Practical Reason are bound to ask themselves how it is possible for them to execute the decree of their will—a decree that originates in the noumenal world—amidst the mechanistic causality of nature which they neither fully know nor control. Humans can find themselves obligated by Practical Reason to perform certain actions that Theoretical Reason declares inconceivable and impossible in a world governed by mechanistic causality. Kant realized that he had to establish the essential unity of Reason in both its capacities as the legislator of the laws of nature and the moral law. In other words, Kant knew that he had to establish the unity of the realm of freedom and the realm of nature.

Part one of this study, which examines the Kantian foundations of modern religious thought, will argue that in his attempts to reunite that which he previously separated, Kant turned to the contemplative idea of the Highest Good. My argument that in this idea of the Highest Good we find both Kant's intended solution to the problem of the unity of Reason and the foundations for a philosophical theology that unfolds throughout the next four chapters of this part.

Chapter two, "Kant's Defense of Rational Faith," presents Kant's justification of faith on the basis of the postulates of Practical Reason, comments on the flaws in his argument, and explains why thinkers like Otto and Tillich felt they had to reject it.

Chapter three, "The Conflict between the Interests of Reason," introduces the conflict between the respective interests of Theoretical and Practical Reason. It argues that the conflict is not resolved by the doctrine of the primacy of Practical Reason and maintains that Kant regarded the solution to this problem an unavoidable task of his critical enterprise.

Chapter four, "The Unity of Reason," is divided into three parts. The first part, which studies Kant's Introduction to the *Critique of Judgment*, argues that Kant defines the unity of Reason as the central problem of the book and outlines the solution he is about to propose. The second part, "The Argument from Taste," reconstructs Kant's setting of the foundations for the solution by establishing an a priori determinability of feeling, that is, by attributing subjective purposiveness to natural objects, thereby justifying a contemplative reference to a designer of nature. The next four parts discuss the notion of the reflective purposiveness of nature. They retrace Kant's further arguments: from the unity of the empirical laws of nature, from organic nature, from Humanity as an End, and from the Highest Good. Through these arguments the contemplative principle of purposiveness gains objectivity and acquires content. I shall argue that through these arguments the ideal of the Highest Good becomes the reflective principle that secures the unity of Reason.

Chapter five, "Religion beyond the Limits of Practical Reason," addresses two issues. First, I show that the *Third Critique* provides an answer to Kant's question, "What may I hope for?" thereby completing his answer to the question, "What is man?" I then argue that these discussions, rather than Kant's official philosophy of religion, had an enormous influence on the philosophies of religion of Otto and Tillich and supply the long neglected clues to their more enigmatic theories.

2

KANT'S DEFENSE OF RATIONAL FAITH

▪ 2.A. Introduction

Having eliminated the concept of happiness from the definition of duty throughout the Analytic of the *Second Critique*,[1] Kant reintroduces it in the Dialectic of that book. An examination of the necessary conditions of the Highest Good leads the discussion from ethics to religion. Toward the end of the Dialectic Kant proudly announces that the *Critique of Practical Reason* was able to establish an object to the regulative Idea of God, a task that could not be accom-

---

[1]Kant argues for the exclusion of happiness from the determination of the will throughout the Analytic of the *Critique of Practical Reason* (trans. Lewis White Beck; Indianapolis: Bobbs-Merrill, 1983) but see especially, Theorem 2 (pp. 20–21/22–23); Theorem 2, Remark 1 (pp. 23–24/24–25); Theorem 2, Remark 2 (pp. 24–26/25–27); Theorem 3, Remark (pp. 27–28/28–29); Theorem 4, Remark 1 (pp. 34–35/34–35); Theorem 4, Remark 2 (pp. 36–38/35–37); see also p. 96/93. The German edition is Immanuel Kant, *Kritik der praktischen Vernunft* (1788; reprinted in *Kants Gesammelte Schriften*, vol. 5).

plished within the confines of the *Critique of Pure Reason*. Kant's discussions of the Highest Good, his moral proof for the existence of God, and the subsequent discussion of the nature of religion were received with mixed feelings. In spite of their awareness of difficulties inherent in these theories, some readers extolled them as the best possible defense of rational religion. Others—like Otto and Tillich—considered them misleading and flawed and refused to accept them as an adequate account of the role of religion in modern life. In this chapter I shall explain what inherent difficulties in Kant's official philosophy of religion make it a weak and dubious foundation for religious thought. I believe that similar compunction led Otto and Tillich to pursue other avenues in defending the rationality of religion.

■ 2.B. Kant's Moral Proof of the Existence of God

Kant's moral proof of the existence of God proceeds in two stages. Kant first tells us that we are commanded by Reason to pursue the Highest Good. Then he argues that the problem of the necessary connection between the two independent components of the Highest Good—virtue and happiness in proportion to it—is resolved by delegating it to an intelligible world governed by a moral being powerful enough to bestow happiness according to merit.[2] The assessment of Kant's defense of rational faith begins with an examination of these arguments. My critique of Kant's argument is twofold: Kant introduces the duty to promote the Highest Good too casually. In fact, this duty is not embodied in any of the formulations of the moral law. In addition I maintain that even if we grant for the sake of the discussion that Reason commands us to pursue the Highest Good, recognition of failure and defeat in moral action need not necessarily lead

---

[2]One of the difficulties of Kant's discussion of the Highest Good is that it is not always clear whether it is our duty to strive for the Highest Good, or actually to realize it. It is the latter possibility that most clearly forces him to postulate divine help, and it is also the interpretation of his views that is generally accepted by the commentators. My discussion of Kant's official philosophy of religion will follow this accepted interpretation.

moral agents to a despair and paralysis that can be resolved only by postulation of an almighty God.

■ 2.C. Examination

The concept of the Highest Good is the concept of the "unconditioned for the practically conditioned"[3]; it is the concept of a "perfect" end which unites all practical ends. As the perfect end it includes not only virtue which is the supreme end of the moral will, but also happiness which is the final synthesis of the diverse purposes of a moral agent and as such is not exclusively moral.[4] While Kant's introduction of the Highest Good in the *Critique of Practical Reason* is sketchy, I find that additional pronouncements in his other writings shed light on his elliptical assertions in this book.

Whereas in the analytic of the *Second Critique* Kant characterized the moral law as a mere form of volition that does not specify what ends are to be pursued in specific situations, the dialectic of the *Second Critique* acknowledges the need to supplement the abstract form of volition—determined by the categorical imperative—with content, and introduces the concept of the Highest Good to direct moral volition. The concept of the Highest Good thus adds both interpretation in terms of the sensible world and direction in the performance of duty. Kant gives a good summary of this argument in *Religion within the Limits of Reason Alone*:

> But although for its own sake morality needs no representation of an end which must precede the determining of the will, it is quite possible that it is necessarily related to such an end, taken not as the ground but as the [sum of] inevitable consequences of maxims adopted as conformable to that end. For in the absence of all reference to an end no determination of the will can take place in man, since such determination cannot be followed by no effect whatever; and the representation of the effect must be capable of being accepted, not, indeed, as the basis for the determination of the will and as an end antecedently aimed at, but yet as an end conceived of as the result ensuing from the will's

---

[3]Kant, *Critique of Practical Reason*, 112/108.
[4]Ibid., 114/110.

determination through the law (finis in consequentiam veniens). Without an end of this sort a will, envisaging to itself no definite goal for a contemplated act, either objective or subjective (which it has, or ought to have, in view),[5] is indeed informed as to *how* it ought to act, but not *whither*, and so can achieve no satisfaction.[6]

Without going into the details of Kant's argument through his discussion of the Antinomy of Practical Reason, we can outline its main points. Kant argues that we "should seek to further the highest good,"[7] because "the moral law commands us to make the highest possible good in a world the final object of all our conduct."[8] He even asserts that "since, now, the furthering of the highest good, which contains this connection in its concept, is an a priori necessary object of our

[5]The subjective end of morality is happiness proportioned to obedience to duty. The objective end which the moral agent ought to have is duty. The combination of the two is the Highest Good.

[6]Immanuel Kant, *Religion within the Limits of Reason Alone* (trans. Theodore M. Greene and Hoyt H. Hudson; New York: Harper & Row, 1960) 4. As I shall show in the following sections, this presentation of the Highest Good, albeit accurate, is very partial. (1) The Highest Good is required by Reason, which Kant portrays time and again as a compulsive unifier. It is not only the case that the will needs direction, it is also the case that Reason requires to synthesize given manifolds. In this case, Reason strives to impose unity on the manifold of moral decisions and actions. (2) As I shall shortly argue, it is not only the weakness of the flesh that requires an ability to believe in the ultimate realization of happiness. The need for the realization of the Highest Good is equally shared by Reason itself, which needs to be able to believe that a moral decree can be realized in the phenomenal realm. I will discuss this last issue in the section devoted to the *Third Critique*.

[7]Kant, *Critique of Practical Reason*, 129/125. Elsewhere Kant says that "the Highest Good is the necessary highest end of a morally determined will and a true object thereof" (119/115). He also says that "it is a priori (morally) necessary to bring forth the highest good through the freedom of the will; the condition of its possibility, therefore, must rest solely on a priori grounds of knowledge" (117/115); that "the achievement of the highest good in the world is the necessary object of a will determinable by the moral law" (126/122); and that "all that here belongs to duty is the endeavor to produce and to further the highest good in the world" (130/126).

[8]Ibid., 134/130.

will and is inseparably related to the moral law, the impossibility of the highest good must prove the falsity of the moral law also. If, therefore, the highest good is impossible according to practical rules, then the moral law which commands that it be furthered must be fantastic, directed to empty imaginary ends, and consequently inherently false."[9] Since we control ourselves with difficulty and certainly do not at all control the laws of nature, we must "postulate a higher, moral, most holy, and omnipotent Being which alone can unite the two elements of this highest good."[10] In sum, Kant argues that the Highest Good is the object that the will must produce through its actions and that the guarantee of future realization of the Highest Good is critical to the moral disposition, even if not to the definition of duty.

Reflecting on the argument as formulated thus far I would suggest that it contains in fact two distinct elements between which we must distinguish. We have to distinguish between the observation that in a volition one does not simply *will* a good disposition (rather one *expresses* a good disposition by willing something more concrete), and the assertion that the agent must pursue the Highest Good through her actions and therefore needs guarantees for the possible realization of the Highest Good. Upon reflection on the first argument I admit readily that while morality prescribes the conditions of moral volition, in the form of the moral law, these conditions remain unfulfilled, as an empty formalism, until the will itself embodies them as the form of an actual moral volition the material of which (while subject to the law) must be acquired through sensibility, that is, through the lower faculty of desire.[11] The claim that we are commanded by Reason to seek to realize the Highest Good and that we need guarantees for its

[9]Ibid., 118/114.

[10]Kant, *Religion within the Limits of Reason Alone*, 4–5.

[11]This point was developed by John Silber in his various articles on the Highest Good. See John R. Silber, "The Copernican Revolution in Ethics: The Good Reexamined," *Kant Studien* 51 (1959) 85–101; idem, "The Ethical Significance of Kant's *Religion*" (second introductory essay), in Kant, *Religion within the Limits of Reason Alone*, lxxix–cxlii; and idem, "The Importance of the Highest Good in Kant's Ethics," *Ethics* 73 (1963) 179–97.

realizability, however, is entirely different and should not be admitted so readily.

As indicated above, Kant's argument concerning the requirement to realize the Highest Good was received critically.[12] In this context I want to present two basic objections. First Kant misleads us if he argues that beyond the command to obey the categorical imperative there is an additional command to further the Highest Good. Second, his postulation of the existence of God, which is based on the supposition that we need guarantees for the realizability of the Highest Good, is unjustified.

2.C.1. First Objection

My first objection is very simple, and since so many commentaries have discussed it, my remarks will be brief. None of the formulations of the categorical imperative embodies the demand to produce the Highest Good.[13] Acknowledgment of the moral law involves the recognition that it is my task to seek to realize virtue. This is as far as my obligation concerning the Highest Good can be stretched. While I have to act out of respect for the moral law, it is not my duty to administer happiness in accordance with merit. The theory of the analytic of the *Critique of Practical Reason* requires Kant to deny that the concept of the Highest Good provides an autonomous motive for the pure will. Admission of happiness into the determination of duty jeopardizes autonomy.[14] Taking into consideration the limita-

---

[12]It is safe to say that this argument was received with almost unanimous disapproval. Allen W. Wood's *Kant's Moral Religion* (Ithaca: Cornell University Press, 1970) is a contemporary exception to the rule.

[13]This argument is developed convincingly by Lewis White Beck in *A Commentary on Kant's Critique of Practical Reason* (1960; reprinted Chicago: Midway Reprints, 1984) 239–58. Indeed Beck is so enraged by Kant's argument that we are committed to realize the Highest Good that he dedicates most of his discussion of the Dialectic to refuting it.

[14]The threat to autonomy here does not arise from a claim that history inevitably leads to the realization of the Highest Good, thereby making the idea of moral efforts futile. We are concerned here with the insertion of a promised happiness into the moral deliberation itself, an insertion that would introduce utilitarian considerations into the pure deontic deliberation.

tions of human nature—the fact that as a sensible creature the moral agent must have an object of volition which is not exclusively moral— the Highest Good can be regarded an incentive, but it should not be a ground or a motive.[15] The possibility of the Highest Good cannot be logically or ethically necessary as a motive to genuine morality; belief in it can be only a legitimate accompaniment to a morality that is pure and autonomous.[16]

2.C.2. Second Objection

Examining Kant's solution to the antinomy of Practical Reason which results in the postulation of a supreme being, I agree that Kant was right in observing a gap between virtuous intention and successful performance. I contend, however, that Kant fails in his attempt to convince us that this gap can be bridged only through moral faith in God's existence. The transition from an acknowledgment of moral frustration to the postulation of God's existence is not convincing.[17]

2.C.2.a. Detailed Discussion

According to Kant every moral act can be seen from two points of view. It can be seen as the moral disposition or determination of the will which takes place in the noumenal realm or as the execution of the moral decree as an event in the phenomenal world. As far as we are concerned with the first, the struggle to obey the moral law is internal to the human mind and does not depend on any external forces. The execution of the moral decree, however, takes place in the natural world which is governed by mechanistic causality that the moral agent does not control. Consequently, when it comes to the

[15]In spite of some elusive hints in this direction, Kant himself (*Religion within the Limits of Reason Alone*, 4) eventually emphasizes this point.

[16]These comments draw upon various objections to Kant's argument by many of his critics. I am especially indebted here to Beck. See Beck, *A Commentary on Kant's Critique of Practical Reason*, 242–45.

[17]A similar argument is developed in William Henry Walsh's essay, *Kant's Moral Theology* (Proceedings of the British Academy 49; London: Oxford University Press, 1963). As I shall indicate in due course, though I am highly indebted to Walsh for some of his perceptive arguments, I differ from him significantly in my overall assessment of the value of Kant's argument.

execution of decision, moral agents cannot ignore the natural circumstances amidst which they must realize their moral decision. When they contemplate the execution of the moral decree as an act in the phenomenal world, moral agents need to estimate the natural circumstances and to anticipate how natural causes may affect the consequences of actions. In carrying out a moral decision in the natural world, moral agents most probably need to count on the behavior of other people (a point that was discussed extensively by Kant in *Religion within the Limits of Reason Alone*).[18] It is probably also safe to assume that moral agents need to expect at least a certain amount of sheer luck in executing their good intentions in the natural world. Moral agents need to be able to hope that natural contingencies will not systematically circumvent their success. Taking these considerations into account, Kant maintains that unless they are firmly convinced that such conditions would be satisfied, moral agents will be paralyzed in carrying out moral projects.

To illustrate this view Kant portrays, in the *Critique of Judgment*, a righteous man whom he, rather ironically, calls Spinoza. Spinoza is a person who apparently studied carefully various philosophical attempts to prove the existence of God, decided that they were all invalid, and found himself unable to hold on to his belief in the existence of God. Nevertheless, Spinoza respects the moral law and wishes to execute its command. Such a man, says Kant,

> does not require that complying with that law should bring him an advantage, either in this world or in another; rather, he is unselfish and wants only to bring about the good to which that sacred law directs all his forces. Yet his effort [encounters] limits: For while he can expect that nature will now and then cooperate contingently with the purpose of his that he feels so obligated and impelled to achieve, he can never expect nature to harmonize with it in a way governed by laws and permanent rules (such as his inner maxims are and must be). Deceit, violence, and envy will always be rife around him, even though he himself is honest, peaceable, and benevolent. Moreover, as concerns the other righteous people he meets; no matter how wor-

[18]See Kant, *Religion within the Limits of Reason Alone*, 86, 88–89, 92.

thy of happiness they may be, nature, which pays no attention to that, will still subject them to all the evils of deprivation, disease, and untimely death, just like all the other animals on the earth. And they will stay subjected to these evils always, until one vast tomb engulfs them one and all (honest or not, that makes no difference here) and hurls them, who managed to believe they were the final purpose of creation, back into the abyss of the purposeless chaos of matter from which they were taken. And so this well-meaning person would indeed have to give up as impossible the purpose that the moral laws *obligated him to have before his eyes* and that in compliance with them he did have before his eyes.[19]

In examining Spinoza's problem we need to determine what factors put him in his precarious situation. In answering this question we must notice that Spinoza not only strives to execute the moral law—as formulated by the Categorical Imperative—to the best of his ability, but also seeks to achieve the particular end of proportioned happiness. Apparently Spinoza agrees with Kant that we have a duty to promote the Highest Good. Spinoza, whom Kant describes as a "righteous man," takes it upon himself to produce the Highest Good. He looks around him and judges that, at least as far as he can observe, it is the wicked who flourish and the just who suffer. Spinoza, the righteous atheist, concludes that he has no reason whatsoever to hope that he will be able to respond successfully to the call of duty and to bring about the Highest Good. On the contrary, it seems to him that he has reason to suspect that all his moral endeavors will end in defeat, that blind natural causes and bad luck will combine to frustrate his moral endeavors. Kant seems to maintain that if Spinoza and those like him insist on remaining atheists then they have no other choice but to renounce morality. Accordingly, Kant concludes that it is possible to adhere to the moral life only by believing in God:

> Alternatively, suppose that, regarding this [purpose] too, he wants to continue to adhere to the call of his inner moral vocation, and

---

[19]Kant, *Critique of Judgment*, 341–42/452. Emphasis mine.

that he does not want his respect for the moral law, by which this law directly inspires him to obey it, to be weakened, as would result from the nullity of the one ideal final purpose that is adequate to this respect's high demand (such weakening of his respect would inevitably impair his moral attitude): In that case he must—from a practical point of view, i.e., so that he can at least form a concept of the possibility of [achieving] the final purpose that is morally prescribed to him—assume the existence of a moral author of the world, i.e., the existence of a God.[20]

2.C.2.b. Comments

Kant's discussion of the need to realize the Highest Good is one of the more ambiguous parts of his Critical enterprise. His position that Spinoza and his like must postulate the existence of God in order not to renounce morality is supported by a psychological observation which Kant does not develop sufficiently. It is not quite clear whether Kant wants to argue merely that religion is rationally defensible or to make a stronger claim that religion is a necessary constituent of rationality. His discussion of Spinoza and his comments in the *Second Critique* can be interpreted as intending to support the latter possibility, but in the next section I shall show that even Kant asserted, elsewhere in the *Critique of Judgment*, that belief in God does not share the universal necessity of the moral law and that inability to believe in God does not excuse us from obedience to morality. Kant's argument in the passage quoted above relies heavily on his belief in the importance of hope. Unlike some of Kant's critics I do not wish to belittle the significance of the notion of hope for moral theories. I certainly do not want my following critique of Kant's argument to be misunderstood as a rejection of his concern for hope. I do not think, however, that Kant's discussion of Spinoza's agony can support the strong argument that religion is an indispensable constituent of rationality.

Granted that the world is governed by a mechanistic causality which is independent of our will and control, it is indeed conceivable that some of our attempts to execute the moral law will end in failure. Kant, however, needs more than this in order to argue, logically or

[20]Ibid., 342/452.

psychologically, that the general possibility of failure culminates necessarily in a moral paralysis that inevitably leads to the declaration of morality as null and void.[21] If Kant is to argue that agents who do not wish to forsake the moral law are left with only one option, namely, to postulate a Supreme Being who will come to the rescue and bring about a state of affairs in which everything is as it should be, he must do more than just assert his claim and illustrate it with the suggestive but hardly persuasive account of Spinoza's adventures. Kant must show either that belief in God is the only possible psychological condition that would make it possible for us to pursue the Highest Good in an indifferent world or that belief in God is required deontologically for pursuit of the Highest Good to be a duty in a world that is inherently hostile to moral ends.[22]

In all spheres of activity, not only in the moral, humans face obstacles and frequently fail. But the general probability of failure, even coupled with the bitterness of defeat, need not force us to seek divine help. Kant suggests that unless humans can enlist divine providence they cannot believe in the possibility of the execution of a moral decree. Kant, the great proponent of human autonomy, seems to give

[21]To convince us that moral agents must postulate the existence of a just and powerful God Kant needs to show that nature is, otherwise, not only indifferent but hostile. Only against the background of belief in an evil God who frustrates all our moral enterprises would Kant's argument be valid. Kant rejected the belief in an evil God in his discussion of evil in *Religion within the Limits of Reason Alone*.

[22]In "The Metaphysical Elements of Justice" (in Immanuel Kant, *The Metaphysics of Morals* [trans. John Ladd; Indianapolis: Bobbs Merrill, 1965; part 1] 127–29/354–55) Kant clarifies that only proof that an end is impossible nullifies our duty to pursue it. Speaking of a political duty to establish international peace regardless of the feasibility of that noble end, Kant explains: "Now it is evident that [although duty may require us to adopt an end as our maxim] it does not require us to conjecture the feasibility of the end in the sense in which such a conjecture is a purely theoretical judgment, and a problematic one as well, for there can be no obligation to do this (to believe something). What duty requires is that we act in accordance with the Idea of such an end, even if there is not the slightest theoretical probability that it is feasible, as long as its impossibility cannot be demonstrated either."

up and assert that without belief in God, morality, the guarantor of human autonomy, is doomed.

2.C.2.c. The Antinomy of Natural Determinism and Freedom

The problem of the Highest Good can be seen as a particular manifestation of a more general problem, that of the general possibility of success in our moral endeavors. At root is the antinomy of natural determinism and freedom. As moral agents we are required to realize the decree of pure Practical Reason amidst a mechanical causality which we neither fully know nor control. I agree with Kant that as moral agents we cannot avoid asking ourselves whether our moral decisions stand the chance of ever being realized. I concede that should we find ourselves necessarily drawn to the conclusion that there is no possibility of ever realizing any of our moral goals, we may find ourselves so paralyzed that we will simply conclude that the whole endeavor is worthless. I maintain, however, that as long as it cannot be argued that of necessity all moral endeavors will fail, hope is still possible though it may require a very special personality. We can still have faith in our own ability, not in a future utopia the exact nature of which we do not and cannot know and which we cannot bring about. To make a stronger case for the necessity of faith Kant has to argue that nature is conducted by evil forces which systematically frustrate all moral effort.[23] Kant holds the view that "ought implies

---

[23]The better to illustrate my argument, I wish to draw a comparison between moral and scientific activities. In both, the human mind armed with its a priori principles, with moral laws and with the supreme laws of the Understanding, faces the contingencies of the phenomenal world. It strives to impose unity on the manifold of sense perceptions and on desires. Like moral agents, scientists confront the unknown and the unexpected. Time and again their efforts are frustrated by unknown factors. Arguing analogically we would claim that scientists too need absolute guarantees to embark upon new experiments. Are we willing to make such an assertion? Are we willing to assert that they must postulate a supreme being who will make sure that the laws of nature conform to their expectations and that their hypotheses will be vindicated by reality? Interestingly, in the *Critique of Judgment* Kant discusses the uniformity of natural laws and suggests that this very uniformity requires us

can" and argues accordingly that since we know a priori that pursuit of the Highest Good is our duty, its realization must also be possible. He tries to show therefore that the possibility of the realization of the Highest Good depends on the existence of a benevolent and omnipotent God. The whole argument seems to require an additional premise of the inherent hostility of nature to moral ends, due to which we are incapable of realizing the Highest Good ourselves. Kant does not argue for the inevitable failure of moral endeavor, and therefore the conclusion that moral agents are doomed to a despair from which they can be relieved only through the postulation of the existence of God is unsubstantiated.

Examining Kant's moral proof we have to conclude that his argument is not compelling. Kant does not prove that the *only circumstance* under which righteous but finite agents could follow the moral law without falling from moral despair to moral paralysis is faith in the help of an omnipotent moral governor of the universe. The conclusion I draw from this assessment is that those who wish to defend the rationality of religion would be advised not to rely on Kant's moral proof of the existence of God.[24]

---

to postulate a divine designer of nature. There is however a crucial difference between the two discussions. In the *Third Critique* Kant bases his proof on the success rather than on the failure of the scientist. The ability to find harmony in nature, an ability which cannot be guaranteed by the supreme a priori laws of the Understanding, is the point of departure of Kant's argument. As I said, I think every agent faces the discrepancy between an ideal and reality. The scientist, the moral agent, and the artist share this problem. If we accept Kant's argument regarding the frustration of the moral agent, we open a Pandora box.

[24]In chapter four, which discusses the *Critique of Judgment*, I shall examine an additional argument of Kant's for the necessity of the Highest Good. There too Kant discusses the antinomy between nature and freedom. However, in the *Critique of Judgment* he describes the problem not as a need for confirmation that moral endeavor will succeed and be rewarded, but as a ground for the ability to judge that spatio-temporal events are purposeful. In the *Third Critique* the Highest Good solves the problem of purposiveness when it is depicted as the governing principle of the designer of nature. It is not intended as an antidote to despair.

▮ 2.D. Assessment of Kant's Phenomenology of Faith

In examining the two stages of the moral proof of the existence of God, I pointed out its difficulties and concluded that religious thinkers should be aware of them. In this section I shall argue that in considering whether to align themselves with Kant's moral defense of faith, religious thinkers must also confront the fact that for Kant belief in God does not share the objectivity of the categories of Reason and of the moral law. Kant's attribution of only subjective validity to rational faith triggered the critique of thinkers like Otto and Tillich and impelled them to look elsewhere for a solid foundation for religion. To make this point clear I shall examine the logical status of a postulate.

2.D.1. The Postulate

In the *Critique of Pure Reason* Kant discusses the concept of God as a speculative concept which, as such, can be neither proved nor refuted. In the *Critique of Practical Reason* the speculative concept of God is introduced on moral grounds that are epistemologically subjective. In his discussion of the postulates of Practical Reason Kant insists that they are founded on a "need of Reason," that is, not on grounds of objective evidence.[25] Consequently the postulates are valid only within the framework of moral action and have no theoretical bearing.[26] In the previous section we saw Kant arguing that belief in the existence of God is of such importance that one cannot discard it and adhere to the moral law. Close examination of Kant's discussion of the postulates of Practical Reason, however, discloses that the moral law demands only that *I believe* in a moral governor of the universe; it does not demand that *I know* this governor to actually exist. The solution of the antinomy of Practical Reason does not justify a theoretical knowledge of God. Furthermore, Kant makes it plain that the recognition of the moral duty does not require the existence of God. Drawing the implications of these assertions, we must conclude that even if God does not actually exist, and we only believe in the ex-

---

[25]Kant, *Critique of Practical Reason*, 130/126, 149/144.
[26]Ibid., 139–42/134–37.

istence of God, the practical consequences for obedience to the moral law are the same.[27] Therefore, a postulate of Practical Reason does not have to be known to be true, and probably does not even have to be true, in order to serve its practical purpose.[28]

Kant introduces his moral proof of the existence of God by examining the practical situation in which people feel the force of the moral obligation to pursue the Highest Good. Belief in God, however, unlike the moral law, is not characterized by Kant as a fact of reason. Indeed Kant himself draws a comparison between the corresponding status of the two and indicates deliberately that belief in God is of inferior status. In the *Critique of Judgment* Kant examines the moral proof for God's existence and asserts:

> This proof, to which we could easily give the form of logical precision, is not trying to say that it is *as necessary* to assume that God exists as it is to acknowledge that the moral law is valid, so that anyone who cannot convince himself that God exists may judge himself released from the obligations that the moral law imposes. No! All we would have to give up [if we could not convince ourselves that God exists] is our *aiming* at that final purpose that we are to achieve in the world by complying with the moral law (in other words, our aiming at the highest good in the world: a happiness of rational beings that harmoniously accompanies their compliance with moral laws); every rational being would still have to cognize himself as strictly bound by what morality prescribes, because the moral laws are formal and command unconditionally without regard to purposes (which are the matter of volition).[29]

[27]Kant, *Critique of Judgment*, 340/451, 366/472–73.

[28]This point is discussed extensively by Beck (*A Commentary on Kant's Critique of Practical Reason*, 262). Otto and Tillich could not adopt this position as a foundation of their own theories of religion since they strove to demonstrate that religious judgments have truth value. When we understand the implications of Kant's position we can see how closely it resembles Wittgensteinian attempts to secure the autonomy of religious discourse by defining faith as an attitude. For Otto and Tillich, religious experiences have objective content and religious statements have truth value.

[29]Kant, *Critique of Judgment*, 340/451. The first emphasis is mine; the second is Kant's.

Religious thinkers must consider whether they can accept these conclusions and still rely on Kant's proof of rational faith as a foundation of their thought. They should ask themselves whether they wish to rely on Kant for a defense of the rationality of faith, especially when Kant himself admits that belief in God—a subjective need of Practical Reason—is ultimately not as rationally necessary as moral duty and is even not as morally indispensable as Kant's discussion of Spinoza's predicament would have us think. Otto and Tillich concluded that Kant made religion the handmaiden of morality, thereby providing flimsy foundations for the rationality of religion. Unable to rely on Kant's moral proof they looked elsewhere for solid foundations for the rationality of religion. As I shall show in subsequent chapters, they thought they found a promising alternative in Kant's *Critique of Judgment.*

2.D.2. The Moral Law as Divine Command

Alongside his justification of moral faith as a necessary correlate of belief in the possibility of the Highest Good, Kant presents another explanation of the phenomenon of religion. He characterizes religion as a "recognition of all duties as divine commands."[30] In *Religion within the Limits of Reason Alone* Kant tells us that "each individual can know of himself through his own reason, the will of God which lies at the basis of his religion."[31] Close scrutiny of this theory of religion finds it an insufficient basis for the rationality of faith. As I shall show immediately, analysis of Kant's argument determines that the real legislator of the "divine commands" is the autonomous moral will. I shall show, furthermore, that the term "divine" really denotes for Kant a "shadowy image" of our conscience. The so-called divine legislator turns out to be a projection of our moral conscience that functions as an internal court of justice, a court whose task is to supervise and guarantee obedience to the moral law.[32] When con-

---

[30]Kant, *Critique of Practical Reason*, 134/130.

[31]Kant, *Religion within the Limits of Reason Alone*, 95.

[32]These arguments make Kant the predecessor of the theory of projection of Ludwig Feuerbach and Sigmund Freud. See ibid., 90–91, 135; and idem, *The Metaphysics of Morals* (part 2) in   James W. Ellington, ed., *Ethical*

fronted by the moral law, this conscience threatens us and keeps us in awe (respect combined with fear). We perceive it as an authoritative figure watching over us, following us like a shadow, addressing us in an awful voice, a figure from which we cannot run away. To function as efficiently as possible our conscience projects itself into the image of God. Kant's graphic description of the process of projection is most instructive. Since this is a relatively neglected argument I shall quote it at length:

> Consider a human being at those moments when his mind is attuned to moral feeling: If, surrounded by a beautiful nature, he finds himself calmly and serenely enjoying his existence, he will feel within him a need to be grateful for this to someone. Or suppose that, at another time [but] in the same frame of mind, he finds himself under the pressure of many duties that he is willing to perform and can perform only through voluntary sacrifice: he will feel within him a need that in performing them he will also have carried out something commanded, and have obeyed some sovereign. Again, suppose that perhaps he has unthinkingly violated his duty, yet without having made himself answerable to [other] people: still, within him he will sternly reprimand himself in words that sound as if they were spoken by a judge to whom he had to account for his action. In a word: he has a need for moral intelligence. . . in such cases the mind has the inclination to expand its moral attitude, and voluntarily thinks an object that is not in the world, so that it may possibly do its duty to that [being] as well. Therefore it is at least possible—and the moral way of thinking even contains a basis for it—to form a presentation of a pure moral need for the existence of a being under which our morality gains either in fortitude or (at least according to our presentation) in range, namely, by gaining a new object to which we can apply it. In other words, it is at least possible to assume a being [that exists] apart from the world, and that legislates morality, and to make this assumption without any concern about theoretical proof, let alone selfish interest, but on a basis that (while indeed only subjective) is

Philosophy [Indianapolis: Hackett, 1983] 438–41/100–103 (§13 "Concerning Man's Duties to Himself Insofar as He is the Innate Judge of Himself"). The German edition is idem, *Die Metaphysik der Sitten* (1797; reprinted in *Kants Gesammelte Schriften*, vol. 6).

> purely moral and free from all foreign influence: on the mere
> recommendation of a Practical Reason that legislates only to
> itself.[33]

Conscience has the peculiar predisposition of making us feel as if
the judge presiding over our internal court of justice is another person. It does so because of the peculiarity of the moral situation in
which we are the legislators, the prosecutor, the defenders, and the
judges. This situation, had it occurred in an ordinary court of justice
would have been absurd. In such a situation, Kant says, the prosecutor would certainly lose every time. Therefore, as far as moral duties
are concerned, our conscience must imagine itself as being judged by
someone else. Such an ideal judge must possess certain qualifications.
Since we are dealing with an internal court of justice, it must be a
searcher of hearts. Since it represents a free legislating will, it must
be regarded as the legislator of the moral law. To make its verdict
effective it must also possess an unlimited power of enforcement.
These are no other than the attributes of the Lord of Heaven and
Earth. To perform its function conscience projects an idea of God as
such a judge, so that when we confront the moral law we see ourselves accountable to an all-knowing God of justice.

The upshot of this interesting piece of fiction is that even as we
feel as if we stand before God, we should keep in mind that we have
no right to suppose that such a supreme being actually exists. We
must remember that this process of projection is done for the sake of
moral benefit but is not absolutely necessary.[34] Most important, we
should always keep in mind that though we feel as if God were a
divine legislator, true morality is autonomous. We have no moral
duties toward God.

> We also have a duty regarding that which lies completely be-
> yond the limits of our experience, but the possibility of which,

---

[33]Kant, *Critique of Judgment*, 334–35/445–46. Kant argues similarly in
Religion within the Limits of Reason Alone, 90–91; 135.

[34]Immanuel Kant, "The Metaphysical Principles of Virtue: The Elements
of Ethics," in idem, *The Metaphysics of Morals* (part 2) § 18, 102.

nevertheless, is to be met with in our ideas, e.g., in our idea of God. This is called the duty of religion, namely, that "of recognizing all our duties as divine commands." But this is not the consciousness of a duty **to** God. For since this idea arises entirely out of our own Reason and is made by us in order, from a theoretical standpoint, to explain the purposiveness of the universe, or, for practical purposes, to serve as an incentive in our conduct, we *do not hereby have before us a given being* **to** *whom we are obligated; for the actuality of such a being would first have to be proved (disclosed) by experience.* But it is a *duty of man to himself* to apply this idea, which offers itself unavoidably to reason, to the moral law within him; in such an application this idea is of the greatest moral fruitfulness. In this (practical) sense, to have religion can be asserted to be a duty *of man to himself.*[35]

The God, the rationality of belief in whom Kant's official theory of religion strives to secure, turns out to be a mere projection of conscience. Sigmund Freud and Ludwig Feuerbach have shown how the notion of projection can be developed and used to criticize and undermine religious belief. Kant's official theory of religion cannot, therefore, provide strong support to the philosophical and theological endeavors of thinkers like Otto and Tillich to defend the rationality of religion in the modern world.

■ 2.E. Conclusion

Kant's discussion of the Highest Good in the *Critique of Practical Reason* might be thought to provide an adequate defense of the rationality of religion. There are writers who consider Kant's moral proof an argument that enables believers to participate in the scientific community while proudly holding on to their religious convictions.[36]

---

[35]Ibid., 107/444. Italics are my emphasis, bold are Kant's.

[36]Walsh, to whose critique of Kant's moral proof of God's existence I am indebted, argues that all the difficulties and even fallacies of Kant's argument notwithstanding, his is probably the best defense of religion a modern believer can have. Walsh writes, "The attraction of the Kantian type of theory is that. . . it keeps the world safe for the scientist without showing the door to the moralist and the religious man. And though the religious man is not

According to them the inclusion of religion within the boundaries of Moral Reason makes religion a legitimate part of the modern world view. The moral proof promises that religion need no longer fortify itself within the walls of irrationality. People of faith need no longer contend that religion and reason are two distinct realms.

Once we examine Kant's discussion of religion closely, however, we realize that Kant's defense of faith is dubious. The arguments he develops to substantiate the rationality of the belief in God are problematic; the status of a postulate makes religious belief inferior to the moral law and the categories of understanding. Since rational faith is recognized as legitimate only for the purposes of ethics, its scope is heavily restricted to this realm alone. Religion turns out to be the handmaiden of ethics and is not recognized as a distinct realm that has to be understood in its own terms. In short, close scrutiny of

---

always grateful for this kind of support—he complains that (a) Kant. . . fails altogether to take account of the cognitive claims which religion involves, or again he complains that they are insensitive to the importance of corporate religious organization and tradition—it may well be that it is the best independent support he can get. Assuming that he does not want to put his trust in blind faith, and in so doing to part company from those of us who find such a step irrational and indeed repulsive, there is probably no better philosophical position he can call to his aid" (*Kant's Moral Theology*, 286). For a recent attempt to defend the rationality of religion on grounds similar to Kant's moral proof, see Ronald M. Green's *Religious Reason* (New York: Oxford University Press, 1970).

An opposing appraisal of Kant's argument is developed by Theodore M. Greene who argues that since Kant was a "typical product of a scientific age and a rationalistic mood," he failed to realize that "the religious experience implies a knowledge of God as real as Kant's own apprehension of the moral law." Consequently, Greene argues, Kant was unable "to recognize a distinctive religious experience, which is akin to that moral experience which he himself describes in such detail, yet is not identical with it." (See Greene, "The Historical Context and Religious Significance of Kant's *Religion*" (first introductory essay), in Kant, *Religion within the Limits of Reason Alone*, lxxvi–lxxvii). These ideas are also found in Theodore M. Greene, *Moral, Aesthetic, and Religious Insight* (New Brunswick, NJ: Rutgers University Press, 1957).

Kant's theory of religion indicates that if we turn to Kant to find a solid foundation for a recognition of religion as an equal participant in the modern world view we shall be disappointed.

The question we must now ask is whether believers who do not wish to trust in blind faith and thereby to part company with the rest of society, who find such a step irrational, must consider Kant's defense of the rationality of faith the best philosophical position on which they can rely. If they find this position untenable, must they reject the Kantian system altogether, or can they still find in it some ground for a philosophical theology?

In the following chapters I shall show that Otto and Tillich believed that they could find in Kant's own philosophy better foundations for the defense of the rationality of religion. I shall show that they subjected religion to a critique, just as Kant subjected ethics, science, and aesthetics to critique. They strove to characterize the distinctive essence of religion and to account for the universality and necessity of religious experience in terms of a distinctive function of reason.

I will show, however, that Otto and Tillich were not interested in merely writing a Fourth Critique. They did not want to present religion as merely an additional realm of meaning. I shall argue that they came to the conclusion that religion cannot be confined to one additional realm of human life. Rather, they felt that religion has the peculiarity that it penetrates into and suffuses every other realm of life. They observe that, to use Coleridge's language, religion is the "total act of the soul."[37]

I suspect that this awareness enabled them to observe a special problem in Kant's philosophy, the problem of the unity of Reason and the realms it constructs. In interpreting their writings I argue that we can understand them properly only if we realize how much their theories of religion draw upon Kant's discussion of the unity of Reason. This problem is ignored by many scholars of Kant, who, I surmise,

---

[37]Samuel Taylor Coleridge, *The Statesman's Manual* (New York: Harper & Brothers, 1853) appendix B, 471.

find Kant's arguments alluding to a supersensible substratum of reality too embarrassing. To defend the rationality of both science and ethics Kant assigned them to different realms. Kant, however, acknowledged the need to unify these realms and restore unity to consciousness. In his struggle with this task, Kant again resorted to the concept of the Highest Good. This time, as I shall argue, Kant provided a more convincing foundation to this concept. I shall examine his argument in the fourth chapter of this part. This discussion will be preceded by a third chapter which provides a general overview of the problem of the unity of consciousness as it is discussed in the *Critique of Practical Reason*. The fourth chapter will reveal a dimension of Kant's thought which, I believe, is his more significant contribution to a theory of religion. I argue further that this dimension, which I call his "unofficial theory of religion," is a source of immense influence on Otto and Tillich, who could not acquiesce with Kant's discussion of the Highest Good and religion in the *Critique of Practical Reason*.

3

THE CONFLICT BETWEEN THE
INTERESTS OF REASON

3.A. Kant's Statement of the Problem of Unity

Examining the structural differences between the first two *Critiques*, Kant, somewhat casually, thrusts upon his readers an intriguing comment:

> Whoever has been able to convince himself of the truth of the propositions in the Analytic will get a certain enjoyment out of such comparisons, for they correctly occasion the expectation of bringing some day into one view the unity of the entire pure rational faculty (both theoretical and practical) and of being able to derive everything from one principle. *The latter is an unavoidable need of human reason, as it finds complete satisfaction only in a perfectly systematic unity of its cognitions.*[1]

[1]Kant, *Critique of Practical Reason*, 94/91. Emphasis mine.

Kant does not pause to dwell on this rather provocative and stimu-
lating comment. He does not tell us exactly what kind of unity he has
in mind or the nature of the "one principle" to be sought. He does not
explain why he speaks of a distant future. Is he implying that he
himself was not yet able to find this principle, or is he just paving the
way for proposing one?

■ 3.B. Clarification of the Problem

One major difficulty in ascertaining the meaning of Kant's reference to the perfect unity to be sought is the fact that the *Critique of
Practical Reason* does not discuss this issue systematically. To shed
light on the nature of the problem I have collected various statements
scattered in different contexts throughout the *Second Critique*. These
statements, I believe, clearly indicate how deeply Kant was concerned
with the problem. It is also important to see that even though the
problem of the unity of Reason arises for Kant as a result of his
bifurcation of our cognitive faculties, the problem is not limited to
the Kantian system. We can all recognize, in various aspects of our
lives, manifestations of the problem that Kant described as a clash
between distinct interests of reason. It is therefore possible to suggest
that the Kantian formulation is an attempt to account for the problem
in systematic terms. In this section I have a dual goal: to reconstruct
Kant's definition of the problem in the *Second Critique* and to present
the acuteness of the problem as it arises in our experience. We shall
proceed to examine several manifestations of clashes of which we are
acutely aware. These examples will illustrate various dimensions of
the Kantian problem and help us appreciate its profundity. Throughout this discussion I wish to emphasize that Kant's obsession with
unity is not merely an artificial architectonic urge to create grand
systems, but an insight into a serious problem. In our discussion of
the *Third Critique* below, we shall see how Kant tried to sharpen his
characterization of the problem of unity and how he proposed to resolve
it.

This chapter explores the problem of unity chiefly through an
examination of Kant's doctrine of the primacy of Practical Reason.
Rejecting various interpretations of the doctrine, I argue that the claim

for primacy should be understood as an attempt to justify, under specific restriction, the acceptance of several metaphysical beliefs that Theoretical Reason could not warrant as necessary for the secure progress of scientific knowledge. In the course of his discussion of the primacy of Practical Reason Kant elaborates on two points that are of importance for us. He (1) discusses the corresponding interests of Theoretical and Practical Reason, and (2) defines the conditions necessary to maintain a balance between the two.

3.B.1. The Interests of Reason

"To every faculty of the mind," Kant argues, "*an interest* can be ascribed, i.e., *a principle which contains the condition under which alone its exercise is advanced.*" Kant goes on to define the corresponding interests of Theoretical and Practical Reason: "The interest of its speculative use consists in the knowledge of objects up to the highest a priori principles; that of its practical employment lies in the determination of the will with respect to the final and perfect end."[2]

Kant, typically, uses the term "interest" equivocally. I understand it to denote both an *end* of the use of a faculty and a *principle* under which its exercise is advanced. I suggest that by focusing on the former we see that for Kant the interest of Theoretical Reason is whatever furthers the exercise of both its function of inquiry to its furthest limits and its relentless striving to find a complete explanation to all phenomena. Its interest is the orderly progress of science. The interest of Practical Reason is to initiate new causal series in the world. In a word, it is to establish its autonomy vis-a-vis the laws of nature.

3.B.2. Balance Between the Interests

Kant explains that in order to secure the function of Reason as such "a relation of balance" must be maintained between speculative and practical reason.[3] Kant insists that any restriction or interference of one function with the interests of the other is a threat to this balance.

---

[2]Ibid., 124/120. Emphasis mine.
[3]Ibid., 147/142.

I propose that Kant's awareness of the acuteness of the problem of conflicting interests underlies the final chapter of the Dialectic of the *Second Critique.* What would happen, Kant asks there, if humans were given the power of insight "which we would like to possess or which some erroneously believe they do possess, what would be the consequence so far as we can discern it?"[4] In other words, what would happen if Theoretical Reason accomplished its goal uninterruptedly and gained total knowledge? Assuming that our psychological makeup remains unchanged, Kant answers that having such knowledge would devastate us:

> But instead of the conflict which now the moral disposition has to wage with inclinations and in which, after some defeats, moral strength of mind may be gradually won, God and eternity in their awful majesty would stand unceasingly before our eyes. . . . Transgression of the law would indeed be shunned, and the commanded would be performed. But. . . most actions conforming to the law would be done from fear, few would be done from hope, none from duty. . . . *The conduct of man, so long as his nature remained as it now is, would be changed into mere mechanism, where, as in a puppet show, everything would gesticulate well but no life would be found in the figures.*[5]

This discussion indicates, more than anything else, Kant's acute sensitivity to the problem of conflicting interests, for it is Kant who announces in the *First Critique* that it is necessary to limit knowledge to make room for moral faith. It is Kant who acknowledges that it is possible to consider the possibility of an uncaused cause, namely, freedom in its negative sense, only due to the limitations of discursive knowledge. Kant, more than anyone else, acknowledges the fragility of the balance between the conflicting interests of theory and praxis. In the *Second Critique,* moreover, Kant goes on to spell out for us the fatal consequences of failure to sustain it:

[4]Ibid., 152/147.

[5]Ibid., 152–53/147–48. Emphasis mine. Kant repeats these ideas in the *Critique of Judgment,* 376–77/481–82. 352/460, 380/484–85.

a conflict of reason with itself would arise, since if the speculative and the practical reason were arranged merely side by side (coordinated), the first would close its borders and admit into its domain nothing from the latter, while the latter would extend its boundaries over everything and, when its needs required, would seek to comprehend the former within them.[6]

In the specific case under discussion (the extension of Theoretical Reason through the concept of the "Highest Good"), Kant thinks that by establishing a subordination of the theoretical to the practical (by extension of the former), a conflict of Reason with itself is avoided and the required balance is maintained.[7]

I propose that the problem of conflicts does not become acute only in futuristic circumstances, such as a completion of knowledge, or in fanaticism. Since by their nature the interests of knowledge and ethics conflict, we encounter borderline cases in almost every aspect of our lives. We do not need to know "God" to reach a stage where knowledge can threaten to paralyze morality. Drawing upon contemporary experience we realize that controversy about public opinion polls is an example of such a conflict of interests. Had social science been able to achieve accurate predictions, what would be the point of elections? The frustration of Californians who still vote when television announces its predictions based on its inquiries in the East Coast anticipates such a danger. Ethical questions concerning genetic engineering and atomic research are additional contemporary examples of a tension created when, in the name of ethical considerations, scientists are asked to repress their endeavor to reach the limits of knowledge. Arguably, these are cases that indicate the fragility of the balance between the two functions of reason and show that a radical solution ought to be found to secure the orderly use of reason.

While genetic engineering and nuclear research encounter ethical objections, these may be considered objections not to the experimentation itself but to possible consequences of it; they may be thought,

---

[6]Kant, *Critique of Practical Reason*, 126/122.

[7]Ibid. I suggest, however, that Kant was aware that the balance between the two interests of Reason remains very delicate and that a conclusive solution ought to be found.

therefore, not to exhibit a genuine clash between ethical value and natural law. A striking example of such a clash can be seen in Bertrand Russell's argument from the second law of thermodynamics against the idea of "cosmic hope." Insofar as morality requires, as Kant says it does, that it be possible for moral agents to believe in the future perfectibility of human nature and in an ultimate realization of the Highest Good, this idea of rational hope clashes with Russell's bleak vision of ultimate human destiny. "The second law of thermodynamics," Russell writes, "tells us that, on the whole, energy is always passing from more concentrated to less concentrated forms, and that, in the end, it will all have passed into a form in which further change is impossible. When that has happened, if not before, life must cease."[8]

The severity of the problem becomes evident once we acknowledge that humans are citizens of both kingdoms. We are scientists as well as moral agents. The conflict between the two interests threatens to frustrate the integrity of our lives. Are we doomed to live in two distinct and unrelated realms? Must we divide our lives into two unintegrated activities? Can we at all afford to live like this? This awareness, I think, underlies Kant's discussion of the required unity. I contend that our text expresses Kant's concern that the respective interests of Practical and Theoretical Reason can threaten to restrict and/or interfere with each other's orderly progress.

[8]Bertrand Russell, *Religion and Science* (London/New York: Oxford University Press, 1961) 218. Russell's case exemplifies a genuine clash between ethical value and theoretical knowledge. It is the theoretical knowledge itself, not its possible consequences, that conflicts with the ethical belief that Kant himself considered vital for moral agency. History abounds with examples of similar clashes. The discovery of irrational numbers by the Pythagoreans was kept secret since it was considered a threat to the rational view of the universe which was the foundation of social order. We have all learned how a religious establishment persecuted Galileo Galilei, whose theory was thought to conflict with the teaching of the church. In more recent history we witness the hostility of religious fundamentalism toward scientific theories and toward the historical analysis of scripture. All these are cases in which knowledge itself, not only its possible practical consequences, conflicts with the outlook of morality. These examples show that Kant's concern for unity is not merely an architectonic obsession; rather it represents a genuine problem with which we can identify today.

In conclusion, I want to observe that the unity of the principles of Reason is an important goal for Kant. Remembering his discussion of the "transcendental unity of the apperception," in the *First Critique*, we realize the particular significance of our subject. According to that discussion, the only means the subject has to comprehend its own unity is reflection on its ability to integrate a given manifold. If an internal division is found within reason, it may be stipulated, then we are doomed to consider ourselves split personalities. As I shall argue in the next chapter, Kant devoted his *Third Critique* to establish the unity of Reason. The fact that he devoted a third *Critique* to this question, shows, I believe, that he did not consider the problem solved by the doctrine of the "Primacy of Practical Reason" which we shall now discuss.

■ 3.C. Evaluation of the Problem

3.C.1. Challenges to the Reality of the Problem

Having argued that Kant expresses his concern with the unity of Reason—that at issue here is a tension between two distinct interests and that resolution depends on a higher principle—we must confront two counterarguments: the first, that the problem is resolved by the "primacy of Practical Reason"; the second, that unity is assured since theory and praxis are two applications of one function.

3.C.1.a. The First Counterargument

It is possible to argue that Kant's quest for unity in the *Third Critique*—his analysis of the problem and the measures he took to resolve it—is superfluous because, as it may be suggested, the conflict between the respective interests of Theoretical and Practical Reason is resolved by the doctrine of the primacy of Practical Reason. It may be argued that this doctrine implies that in moments of conflict the theoretical interest should give way to the interests of Practical Reason.

Since the ambiguity of Kant's language lends itself to diverse interpretations we need to ascertain the exact scope and nature of Kant's position. Several optional interpretations suggest themselves and all

are widely represented in the literature on Kant.[9] Kant could be interpreted as saying that Practical Reason has a closer affinity with the
spontaneity of Reason; he could also be interpreted as arguing that
Practical Reason protects the metaphysical interest of Reason by securing objectivity to the regulative ideas; or he could perhaps be
understood as asserting that moral action brings us closer to the
noumenon.

In untangling this ambiguity we first need to establish whether
Kant argues that practical knowledge has a primacy over theoretical
knowledge or whether he argues that action is superior to knowledge
(see Kroner). On the one hand, Kant could claim that the metaphysical interests of Reason find satisfaction in practical knowledge (see
Yovel). On the other hand, he could hold that action is superior to
knowledge in that action is purely spontaneous while knowledge is
limited by the givenness of intuition (see Caird). On the basis of such
arguments it could be suggested that the quest of Reason for the
"unconditioned for every conditioned" culminates in the establishment
of the practical ideal of the Highest Good.

We shall now examine the argument to this effect as it is advanced
by the various thinkers. In his book *The Critical Philosophy of
Immanuel Kant*, Edward Caird argues that "perhaps we may say—
though Kant does not say it in so many words—that just because
reason cannot find its ideal realized in the world, it seeks to realize
that ideal for itself."[10] Richard Kroner argues in *Kant's Weltanschauung*
that "Kant holds that the recognition of an imperative, guiding us not
only when we seek the truth but guiding our will as its highest mea-
sure and goal, brings us nearer to the ultimate meaning of the world
than any speculative or theoretical knowledge possibly could. If you
follow the voice of your conscience, if you fulfill your duty, however
large it may loom, then you will penetrate farther into the unknown

---

[9]The next three options were presented, respectively, by Richard Kroner,
Kant's Weltanschauung (trans. John E. Smith; Chicago: University of Chicago Press, 1956); Yirmiahu Yovel, *Kant and the Philosophy of History*
(Princeton: Princeton University Press, 1980); and Edward Caird, *The Critical Philosophy of Immanuel Kant* (2 vols.; New York: Kraus, 1968).

[10]See Caird, *The Critical Philosophy of Immanuel Kant*, 2. 164.

sphere of the supersensible than any kind of thought could do."[11] Yirmiahu Yovel says in *Kant and the Philosophy of History* that "the unconditioned and the total, which we cannot approach by knowledge, can be *created* by moral action and by the totalization of the particular acts in light of a comprehensive historical goal. The unconditioned takes the form of the *absolute law* of the will, the categorical imperative, and the total is given in the form of the *ultimate end* of the will, the highest good."[12]

These interpreters claim that the *vita activa* is superior to the *vita scientia*. At the heart of their opinion we find the view, sometimes expressed only tacitly, that ultimately knowing is a mode of acting. The logic of such an argument should be formulated as follows: Reason is essentially spontaneous, spontaneity is creation, and creation is a practical activity. Accordingly, Reason is practical by its very nature.[13] Kroner gives an illuminating expression of this opinion when he argues that

> man is, in the true sense, a subject only in so far as he wills and acts. This is true even of the subject which seeks scientific knowledge, for we can know nature only through voluntary and active investigation of her dynamic activity. . . . From the practical perspective theoretical knowledge itself is determined by the will—the will to know the truth. . . . Science is basically an ethical undertaking; this is its ultimate and most exalted conception. The ethical ideal thus penetrates the theoretical sphere itself and appears within it as its supreme master and interpreter."[14]

This is truly an exalted formulation of a view that is shared today by many of pragmatic inclination, who ascribe no inherent interests to the project of science and attribute the goals of scientific inquiry to general social and cultural interests. It is not, I believe, a valid pre-

---

[11]Kroner, *Kant's Weltanschauung*, 21

[12]Yovel, *Kant and the Philosophy of History*, 290.

[13]I am indebted to Nathan Rotenstreich's formulation of this view (to which he objects). See his *Experience and its Systematization: Studies in Kant* (2d ed.; The Hague: Nijhoff, 1972) 120.

[14]Kroner, *Kant's Weltanschauung*, 83–84.

sentation of Kant's position, since Kant thought that Theoretical Reason is spontaneous and autonomous in its quest for a unified explanation of all natural phenomena.

These interpretations rely on two distinct arguments: (1) that Practical Reason is a direct expression of or is identical with the spontaneity of Reason, and (2) that in realizing the ideal of the Highest Good, Practical Reason must be ranked higher than Theoretical Reason. Kant, I believe, had good reasons to reject both. His intended argument in the doctrine of the primacy of Practical Reason is a restricted one. Kant wanted to prevent an internal contradiction in Reason that would arise had Theoretical Reason denied the content of freedom, immortality, and God, the objectivity of which Practical Reason affirms as conditions for the realization of duty.[15] To prevent a disintegration of the system of reason and to avoid a theory of a double truth, Kant introduced the idea of the primacy of Practical Reason. He wanted to establish that Theoretical Reason does not conflict with the postulates of Practical Reason and permits practical belief in them.[16]

(1) An implicit assumption of the interpretations I am examining is that Practical Reason is superior to Theoretical Reason since it is a direct expression of the spontaneity of Reason. In considering this issue it is crucial to remember that for Kant both Practical and Theoretical employments of Reason are expressions of the spontaneity of reason. The *Critique of Pure Reason* states clearly that the status of the categories of the Understanding is grounded in the spontaneous capacity of reason. Therefore, the mere spontaneity of moral activity cannot justify a claim for superiority of the practical employment of reason. Furthermore, had we argued that spontaneity is the exclusive property of Practical Reason, we would have implied that Theoretical

---

[15]We should remember that whereas freedom is the transcendental ground of the good will which determines itself in obedience to the Categorical Imperative, immortality and God are merely postulates that facilitate belief in the realizability of the Highest Good.

[16]My point is that Kant wanted to stress that Practical Reason is indeed Pure Reason and not merely rational self-interest. His argument is not that Theoretical Reason has no interest, but rather that Practical Reason has interests of its own which must be respected.

Reason is essentially passive. Kant, however, clearly rejects the view that Theoretical Reason gives us only a copy of the world. The spontaneity of Reason is manifest in both its functions; the spontaneity of the practical does not support a claim for primacy.[17]

(2) The other argument for primacy is that whereas Theoretical Reason legislates to the phenomena, Practical Reason legislates to the will—understood as a noumenal being. While the Understanding is in touch with merely phenomenal objects, Practical Reason is in touch with the noumena. This observation could support ascribing some primacy to Practical Reason. The introduction to the *Third Critique* which maps the "domains of reason," however, poses a major obstacle to a theory of a substantial primacy of Practical Reason that holds that the interests of Reason are satisfied in practical ideals. Kant's mapping of the domains of Reason shows that while Practical Reason autonomously legislates what ought to be and demands that its legislation take effect in the world of sense, the determination of what ought to be does not guarantee that things are as they should be. The execution of the moral decree takes place in the midst of a mechanistic causality which the moral agent neither fully knows nor controls. Furthermore, even if the demands of Practical Reason were in fact spatio-temporally realized, neither Practical Reason nor the Understanding could be aware of it.[18]

These observations will be examined at length in a later chapter of this part. That section will show that the fact that Practical Reason cannot know the realization of its ideals, along with the fact that the Understanding can have no experience of values, directs Kant away from considering either of these as supreme. The Understanding is free in its spontaneous systematization of experience but is limited to the phenomena. Practical Reason is free in its legislation to the will but cannot know the act that proceeds from its willing. Both, from this perspective, are seen as partial. Each requires completion from

---

[17]See Rotenstreich, *Experience and its Systematization*, 121–23; and idem, "Is There a Primacy of Practical Reason?" in Irwin C. Lieb, ed., *Experience, Existence and the Good: Essays in Honor of Paul Weiss* (Carbondale, IL: Southern Illinois University Press, 1961) 247–59.

[18]See especially Kant's discussion in *Religion within the Limits of Reason Alone*, 17, 63, 65, 71.

outside of itself, a completion they cannot supply for each other. It is for these considerations that Kant is led to a position that we can only characterize as the supremacy of contemplation over both practical and scientific concerns. Rather than adopting a supremacy of the practical life, a supremacy that the doctrine of the primacy of Practical Reason seems to imply, Kant shows that the ideals of both science and morality can only be contemplated from the point of view of the spectator who, freed from involvement in their respective interests, reflects on their achievements. Kant suggests therefore an ideal of a contemplative life, an ideal no longer understood as the supremacy of scientia but of reflection.[19]

3.C.1.b. The Second Counterargument

A different interpretation of the doctrine of the primacy of Practical Reason may suggest that Kant intends to establish the internal unity of Reason by demonstrating that theory and praxis are two functions of one faculty, that Practical Reason is pure Reason and hence that Kant has no cause to worry about the internal unity of Reason. Kant's higher ranking of Practical Reason would then be explained in light of his opinion that Practical Reason establishes objects to the empty regulative ideas of the *First Critique*. Along these lines it could be maintained that the faculties of Understanding and of practical reasoning are both instruments of unification and that the ideas which guide them are the same. From this a conclusion might be drawn that science and morality are but two applications of the same faculty. Consequently, no reconciliation is needed.[20] The counterargument, as I see it, would run as follows. Even if there were

---

[19]A similar understanding of Kant's position regarding the supremacy of contemplation can be found in Ernst Cassirer, *Kant's Life and Thought* (trans. James Haden; New Haven: Yale University Press, 1981); and in Hannah Arendt, *Lectures on Kant's Political Philosophy* (ed. Robert Beiner; Chicago: University of Chicago Press, 1982), esp. lectures 8–10.

[20]The main threads of such an argument can be found in Beck, *A Commentary on Kant's Critique of Practical Reason* 47–51. Beck acknowledges that the argument is problematic, but claims that we can find a solution to the problems in Kant's text.

a problem in the fact that in its distinct applications Reason legislates two different laws, Kant rather easily overcomes a suspicion of a split in reason.

If we regard the moral law as necessary, objective, internally consistent, and binding, and if we maintain that the objectivity and the necessity of the law are not grounded in the same source that grounds the objectivity of the laws of nature and of science, then the unity of Reason is threatened. In order to overcome this suspicion and to demonstrate the essential unity of reason, Kant would have to show that far from there being an opposition between Theoretical and Practical Reason, there is but one Reason that carries out the same function in two different applications.

Kant then has to establish two points: The first point is that Reason functions similarly in the realms of nature and of ethics. To demonstrate this it can be argued that in both its employments Reason's function is the same: to unify, integrate, systematize, and universalize; and that in this activity Reason is driven by its demand to find the "unconditioned condition for all conditions." The second point is that in both realms the unconditioned condition sought for is the same. This can be substantiated by pointing out that in the *Second Critique* Kant argued that he was able to establish the objective reality of the regulative but empty ideas of the *First Critique*. The main thrust of this argument is as follows. In experience Reason's demand to find complete unity cannot be met because of the limitations of discursive thinking and because of Reason's dependence on experience. This unrealized demand leads to theoretical speculations about an unconditional thing-in-itself, an unconditioned substance, and an unconditioned cause. In the theoretical realm, however, the Ideas used for the purpose of unity are only regulative and provide mere maxims for the conduct of inquiry without determining its outcome or being necessary (for inquiry itself is not necessary). These Ideas are only assumptions, not cognitions, and no theoretical conclusions can be drawn from the fact that we assume them for the guidance of inquiry. In the *Second Critique* Kant asserts that "through an apodictic practical law, they, (the soul, an intelligible world and the Supreme Being) as necessary conditions of the possibility of that which this law requires to be made an object, acquire objective reality. That is to say, they show by this that they have objects."[21]

Maintaining that the ideas needed by Speculative Reason for its own purpose are the same ideas needed by Practical Reason, it could be concluded that the unity of Reason is not threatened and that there is no need for a third, reconciling principle. I do not think that this is the case.

3.C.1.B.(1) Examining this twofold argument I conclude that neither of its parts properly addresses our dilemma and consequently that the problem of conflicting interests continues to demand solution. Let us focus now on the first part of the argument. If it is maintained that Kant does not have to establish the unity of Theoretical and Practical Reason since he presents both as unifying and synthesizing faculties, I shall argue that this formal similarity will not suffice to prevent oscillations between the two concrete ways in which these unifying activities proceed. To illustrate the dilemma confronting a person who needs to decide upon which course of conduct to embark, the ethical or the theoretical, let us imagine such a person standing in front of a filing cabinet each drawer of which is organized according to a different method. The files in one drawer are organized alphabetically, in another they are organized according to their size, and in yet another drawer the files are organized according to their colors. Knowing that ultimately all my files are organized does not help when I need to find a specific file. To work efficiently, I need to know more than that all my files are organized according to various systems. I need specific indications as to which drawer to open when I need a specific file; I need to know how to use them all.

To unite the faculties of Reason into a unified personality, into a unified and harmonious way of life, I need to know more than just the fact that the faculties are all synthesizing and unifying functions. I need more specific guidelines as to how to coordinate their employment. Even if I acknowledge that each activity of Reason is driven by a desire to unify, I still confront a variety of particular options, each guided by different criteria. In order to complete its task of unification Reason has to be able to unify itself, to unite the various modes

[21]Kant, *Critique of Practical Reason*, 140/135.

of unity into an integrated personality. We need to be able to point to a concrete common denominator that will provide concrete guidelines for conduct, a principle of unifying the various modes of unification.

Kant does not just assert that in each realm of activity Reason's goal is unity. Kant aims to indicate the specific principles that guide these activities. Similarly, confronting the variety of modes of unification, Kant needs to indicate a specific principle of unifying and integrating the different modes by which Reason operates to unify. He needs to define and to give concrete content to the superior principle that would integrate the particular principles of the different functions of reason.

3.C.1.b.(2) Focusing now on the second part of the argument, I would like to maintain that the claim that there is no opposition between Theoretical and Practical Reason since there is only one Reason that carries out the same function in two different applications—this function being to search out the unconditioned conditions—and that ultimately the Ideas needed by Speculative Reason for its own purpose are the same as those needed by pure Practical Reason does not address a serious problem in Kant to which I want to turn our attention. Even if we grant, for the sake of the argument, the alleged identity of the regulative ideas, we still have to confront the implications of the fact that these ideas regulate two distinct activities the corresponding interests of which are, I propose, in conflict.

Consider the following difference. Choosing a path leading to "God," guided by belief in radical determinism, you develop a personality that is quite different from the personality you would have developed had you embarked on a route the underlying guideline of which is an uncompromising belief in radical freedom. Consequently it cannot be alleged that since ultimately all the roads lead to the same end, the choice between two different courses of conduct is inconsequential and unimportant. To argue that since in its two functions it is guided by the same ideas, Reason is a united faculty whose functions do not oppose each other or conflict, you have to prove that the implications of choosing either route are the same. If we look at Kant's text that discusses a similar problem of deriving distinct principles from one source, we realize that Kant himself is aware of the problems involved.

In his *Grounding for the Metaphysics of Morals* Kant presents several formulations of the Categorical Imperative. Since all are formulations of the supreme law of ethics, Kant insists that the same laws can be derived from any formulation. Even if we grant Kant the equivalence of the formulations, that the same particular laws can be derived from the formula of the "End in Itself" and from the formula of "Universal Law," it is quite obvious that the character of a person guided by the first formulation of the law will differ significantly from that of a person guided by the second formulation. The moral disposition, the moral struggle undertaken by a person who respects other humans as ends in themselves will differ considerably from that of a person who calculates his maxims in his striving to universalize them. In the first course of action we have in mind humans whose dignity is of utmost importance to us; in the second we have our own rationality in mind, guided by the abstract law of universalization. It seems to me that Kant's awareness of this crucial difference brings him to synthesize both formulations in the formula of the "Kingdom of Ends." This formula brings the interests of a systematic rationality of the will to apply to all humans considered as ends.[22] Similarly, I want to argue, once the differences in interests of Reason's distinct faculties are acknowledged, Kant realizes that a third principle is needed to ground the two interests and to facilitate an uninterrupted employment of reason.

3.C.2. Does the *Second Critique* Solve the Problem?

It may be possible to consider the theory of religion that Kant develops in the *Second Critique* as an elaboration of what he had in mind as he called for unity. Kant argues that as Pure Reason, Prac-

---

[22]This interpretation follows Herbert James Paton's excellent discussion of the relations between the formulations of the Categorical Imperative, their derivation from each other, and the necessity so to derive them—Kant's insistence on the strict equivalence of the formulae notwithstanding. See Herbert James Paton, *The Categorical Imperative* (1st ed.; Philadelphia: University of Pennsylvania Press, 1971) 185–98.

tical Reason seeks the unconditioned condition for its decisions in the quest for the Highest Good, the totality of the object of morality. Kant argues, we recall (see 2.C.2.b.), that we are commanded by Reason to seek to realize the Highest Good, so that if the Highest Good were not possible, the moral law would be null and void. To rescue morality Kant argues that the *possibility* of the Highest Good is established when we *assume* (postulate) that there is an intelligible world governed by a moral being with the power to administer happiness in accordance with virtue.

Examining this contention from the perspective of our current concern we might think that therein lies the core of Kant's solution. This hypothesis recommends itself particularly because of Kant's language. Let us examine the following assertion:

> Therefore it cannot be a matter of unconcern to morality as to whether or not it forms for itself the concept of a final end of all things (harmony with which, while not multiplying men's duties, yet provides them with a special point of focus for the unification of all ends); for only thereby can objective, practical reality be given to the *union of the purposiveness* arising from freedom with the purposiveness of nature, *a union with which we cannot possibly dispense.*[23]

The argument could proceed as follows. Kant acknowledges that Reason is ever restless in its quest for an ultimate unity. Reason is unable to acquiesce in the apprehension of a world that is indifferent to our moral judgments or to laws of duty that appear to prescribe courses of action that, under the conditions of the laws of nature, cannot hope to succeed in achieving their objects. The unity of the moral and the natural spheres could not be established by Theoretical Reason, but it may be apprehended by moral faith. Rational faith in a supreme being who will harmonize the kingdom of nature and the kingdom of freedom provides us with the principle that grounds the reconciliation

---

[23]Kant, *Religion within the Limits of Reason Alone*, 5. Emphasis mine.

between the conflicting ideals or interests of Theoretical and Practical Reason and thus satisfies the quest for an ultimate unity.[24]

This theory is certainly interesting. When we examine it from the viewpoint of our interpretation of Kant's dilemma, however, we have to conclude that it does not provide a satisfactory solution. Two arguments can be advanced to support this conclusion. The first refers to Kant's discussion of the restriction of belief to the realm of morality, the second to his discussion of the nature of morality.

3.C.2.a.

Kant maintains that without (justified) hope in our ability to realize the ends of Practical Reason in the realm of natural contingencies, we shall find it very difficult to act morally. If, however, we seriously attempt to carry out the decrees of the moral law, trusting that our efforts are not in vain and will somehow succeed, this trust of ours should be understood as practical belief in God. The question we must then ask is what exactly belief in God is supposed to do for a person who faces a situation of conflicting interests.

Kant does his best to convince us that the concept of "God" has no theoretical application. It is given substance only in the context of deliberation about what we ought to do. It is true that Kant often makes assertions that go beyond these subtle distinctions. Admittedly, Kant asserts that due to the context of practical deliberations there is "an extension of theoretical reason and of its knowledge with respect to the supersensuous in general, inasmuch as knowledge is compelled to concede that there are such objects."[25] Kant, however, hastens to qualify this bold claim, saying, "without more defining them, and thus without being able to extend this knowledge of objects given to it *only on practical grounds and only for practical use.*"[26]

The main thrust of this argument is that even if theoretical knowledge is "justified in assuming" the concept of "God" because "prac-

---

[24]I read Clement Charles Julian Webb's *Kant's Philosophy of Religion* (Oxford: Clarendon, 1926) and Kroner's *Kant's Weltanschauung* as advancing this theory.

[25]Kant, *Critique of Practical Reason*, 140/135.

[26]Ibid.; I would especially emphasize "only for practical use."

tical reason inexorably requires the existence of these objects for the possibility of its practically and absolutely necessary object, the highest good," "this extension of the theoretical reason. . . is not an extension of speculation. That is, *a positive use cannot be made of those objects for theoretical purposes.*"[27] The implication of this discussion for our dilemma is that for theory the existence of God is not a fact at all. "God" is merely the object of a regulative idea. The claim "God exists" gets its meaning from deliberation about how things ought to be. It has nothing to do with the way the world is. Belief in God is inexorably bound with action; it expresses a practical attitude and is meaningless outside of deliberation.

People who confront our dilemma and consider whether this theory of "religion as unity" is useful or not must ask what difference postulating God's existence can make for them. Taking Kant's admonitions seriously, one cannot ask *how* God operates, since that is a speculative question ruled out by the *First Critique*. God, the rationality of a belief in whom was established, was not meant to solve theoretical puzzles. If talk about God is to make sense, it must do so within the context of action. Consequently, the only answer provided by this theory is that such postulation enables us to feel confident that our *moral effort* will not be in vain. Thus, examining the theory of "religion as unity" in light of the preceding deliberation, we have to conclude that it does not suffice to solve our problem.

Examining the content of the solution, its promise of hope, we must realize that the problem of a person oscillating between two conflicting interests demands a solution here and now (i.e., some concrete guidelines for conduct in the present) and hence cannot be solved by the thought of some utopia in which everything is as it should be.

If we examine the logical status of the solution we have to admit that a postulate that we are justified in holding within the framework of one point of view cannot function as a principle from which "everything should be derived." The validity of this postulate depends on the adoption of one of the two points of views in conflict. When a conflict of interests arises we need an "impartial moderator," a prin-

---

[27]Ibid., 139/134. Emphasis mine.

ciple the justification of which does not depend on the adoption of one of the viewpoints in conflict. We have to conclude that a postulate that depends on one point of view cannot be our principle. We need a third principle, higher in its degree of abstraction, that will be able to reconcile the differences in interests. We end our discussion with the conclusion that the idea of harmony between kingdoms does not fulfill the expectation of "bringing some day into one view the unity of the entire pure rational faculty (both theoretical and practical) and of being able to derive everything from one principle."

3.C.2.b.

When we examine the possible consequences for morality of making the Highest Good our supreme principle we have to conclude that instead of reconciling science and ethics, this will abolish morality. Two arguments will show this point from different perspectives.

3.C.2.b.(1) Let us examine our problem again. We acknowledge the fact that the respective interests of theoretical knowledge and of ethics can conflict. To restore harmony, we are looking for a third principle that can unite these interests. Kant argues that we need a third principle from which to *"derive* everything." Our question is: Can it be argued, within the context of Kant's theory, that morality can be derived from the concept of the Highest Good? Can this concept serve as the ground of morality? Undoubtedly, once we focus on this aspect of the alleged solution to the problem of "unity," the answer is unmistakably in the negative. If we take the Highest Good as our supreme principle from which morality is to be derived, and which consequently can guide our oscillation between the corresponding interests of ethics and science, morality will in fact be destroyed.

According to Kant, the Highest Good, and especially proportional happiness, should *never* be the determining ground of the moral will. Happiness is the object of the inclinations, and to elevate it to the status of a supreme principle, from which the principle of ethics is derived, will transform Kant's deontic morality into consequentialism. Accordingly Kant tells us that although ethics leads to religion, the latter should not be made the ground of the former. The hope for the Highest Good may be a necessary incentive to do that which duty prescribes but which in itself duty cannot move humans to execute.

Establishing the hope for the Highest Good as the determining ground of conduct, however, will abolish autonomy.

3.C.2.b.(2) A similar rejection of this solution can be reached when we illuminate the case from a slightly different angle. Kant seems to argue that humans who acknowledge the binding force of the moral law need some promise that hostile nature will not sabotage their attempts to execute the legislation of Practical Reason. To rescue moral agents from such threatening paralysis, Kant suggests, humans can justifiably postulate the help of a benevolent and powerful "Supreme Being" who will cooperate with them in bringing about the "Kingdom of God." Granting for the moment that this proposition is valid, we must nevertheless notice that there is a difference between postulating the Highest Good in order to bolster the moral activity and making this postulate the ground of this activity. When the hope for proportional happiness is introduced into one's considerations, the conflict between inclinations and duty, a conflict which is the core and essence of morality, dissipates. Instead of executing the legislation of Practical Reason out of respect for the law, humans can still act according to the law, but they will do so because they follow their inclinations, their expectations for proportional happiness. This hope may be necessary as an end or goal of the moral action, but it cannot be its supreme principle. Thus, for all the above reasons, we have to dismiss as insufficient the suggestion that Kant's official discussion of religion provides a solution for our dilemma. In the following chapters I shall argue that the *Critique of Judgment* reopens the discussion of the Highest Good. This time, the foundations for this concept are laid jointly by physical teleology and moral teleology. As a reflective principle the Highest Good no longer threatens the autonomy of morality, but instead suggests itself as an interesting solution to the problem of unity.

4 ⊠

THE UNITY OF REASON

▰ 4.A. The Quest for Unity in the Introduction to the *Critique of Judgment*

We have thus far discussed the contest between Practical Reason and Understanding as a conflict between their respective interests and learned that the desired solution must reconcile the two without infringing upon their autonomy. The present chapter will continue to show that Kant considered the problem of unity inherent to the critical project and believed that conclusion of his critical investigation of our cognitive powers requires its resolution. Accordingly, I shall argue, the *Critique of Judgment* should be understood as an integrated work devoted to establishment of the unity of Reason.[1] My argument

---

[1]It is sometimes argued that the *Third Critique* is a collection of loosely related discussions. For example, William Henry Walsh argues ("Kant," *Encyclopedia of Philosophy* 3–4 [1967] 319) that "the *Critique of Judgment* contains some fresh ideas of remarkable power, but it constitutes a series of appendixes or addenda to Kant's earlier work rather than something wholly new. It should be seen as three or four separate essays whose connecting link

is that in the *Critique of Judgment* Kant refocuses attention on the problem as he addresses a fundamental question regarding the possibility of a moral act.[2] I demonstrate that the quest for unity culminates in the concept of the Highest Good, which the *Third Critique* considers a reflective principle. My introduction to this chapter will provide an overview of the problem and Kant's method of solving it. I shall do so through an analysis of the Introduction to the *Third Critique*.[3] Kant's Introduction is a very dense text, laden with "faculty language" and allusions to a "supersensible substrate" ("übersinnliches Substrat") of reality. These factors may be the reason for the unfavorable treatment it has sometimes received.[4] In fact, however, the In-

---

is the concept of purpose." Having noticed that the *Third Critique* is a sustained argument to establish the unity of Reason, I was surprised to see almost no attention to this argument in the various commentaries. As we proceed, I shall suggest that Otto and Tillich understood that the subject of the book is the unity of Reason, as did Jakob Fries. I was glad to find a similar understanding of the purpose of the book—although never a systematic interpretation of the structure of the argument or of Kant's solution—in Wilhelm Windelband, *Renaissance, Enlightenment and Modern, A History of Philosophy* (New York: Harper & Row, 1958); Cassirer, *Kant's Life and Thought*; Lewis White Beck, "Editor's Introductions" to *Kant: Selections* (ed. Lewis White Beck; Great Philosophers Series; New York: Macmillan, 1988) 331–34; James Hoyden Tufts, *The Sources and Development of Kant's Teleology* (Chicago: University of Chicago Press, 1892).

[2]The reader should notice that at issue is a possibility of actions, not of decisions. The possibility of the moral will was established in the *Critique of Practical Reason*. In the *Critique of Judgment* Kant addresses the further issue of the execution of the moral decree in the natural world. This is a problem that many Kantian ethicists fail to recognize. I elaborate on this issue in section 4.A.1 below.

[3]My analysis focuses on Kant's second Introduction (the one he chose to publish). This version is better written than the first; it is shorter and omits nothing of substance.

[4]John D. McFarland's widely quoted commentary on the second part of the *Third Critique* (*Kant's Concept of Teleology* [Edinburgh: University of Edinburgh Press, 1970]) is an example of such reservations. Commenting on the Introduction, he writes, "I can think of no passage of comparable length in the Kantian corpus which is more thoroughly architectonic and riddled with faculty-talk than the Introduction to the *Critique of Judgment*. For much of the time Kant seems to be interested in little else than making neat divisions

troduction provides a concise statement of Kant's understanding of the problem of unity and its required solution.

4.A.1. Introduction

Kant reintroduces the problem of unity as he discusses the problem of the possibility of moral acts. To understand this problem we need to recall that all spatio-temporal events, including our bodily movements, are necessarily governed by causal laws according to the a priori legislation of the categories of the Understanding. Kant has shown that this must be the case in the famous transcendental deduction of the *First Critique*. The *Grounding* and the *Second Critique*, in which Kant's moral theory is developed, are concerned with showing that a moral decision is possible and that beyond the psychosomatic influence of natural inclinations on the will there is also a possibility of a motivation of the will by the legislation of Reason.

To clarify my argument I need to emphasize here that Kant's project in these works is misunderstood if it is taken to be trying to show that moral *action* is possible.[5] Its goal is much more limited. It aims

---

among mental and cognitive faculties, assigning principles to them, and setting out the areas of experience within which the principles apply" (p. 70). Consequently, McFarland does not think that in commenting on the book he can gain "any great value" from a detailed examination of the "architectonic division" of the Introduction (ibid.). I suspect that the reservations with which the Introduction was received prevented many good scholars from appreciating its real topic, the unity of Reason.

[5]Whoever misunderstands Kant's task to be to prove that free action is possible will have to play down the significance of the opening argument of the *Grounding* concerning the good will as the only good in itself, defending it from any unintended failure of realization. Doing so one can only be disappointed with the proof of the third section that the will must necessarily regard itself as free, for this argument implies nothing about the possibility of free spatio-temporal actions. The distinction is necessary for Kant's project, and he draws it explicitly in *Religion within the Limits of Reason Alone*: "The term 'act' can apply in general to that exercise of freedom whereby the supreme maxim (in harmony with the law or contrary to it) is adopted by the will (*Willkür*), but also to the exercise of freedom whereby the actions themselves (considered materially, i.e., with reference to the objects of volition [*Willkür*]) are performed in accordance with that maxim" (pp. 26–27). Kant distinguishes accordingly between "intelligible action, cognizable by means of pure reason alone," and "sensible, action, empirical, given in time" (ibid.).

to show that *a good will* is possible. Naturally, a good will is a will that not only decides well but also strives to realize its decisions. The question of the realization of the decision of the good will, however, is beyond the scope of the *Critique of Practical Reason*. While theoretical knowledge necessarily leaves no room for spontaneous interventions of a noumenal will in the scheme of nature, Practical Reason can merely legislate to the will but can never know that its goal is realized; it has no knowledge of the phenomenon. Unable to admit teleological causes into scientific method, the Understanding is limited to causal explanations of human acts and cannot identify moral acts as such. This dual limitation of the faculties of Reason calls into question the possibility of our ever knowing that a moral act was performed.[6] It is not only that we cannot know if our motives in acting were not merely according to the moral law but out of respect for it; we cannot even know if a free will was effective in bringing an event about.[7] Our moral life, however, evidently involves a recognition that moral acts, worthy and vicious, do take place. This recognition is essential to our understanding of ourselves as moral agents responsible for our actions. From our preceding discussion it should be clear that neither Theoretical nor Practical Reason can account for this central recognition; to account for it is a task Kant sets himself in the *Critique of Judgment*. He can only achieve this task, as he clearly says, by establishing a fundamental unity of the faculties of Reason or, in other words, by discovering the transcendental unity of the realms of freedom and nature.

We need to emphasize again that the problem that defines the task of a critique of Judgment arises from morality but cannot be answered within morality or within natural science. It is not a moral problem but a problem of morality as such. It addresses not the proper questions of morality as defined in the *Second Critique* and in the *Grounding*, questions concerning what I ought to decide to do, but questions concerning whether it is possible to say that moral decisions are in fact realized. It is a problem that can only be answered,

[6]Kant discusses the necessity to limit knowledge for the sake of morality at the end of the *Second Critique*. I discussed this issue in a previous subsection (3.C.2.b.2.)

[7] See Kant, *Religion within the Limits of Reason Alone*, 17, 63, 65, 71.

as Kant will argue, through a teleological conception of the totality of nature which involves a philosophy of history. In other words, the problem of morality can only be solved from the point of view of a conception of the end of history in light of the rational Ideal of the Highest Good and the postulate of a divine agent who designed nature according to this principle. The problem of the unity of Reason which is identified in the problem of the moral act finds its solution in what I venture to call, with the theologians whose work this volume studies, a religious domain of Reason.[8]

The question of the goal of history and the possibility of worthy human existence, questions which explicate the third of Kant's three great questions in the *First Critique*—what can I know, what ought I to do, and what may I hope for—are traditionally the questions that religion seeks to address. It is therefore fitting to designate the realm in which these Kantian questions find their solution the realm of religion. This as I shall argue in later chapters, was the fundamental Kantian insight that major theologians like Otto and Tillich developed in their theories of religion. It is because of this factor at least that Kant should be seen, perhaps against his will, as the forefather of liberal theology.

4.A.2. Reflective Judgment

Kant hedges when discussing the problem of unity in the Third Critique. His solution is therefore never quite conclusive and straightforward. Nevertheless, from his various partial attempts to address the issue it is possible to recognize the solution he never refined.[9] To

---

[8]It already becomes clear from these brief remarks that, as the unifying domain of Reason, religion exists on the basis of the achievements of the Understanding and Practical Reason. Its only object is to bring them into harmony in light of its contemplation of a structure of reality that transcends them but to which they are ultimately attuned. It is from these Kantian Ideas, I presume, that Jakob Fries and Leonard Nelson concluded that the religious life is based on science and morality and can never be divorced from them without becoming thereby a superstitious fanaticism.

[9]This section concisely presents the problem of unity, as Kant presents it, and outlines the structure of Kant's solution. Further elaboration will follow in the subsequent sections.

reconcile the opposition between natural determinism and freedom, without surrendering either, the *Critique of Judgment* presents a new realm of judgments, distinct from the theoretical as well as the practical. The concept of purposiveness, a concept that indicates a harmonious interplay and interdependence of the parts of the whole, is presented by Kant as the link between the practical and the theoretical. Implicit in this suggestion is the recognition that the problem of mediation cannot be solved by insertion of a third domain between nature and freedom. The solution is to be found in a type of contemplation[10] that participates equally in the principle of empirical explanation and the principle of ethical judgment.[11] Kant asserts that "judgment will bring about a transition from the pure cognitive power, i.e., from the domain of the concepts of nature to the domain of the concept of freedom, just as in its logical use it makes possible the transition from understanding to reason."[12]

Kant presents the faculty of Judgment as a third faculty of the mind which links Reason, the faculty that legislates to the faculty of desire through the moral law, and Understanding, the faculty that legislates for empirical cognition in providing natural law.[13] Kant proposes that as both Reason and Understanding have a priori functions, it is plausible to assume that there may be a priori principles to the faculty of Judgment too. Beside the triad of cognitive faculties (Reason, Understanding, Judgment) Kant recognizes a triad of mental faculties in general: cognition, desire, and feeling. Thinking analogically, Kant suggests that we find here more than a mere formal parallelism and argues that judgment and feeling are closely related. If so, there may be an a priori condition for the determination of feeling. This condition will be the concept of purposiveness.

---

[10]The term "contemplative" (*kontemplativ*) is used in the sense Kant gives it as a thought that is indifferent to the existence of its object. It considers only the character of the object as we come to think of it. The nature of contemplative thought will be clarified later on in our discussion.

[11]I show in the second part of this study the important role that this insight played in Tillich's theology.

[12]Kant, *Critique of Judgment*, 18/179.

[13]In the *Third Critique* Kant tends to use the term "Reason" to refer to the faculty that, in the *Second Critique*, he called "Practical Reason."

Kant proposes that in science, especially in biology, it is necessary to make use of the concept of purpose in the discovery of mechanical causes themselves. Likewise, in thinking of moral actions and historical events we need to employ the concept of final end (purpose), otherwise we would be unable to see unity and systematization in this domain. The *Critique of Practical Reason* and the *Grounding* have already taught us that only one thing, a moral agent, can be thought of as an end in itself. Accordingly Kant contends that the final purpose of the world, that which is an end and should not be merely a means, is humans who see themselves obligated to pursue the Highest Good, a concept that unites the lawfulness of nature and the purposiveness of freedom. Armed with this contemplative principle, humans can interpret the world itself as the stage for moral evolution and not just as the scene of blind mechanical causality. All these issues will be further explored below.

Kant studies the faculty of Reflective Judgment and its contribution to the solution of the problem of unity through discussions of three distinct topics: the universality of aesthetic judgment, the unity of empirical laws of nature, and the method of biology. All three discussions conclude with an allusion to a contemplative idea of a supernatural substrate of reality that bridges the gap between freedom and nature. In order to understand Kant's solution we shall detour briefly, in subsequent sections devoted to these discussions, for a concise examination of these issues. Due to the limits of this study I shall not examine all the aspects of Kant's argument.[14] My limited goal is to demonstrate that the underlying common denominator of these discussions is the search for a unifying principle for the realms of freedom and nature and that Kant's suggested solution is the contemplative principle of a moral designer of the universe whose design

---

[14]Extensive literature has been devoted to critical evaluation of many of Kant's specific arguments in these sections. For the sake of brevity I shall not assess the validity of these arguments one by one. I shall focus instead on the general structure and overarching goal of Kant's argument, which have generally been overlooked. Occasionally, however, I shall devote some space to exegesis of arguments that were neglected by the commentators and that I find crucial for the development of the overarching argument of the *Third Critique.*

is guided by the idea of the Highest Good.[15] I shall argue that Kant's search for unity culminates in religion. His discussion of religion, however, is at best partial. I suggest that Kant's deep suspicion of positive religion prevented him from conducting a systematic critique of religion, even though he recognized the theological significance of his solution.

Before proceeding with our exposition let us recapitulate the structure of our central argument. In the introduction to the *Third Critique* Kant tackles the problem of the unity of the practical and the theoretical by indicating that this is a problem inherent in Reason itself. The problem, which defines the task of a critique of Judgment, arises from morality but can be answered neither within morality nor within natural science. The *Third Critique* sets out to confront questions concerning whether it is possible to say that moral decisions are in fact realized. My argument is that Kant sees this as a problem that can be answered only with a teleological principle, from the point of view of a conception of the end of history in light of the rational Ideal of the Highest Good. The problem of the unity of Reason, which is identified in the problem of the moral act, finds its solution in religion.

4.A.3. The Problem of Unity in Sections Two and Nine of the Introduction

Kant states the problem first in section two of the Introduction, entitled "On the Domain of Philosophy in General" and then in section nine entitled "How Judgment Connects the Legislations of the Understanding and of Reason." Kant presents the problem through a metaphor of government, which he takes from political science. The subject is the realm of philosophy in general, including all that can be thought, imagined, desired, etc., whether it exists or not, whether it

---

[15]As I mentioned earlier, many do not read the *Third Critique* as a systematic work. Instead they see it as an aggregate of three loosely related discussions. It is my view that their difficulty results from a failure to notice that the one overarching concern of the *Critique* is to address the problem of the unity of Reason. It is this concern that supplies the common thread of systematic unity to this book.

can be known or not. Within this unlimited realm there is a region in which cognition is possible for us. This includes all that can be known, a priori and a posteriori. This region of all that can be possibly known is called by Kant the "territory (*Boden*) of philosophy." I believe that Kant intends to include here both theoretical and practical cognition; unfortunately he does not specify it. Within the territory of philosophy there is a more limited region in which Reason has legislative authority. Kant calls this region the "domain (*Gebiet*) of thought." This is the area in which a priori cognition is possible. Using this metaphor, Kant explains that our cognition has two domains: the domain of the concepts of nature and the domain of the concepts of freedom. Both are domains because Reason in its twofold function as theoretical and practical legislates in them a priori. Legislation by the Understanding through the concept of nature is theoretical. Legislation through the concept of freedom is practical.[16]

This metaphorical description should suffice to alert us to a possibility of conflict between two legislators. Kant draws from it the conclusion that the Understanding and Practical Reason behave as two distinct sovereigns legislating to the same territory of experience. The ensuing problem is twofold: first is the problem of the unity of Reason itself, second is the conflict in the effects of the separate legislative acts. Kant comments here that the first problem, understood as the coexistence of two a priori powers of legislation in the same subject, has already been dealt with in the Third Antinomy of the *Critique of Pure Reason*. The preliminary conclusion of that discussion was that "it is possible at least to think without contradiction"[17] of the coexistence of the two. A contradiction between them is avoided insofar as the subject keeps them absolutely apart, legislating once according to the one and then according to the other. The theoretical self and the practical self can coexist as long as they never meet. This is possible since "for just as the concept of nature has no influence on the legislation through the concept of freedom, so the

[16]It is interesting to note here that Kant says of this legislation of Reason that it is "*merely* practical," an emphasis that I understand to exclude any possibility of upholding the primacy of Practical Reason as the solution to the problem of unity.

[17]Kant, *Critique of Judgment*, 13/175.

latter does not interfere with the legislation of nature."[18] We must comment that this solution is at best partial, for while it prevents an internal contradiction in the subject, it does not secure its unity. This in fact is the problem dealt with in chapter three of this part.

The conflict reemerges however in the outcome of the distinct legislating acts. If the two legislative acts do not contradict each other in themselves, they are still two different legislators ruling "one and the same territory of experience."[19] Both nature and freedom determine what is to occur in the world of sense. Since this discussion of unity is usually ignored by Kant's commentators I quote it at length:

> The understanding legislates a priori for nature, as object of sense, in order to give rise to theoretical cognition of nature in a possible experience, Reason legislates a priori for freedom and for freedom's own causality, in other words, for the supersensible in the subject, in order to give rise to unconditioned practical cognition. The great gulf that separates the supersensible from appearances completely cuts off the domain of the concept of nature under the one legislation, and the domain of the concept of freedom under the other legislation, from any influence that each (according to its own basic laws) might have had on the other. The concept of freedom determines nothing with regard to our theoretical cognition of nature, just as the concept of nature determines nothing with regard to the practical laws of freedom; and to this extent it is not possible to throw a bridge from one domain to the other. And yet, even though the bases that determine the causality governed by the concept of freedom (and by the practical rule contained in this concept) do not lie in nature, and even though the sensible cannot determine the supersensible in the subject, yet the reverse is possible (not, indeed, with regard to our cognition of nature, but still with regard to the consequences that the concept of freedom has in nature); and this possibility is contained in the very concept of a causality through freedom, whose *effect* is to be brought about in the world [but] in conformity with formal laws of freedom. It is true that when

[18]See the Third Antinomy in Immanuel Kant, *Critique of Pure Reason* (trans. N. K. Smith; New York: St. Martin's Press, 1965) 409–15/A444–51=B472–79, and its solution (464–79/A532–58=B560–86). For the German edition, see idem, *Kritik der reinen Vernunft* (1st ed., 1781; 2d ed., 1787).

[19]See Kant, *Critique of Judgment*, 13/175.

we use the word *cause* with regard to the supersensible, we mean only the *basis* that determines natural things to exercise their causality to produce an effect in conformity with the natural laws proper to that causality, yet in accordance with the formal principle of the laws of Reason as well. Though we have no insight into how this is possible, the objection that alleges a contradiction in it can be refuted adequately. The effect [at which we are to aim] according to the concept of freedom is the final purpose which (or the appearance of which in the world of sense) ought to exist; and we [must] presuppose the condition under which it is possible [to achieve] this final purpose in nature (in the nature of the subject as a being of sense, namely, as a human being).[20]

The conflict on the level of the effects of the distinct acts of a priori legislation can be understood quite easily if we consider the nature of a moral act. The supreme laws according to which a moral decision is to occur are determined freely by Practical Reason (this is the subject of the *Second Critique* and the *Grounding*), but the moral act itself must be performed by a spatio-temporal agent acting in the world of sense under the a priori concept of (deterministic) nature. If a moral act can be possible, it must be possible as a natural event determined by the causal laws of nature which recognize no moral ends. The reality of our experience of moral acts makes it necessary to inquire whether it is possible to conceive of some unity between nature and freedom, a unity in which the autonomy of both will be preserved.

It must be realized that if it were possible for Practical Reason, of itself, to bring about a moral act, this act would of necessity be viewed from the point of view of the Understanding as a miracle, an inexplicable event that violates the a priori legislation according to the concept of nature. Conversely, if an act is naturally realizable, it must have sufficient natural causes, and it is impossible to see how the laws of freedom could intervene with the conduct of nature. Insofar as freedom and nature are kept apart to prevent internal contradictions, no moral act seems possible. If it is possible to think of any

[20]Ibid., 35–36/195–96.

act as a moral act, and this must be possible if moral duty is to have any real validity, then, Kant says, "it must be possible to think of nature as being such that the lawfulness in its form will harmonize with at least the possibility of achieving the purposes that we are to achieve in nature according to the laws of freedom."[21]

It is important to notice what Kant sets as the goal of his ensuing study, namely, to show a possibility, a possibility to think, not to know. What the *Critique of Judgment* has to show, if it is to solve the problem of unity just depicted, is that it is at least possible to think of nature as in harmony with freedom. The task is neither theoretical nor practical, but contemplative. It is to show that there is a perspective from which we can think of nature as teleological.

Throughout the *Third Critique* Kant repeatedly refers to the supersensible. He says that "an immense gulf is fixed between the domain of the concept of nature, the sensible, and the domain of the concept of freedom, the supersensible,"[22] and argues that the problem is to show that a harmony between them can nevertheless be thought. His suggestion is that there must be a common basis that unites "the supersensible that underlies nature and the supersensible that the concept of freedom contains practically."[23] It will be noted that there is no appeal here to a supersensible that unites the two supersensibles. It is precisely the unity between them that is Kant's quest. The *Third Critique* will have to show how a unity between two distinct transcendental grounds for the distinct applications of Reason can be thought.

In my interpretation I shall try to explain how Kant thinks this can be achieved. I shall argue that when Kant seeks "a basis uniting the supersensible that underlies nature and the supersensible that the concept of freedom contains practically, even though the concept of this basis does not reach cognition of it either theoretically or practically. . . though it does make possible the transition from our way of thinking in terms of principles of nature to our way of thinking in

---

[21]Ibid., 15/176.
[22]Ibid., 14/175.
[23]Ibid., 15/176.

terms of principles of freedom,"[24] this basis will be found in the reflective concept of the Highest Good. It is crucial to emphasize that the solution is not achieved from the point of view of the divine designer who is responsible for the realization of the Highest Good in history. This would not be a solution from any perspective that is humanly possible. As I see it, the solution is achieved from the point of view of Reflective Judgment that sees the Highest Good as the uniting principle of nature and freedom. According to my interpretation the solution is achieved within Reflective Judgment and the faith that it involves (as a postulate) remains within Reason.

In interpreting Kant's solution it is important to avoid a mistaken reading that would ascribe to him the argument that the problem of unity is solved only in the supersensible.[25] Kant's language lends itself at times to such interpretation. Had this been the argument, however, his solution would have been far from satisfactory. Kant would be interpreted as arguing that it is from God's point of view that necessity and freedom become one, that the distinction between "is" and "ought" is dissolved and that the opposition of nature and freedom is resolved. It should be noticed immediately that this is not a perspective that we can inhabit, but believing in its existence, as in a postulate of thought, we can rest assured that somehow the conflict is dissolved.

The main disadvantage of such a reading is that it locates unity in the supersensible structure of reality and not in consciousness. Kant's continued references to the supersensible structure of reality may lend themselves to such interpretation, but I believe that in the final analysis they do not support it. I argue that Kant's solution is a solution in Reason on the basis of the rational ideal of the Highest Good. It

---

[24]Ibid.

[25]Werner S. Pluhar's introduction to his translation of the *Third Critique* is an example of such an interpretation. He writes, "As Kant sees it. . . , the three *Critiques* cannot form a system (and thus be scientific), unless not only the mental powers but also those "worlds," especially as they are in themselves, are shown to form a system." See Werner S. Pluhar, "Translator's Introduction," in Kant, *Critique of Judgment*, lxxxviii.

seems to me that if a solution can be found within Reason, supported by Kant's explicit text, it is to be preferred.

Had we believed that the problem of unity of Reason was resolved by Kant through the doctrine of the primacy of Practical Reason, we might have been tempted to interpret the *Third Critique* as trying to proceed beyond that resolution to demonstrate that the world is unified in itself. Assuming that the doctrine of the primacy of Practical Reason solves the problem of the unity of the diverse functions of Reason, we could interpret Kant's argument in the *Third Critique* as striving to show that although the conflict between the "ought" and the "is" is irresolvably real to finite human Reason, it is not impossible for us to believe that there may be another infinite Reason for which the distinction does not exist. In the mind of such an intelligence the supersensibles that underlie nature and morality are united. Accordingly Kant would be read as maintaining that there is inherently no real contradiction between the two modes of legislation of Reason, and the unity of Reason is not threatened.[26]

My objection to this reading is that since it appeals to a unity in the supersensible structure of reality, it is a solution for a divine Reason and not for us. It is hardly any help for a human agent, who decides to act morally and does not know how such an act is possible in the world of nature, to believe that if God were to act nature would automatically obey.

Nowhere in the Introduction does Kant assert the *existence* of the supersensible in which a unity of nature and freedom may be found. Kant is careful to relegate our mere thought of a supersensible to the realm of concepts "which we refer to objects without considering whether or not cognition of these objects is possible."[27] While we are incapable of knowing a supersensible, we are capable of thinking about it. Kant is interested in showing that these thoughts are not necessarily idle speculation, but that a certain minimum is justified as a necessity of the reflection of Reason on its own powers. Insofar as

[26]I have already argued that the unity of Reason is not secured by the primacy of the practical, and it remains for the *Critique of Judgment* to establish it. Once this is granted, we could not seek a further speculative object for the *Third Critique*.

[27]Kant, *Critique of Judgment*, 12–13/174.

our idea of the supersensible acquires justified content, it is sanctioned by what we should think of as a postulate of reflective judgment.

In mapping the functions of Reason, Kant designates the two domains of nature and freedom as independent legislative powers which nevertheless clash as they legislate to the objects of sense. One domain, governed by the concept of nature, is capable of knowing its object in intuition but only as mere appearance. A second domain, governed by the concept of freedom, is capable of presenting its object as a thing in itself but provides no intuition of it. If it were possible for the two to be unified, the result would have been "a theoretical cognition of objects as things in themselves."[28] Neither the concept of nature nor the concept of freedom can secure this knowledge which therefore remains a mere idea. Yet our thought about a supersensible object is not merely a frivolous idea, for it is required as the basis for both the possibility of the objects of appearance and the possibility of the actualization of the purposes of freedom, a requirement that can never become a cognition.

It is in this thought about a supersensible at the basis of nature and of a supersensible at the basis of freedom and in the thought about the possible unity of these ideas of the supersensible that Kant seeks to find the reflective unity of nature and freedom.

> It is judgment that presupposes this condition a priori, and without regard to the practical, [so that] this power provides us with the concepts that mediate between the concepts of nature and the concept of freedom: the concept of a purposiveness of nature, which makes possible the transition from pure theoretical to pure practical lawfulness, from lawfulness in terms of nature to the final purpose set by the concept of freedom. For it is through this concept that we cognize the possibility of [achieving] the final purpose, which can be actualized only in nature and in according with its laws.[29]

[28]Ibid., 14/175.

[29]Ibid., 36–37/196. This language of Kant's arguments should be noted. Kant speaks here of a concept that mediates between the concepts of nature and freedom. This precluded an interpretation that the solution is to be found in the supersensible.

In sum, Kant sought a concept of a basis for this unity, not merely the conditions for its logical possibility. He sought the possibility of contemplating this concept and not the metaphysical commitment that the unity exists for God.

4.A.4. Reference to the Supersensible in Section Nine

In order to understand better Kant's claim that the bridge between nature and freedom is to be found in a reflective reference to the supersensible, we must interpret it in light of his dense explication of the issue in section nine of the Introduction. As I understand it, this section encapsulates the whole theme of the *Third Critique*. We know, from previous discussion, that the Understanding and Reason are incommensurable with regard to their legislation. One legislates to nature, the other to freedom. This is all that we can know, but it is not all that we are aware of. Considering myself a moral agent, I am aware of myself as determining in freedom, what I ought to do. I am also occasionally aware of myself as performing what I had previously decided to do. Considering this awareness in light of the absolute separation between the worlds of freedom and nature, there should be on the one hand knowledge of a rational decision and on the other knowledge that a certain event in which I am involved has occurred. At most, these bits of knowledge could be related by a judgment of Practical Reason that the act is lawful, that it conforms to the moral law. It seems impossible, given the separation, to be aware of the act as performance of a decision. At most we could speculate that the two correspond due to either a preestablished harmony or beneficial chance.

Kant's whole argument depends on the fact that the awareness that the separation of nature and freedom makes seemingly impossible is in fact the awareness we do normally have. We are not normally aware of having decided morally, and then aware that we did something, and finally relate the two as fitting one another (though this too can happen in moments of conscientious self-judgment). We are normally aware that we are doing what we have decided. How then is it possible for us to be so aware? Kant supports his analysis of the necessary conditions of our awareness of our ability to act on free decisions, with an examination of the ultimate conditions of our ability to judge biological entities to be teleologically organized.[30] He suggests that, since freedom and nature do not intervene with each other, the only way in which it can be possible for the one to reflect the other would be if the lawfulness of nature were determined by freedom. While it is impossible for a decision in freedom to intervene in the course of nature and violate its lawfulness, it is possible for the lawfulness of nature to be determined in harmony with the purposiveness of reason.

Let us consider the situation from the point of view of the subject who is aware of having decided and having acted accordingly. As a moral agent the subject determines what ought to be in the world of freedom, and as such is aware of herself as a noumenal being. As a discursive examiner of nature the subject is aware of her act as causally determined in a spatio-temporal world. As students of Kant's *First Critique* we know that the spatio-temporal world, which we organize according to the categories of the Understanding, is merely phenomenal and implies an unspecifiable dependence on a noumenal substrate. In the case of moral action however, we are directly aware of this noumenal substrate that underlies the possibility of our spatio-temporal action; it is the subject as a free being. We therefore also know the rational structure of this noumenal substrate; it is the moral law. We can thus be aware not only of having decided and acted but also that our decision is so ontologically situated as to be the ground of the possibility of the act.

The situation of the subject of both moral decision and moral action provides a model for projecting the relation between Reason and nature as such. Our ability to judge that a biological entity is teleologically organized, regardless of the demand of the Understanding that it be accounted for in terms of purely efficient causes, can only be possible on the basis of an awareness that the scientific account relates to a phenomenal realm, which is in itself dependent in some way on a noumenal substratum, and that its lawfulness reflects a purpose. Our ability to judge that moral actions take place and that biological organisms exist, together with our awareness that natural phenomena

---

[30]Further discussion follows in section 4.D below.

are dependent on noumenal substrata, therefore constitutes a bridge between the distinct realms of nature and freedom.[31]

The relation between nature and freedom cannot consist in a free determination of natural events that would amount to a miracle, a violation of the lawfulness of nature, nor can it consist in a natural determination of the will which would violate the latter's autonomy. If such a relation does exist, as our moral experience seems to show, the connection should be sought elsewhere. Kant's argument is that it can be found only in our reflection on the supersensible substrate of reality. The supersensible substrate is implied by the phenomenal world and determined by freedom. The Understanding leaves the supersensible substrate undetermined; it has no intuition of it. Freedom determines the supersensible but has no intuition and cannot realize it as an object of cognition. Such realization would be the exclusive privilege of an Archetypal Reason if one were to exist. Reflective Judgment is aware, however, through its concept of purposiveness, of a profound lawfulness that underlies the empirical laws of nature and cannot be accounted for in terms either of the Understanding or of sense. All that remains, Kant believes, is to assume that the ground of this deeper lawfulness is the supersensible which is implied by the world of the Understanding and is determined by freedom. Hence the concept of purposiveness bridges the gap between the lawfulness of nature and the purposiveness of freedom; it accounts for our ability to identify moral acts and teleological beings, and finally to judge history as the arena of moral success and failure. It is crucial to note that the bridge between nature and freedom is not the supersensible itself but a reflective principle that enables us to construct a contemplative thought of a supersensible, a thought which we entertain regardless of whether or not it has an object. Kant in no way oversteps the limits of his transcendental philosophy.

---

[31]Kant's discussion assumes, of course, a pre-Darwinian biology, but his analysis of the relation between mechanistic and teleological explanations is, even today, of not merely historical interest. Kant clearly believed that mechanistic biology should in principle be possible and saw some hope for one. Yet he argues that no mechanistic explanation in biology would be the complete story (see Kant, *Critique of Judgment*, 303–304/418–19).

Having outlined the structure of his solution, Kant turns to establish it systematically in a series of arguments, one paving the way for the next, through analyses of reflective judgments. I call the various stages of the argument, respectively, an argument from taste, an argument from the unity of the laws of nature, an argument from organic nature, an argument from Humanity as an End, and an argument from the Highest Good. In the following sections we shall examine these arguments one by one. We shall see that Kant argues that the ultimate solution to the problem of unity is achieved through a cooperation of physical and moral teleology. The result of this cooperation is the establishment of the contemplative concept of the Highest Good as the underlying principle of Creation. Kant's search for unity culminates in religion. My argument is that this discussion with its religious conclusions provided significant material for the theories of religion of Otto and Tillich. Whereas, for the reasons specified in chapter two of this part, they rejected Kant's official theory of religion, in his *Critique of Judgment* Otto and Tillich found ideas of utmost importance for their theories of religion.

■ 4.B. The Argument from Taste

We have thus far seen that in the introduction to the *Third Critique* Kant tackles the problem of the unity of the practical and the theoretical by indicating that the problem is inherent to Reason itself. The problem that defines the task of a critique of Judgment arises from morality but can be answered neither within morality nor within natural science. The *Third Critique* asks whether and how it is possible to judge spatio-temporal events as purposive. My argument was that Kant sees this as a problem that can only be answered through a teleological principle, from the point of view of a conception of the end of history in light of the rational Ideal of the Highest Good. The problem of the unity of Reason, which is identified in the problem of moral action, finds its solution in religion. We shall now follow the major steps in the gradual unfolding of Kant's argument toward the establishment of unity between Practical Reason and Understanding and their respective realms.

My examination of Kant's argument begins with his analysis of aesthetic judgment.[32] Kant's analysis of judgments of taste aims to demonstrate that there are subjective judgments that are universal. I intend to show that Kant argues that the highest transcendental condition of our ability to discern beauty in natural objects is a thought about a supersensible will who designed nature in a way which pleases us. Kant argues that our faculties of Imagination and Understanding respond to the harmonious interconnection we discern in natural beauties with a harmonious interplay of their own and that we become aware of this interplay through the "feeling of life" (*"Lebensgefühl"*).[33] This analysis strives to show that in contemplating beautiful natural objects we gain an awareness of something beyond nature. Having established this stage of Kant's argument, I shall show that for Kant judgments of taste have a close affinity with teleological judgments concerning the unity of the empirical laws of nature. As does awareness of natural beauty, so too does awareness of the unity of empirical laws elicit our pleasurable response. Unlike the former, however, judgment concerning the laws of nature brings pleasure to a small minority of people. Kant thinks that, unlike the ability to apprehend the unity of empirical laws, the aesthetic sensibility is common to everyone. He expects that a critique of aesthetic judgment will support his analysis of teleological judgments regarding empirical laws.

Kant accounts for the universal validity of judgments of taste in terms of the concept of the "supersensible substrate" which he defines as "something that is both in the subject himself and outside him, something that is neither nature nor freedom" but is their common

---

[32]My intention is to present the structure of Kant's argument and to show that it serves as a first stage in the larger argument of the *Critique of Judgment* which strives to secure the unity of freedom and nature. Extensive literature has been devoted to the details of Kant's theory of taste, and there is no need to add to it here. I shall focus instead on those elements of the theory that have not been duly recognized and on aspects of it that are important for understanding Otto's theory of religious experience.

[33]Although I prefer to translate *"Lebensgefühl"* as "life-feeling," I use Pluhar's rendering both in quotations and in my text in order to prevent confusion.

underlying ground.[34] The analysis of taste thus becomes a decisive stage in the restoration of unity to our cognitive powers.[35] According to my interpretation of the first part of the *Third Critique*, the task of the analysis of judgments of taste is analogous to the "aesthetic" of the *First Critique*. Like the discussion of space and time, the analysis of judgments of taste is a propaedeutic. It paves the way for the study of teleological judgments of organisms, a study that strives to establish the ultimate unity of nature and freedom.

4.B.1 A Priori Determination of Feeling

The "Analytic of Aesthetic Judgment" sets out to discover the necessary conditions for calling an object beautiful. Kant analyzes the various elements of judgments of taste in order, on the one hand, to differentiate them from moral and scientific judgments and, on the other, to establish their a priori and universal validity. Kant argues that the foremost characteristic of any judgment of taste is its subjective universality. The "Dialectic of Aesthetic Judgment" accounts for this subjective universality in terms of the concept of the supersensible substrate of nature and reason. The critique of aesthetic taste as a whole is a first decisive step in Kant's elaborate attempt to solve the problem of unity. My interpretation will focus on these arguments. I shall first analyze the Analytic's claim for universality and then the Dialectic's discussion of the concept of the supersensible.

My examination of Kant's investigation of judgments of taste is somewhat lengthy and detailed because several elements of it, especially Kant's analysis of the a priori determinability of feeling, are presupposed by Otto's theory of religion and therefore crucial for understanding it. I believe that ignorance of these discussions has led, for example, to a complete misunderstanding of Otto's analysis of the a priority of the numinous consciousness. To redeem Otto from the charges of methodological confusion, I need to explain how his theory is grounded in the Kantian corpus.

Heretofore the critical corpus did not discuss subjective universality. In the *Third Critique*, through his discussion of teleological prin-

---

[34]Kant, *Critique of Judgment*, 229/353.
[35]Ibid.

ciples as a priori subjective principles of reflection, Kant sheds new light on what he calls "feeling of life." Hitherto in the Critical corpus feeling was considered totally empirical, completely private and arbitrary, a mental element that distinguishes rather than unites humans.[36] Now Kant includes feeling in the domain that can be determined a priori and has a cognitive function.[37] I shall demonstrate in the chapter on Otto that this discussion of the role of feeling and its status in the economy of consciousness is the clue to understanding Otto's theory of the numinous consciousness.

[36]An interesting exception to this rule is the feeling of respect for the moral law about which Kant says that it "is one which can be known a priori. Respect for the moral law, therefore, is a feeling produced by an intellectual cause, and this feeling is the only one which we can know completely a priori and the necessity of which we can discern" (Kant, *Critique of Practical Reason*, 76/74). Because this feeling can be known a priori and requires no external stimulus, the feeling of respect is not an instrument of cognition. Aesthetic feeling is determined a priori in response to an encountered internal purposiveness and serves to identify it. It is interesting to compare the Kantian position to that of Nelson Goodman who says that "in aesthetic experience the *emotions function cognitively*" (*Languages of Art: An Approach to a Theory of Symbols* [Indianapolis: Bobb-Merrill, 1968] 248). Goodman objects, however, to Kant's insistence on the disinterestedness of the aesthetic.

[37]In the *Critique of Judgment* Kant explicitly changes the opinion he pronounced in the *First Critique* where he declared that feelings of pleasure and pain can never furnish a priori laws: "The Germans are the only people who currently make use of the word 'aesthetic' in order to signify what others call the critique of taste. This usage originated in the abortive attempt made by Baumgarten, that admirable analytical thinker, to bring the critical treatment of the beautiful under rational principles, and so to raise its rules to the rank of a science. But such endeavors are fruitless. The said rules or criteria are, as regards their chief sources, merely empirical, and consequently can never serve as determinate a priori laws by which our judgment of taste must be directed. On the contrary, our judgment is the proper test of the correctness of the rules" (*Critique of Pure Reason*, 66/A21=B35). Having reached the conclusion that the universal laws of the Understanding are necessary but insufficient conditions of scientific experience, Kant furthers his investigation to find the transcendental conditions that ground the lawfulness of the particular and seemingly contingent.

4.B.2. Beauty—Purposeless Purposiveness

It sometimes happens to us, when we focus our attention disinterestedly on particular objects, such as a beautiful flower, that we perceive them as harmonious wholes. Without trying to understand the purpose that this flower may serve—without, for example, understanding it as the reproductive organ of a plant—we perceive in the flower an internal design. The flower seems to us to be constituted as if it were actually designed by someone who wished to please us. The parts of such objects are intimately interrelated and harmoniously interconnected in such perfect fitness that we must think of them as if they have an internal design, and we attribute this design to them without trying to find out whether there is indeed such a designer and what the purpose of such design might be. We call such a flower beautiful and we mean by this term "an object's form of purposiveness insofar as it is perceived in the object without the presentation of a purpose."[38] To understand Kant's definition of the beautiful we need to examine his characterization of the internal design in terms of purposeless purposiveness.

> What is a purpose? If we try to explicate it in terms of its transcendental attributes (without presupposing anything empirical, such as the feeling of pleasure), then a purpose is the object of a concept insofar as we regard this concept as the object's cause (the real basis of its possibility); and the causality that a concept has with regard to its object is its purposiveness.[39]

The meaning of this abstract definition can be made clearer by an example. A claim that the purpose of the eye is to see is taken to mean that the eye would not have existed had it not been for the function it fulfills. According to Kant, seeing is a real ground for the existence of the eye. The causality of the concept of seeing, in respect

---

[38]Kant, *Critique of Judgment*, 84/236. Beautiful objects, like organisms, are interrelated wholes. Unlike organisms, they do not have functions.
[39]Ibid., 64–65/220.

of its object, is called "purposiveness." The eye would not exist but for the purpose it serves. We ascribe causality to the concept of the purpose, seeing, and claim that the concept has made the existence of the eye possible. The object is an effect that owes its being to its real ground—its purpose. Kant here portrays a reciprocal causality that differs in nature from mechanistic causality. While in the latter only the effect depends on its cause, in this new causality the cause itself depends on its effect. "Hence we think of a purpose if we think not merely, say, of our cognition of the object, but instead of the object itself (its form, or its existence), as an effect that is possible only through a concept of that effect. In that case the presentation of the effect is the basis that determines the effect's cause and precedes it."[40]

In considering an object purposeful we maintain that the being who brought it into existence would not have done so had it not been for the purpose that can be realized by bringing this object into existence. The cause is determined in its action by the presentation of the desired effect. In section sixty-five of the *Critique of Judgment* Kant illustrates this idea with an example of a house that is built in order to provide its builder with income from rent.[41] The house is the cause of receiving rent, but the rent itself is the cause of building the house. Had we not desired this effect, we would not have bothered to build the house in the first place. Purposiveness thus is a relation in which cause and effect are so interdependent that the presentation of the effect is the determining ground of its cause.

Kant addresses the question of whether we are in fact entitled to ascribe such purposiveness to nature in the "Critique of Teleological Judgment."[42] Here Kant is interested merely in subjective purposiveness:

> On the other hand, we do call objects, states of mind, or acts purposive even if their possibility does not necessarily presuppose the presentation of a purpose; we do this merely because

[40]Ibid., 65/220.
[41]Ibid., 251–52/372.
[42]Ibid., 65/220. Emphasis mine.

we can explain and grasp them only if we assume that they are based on a causality [that operates] according to purposes, i.e., on a will that would have so arranged them in accordance with the presentation of a certain rule. Hence there can be purposiveness without a purpose, insofar as we do not posit the cause of this form in a will, and yet can grasp the explanation of its possibility only by deriving it from a will. Now what we observe we do not always need to have insight into by reason (as to how it is possible). Hence we can at least observe a purposiveness as to *form* and take note of it in objects—even if only by reflection—without basing it on a purpose (as the matter of the *nexus finalis*).[43]

Kant argues then that we cannot perceive beautiful objects without accounting for their form (of purposiveness) in terms of the idea of a causality according to purposes. Kant argues that in the case of judgments of taste such purposiveness is merely subjective. He maintains that in judging an object beautiful we do not concern ourselves with the object as such. Rather, in declaring an object beautiful, we merely state that we take pleasure in it. "Here the presentation is referred only to the subject, namely, to his *feeling of life*, under the name feeling of pleasure and of displeasure (*Gefühls der Lust oder Unlust*), and this forms the basis of a very special power of discriminating and judging."[44]

Perceiving a beautiful object, we are interested only in the mere form of the object and its relation to our cognitive faculties. If we ascribe purposiveness to the object we mean that it is purposive only in relation to our own minds. What we judge purposive is not the object itself, we do not consider a beautiful flower a purpose of nature, rather, we judge as purposive the presentation whereby the object is given to us. As we shall see shortly, Kant will argue that we call objects beautiful not because we consider them purposes of nature; we do so because contemplating them makes us conscious of the harmonious interplay of our cognitive faculties.

[43]Ibid. Emphasis mine.
[44]Ibid., 44/204. Emphasis mine.

4.B.2.a. The Disinterestedness of Aesthetic Judgment

Focus on the effect the beautiful object has on our cognitive faculties provides Kant a means for distinguishing judgments of taste from scientific and moral judgments. Kant observes that unlike these forms of judgment, judgments of taste are disinterested. The judging subject must have no interest whatsoever in the existence or otherwise of the beautiful object. In maintaining that the aesthetic moment is disinterested, Kant means that it does not share the interests of Theoretical and Practical Reason.[45]

Theoretical Reason is interested in an objective explanation of the object in terms of the causal relations of its components. Practical Reason is interested in the realization of its object according to its objective demand and conceives everything in terms of ends and means.[46] Both strive for pure objectivity, abstracting as much as

---

[45]The universality of aesthetic judgments differs from both that of moral and that of scientific judgments. Unlike the former, the judgment of taste does not indicate how the subject should act, and unlike the latter, it does not demand that everyone should attribute the same properties to the object of taste since it is not concerned with these properties. Unlike empirical judgments, the judgment of taste does not predict, on the basis of empirical experimentation, that everyone will agree with my judgement that an object is beautiful, rather it conveys my conviction that everyone *ought* to agree with me. Kant calls the necessity of aesthetic judgments exemplary (ibid., 54/211, 56/213, 88–89/239).

[46]The quality of disinterestedness provides Kant with a means for distinguishing judgments of taste from moral judgments. Kant is convinced that we are necessarily interested in the existence of the moral good and that therefore when we perform a moral action we take delight in our ability to bring into existence an object of the moral will, an object in the existence of which we necessarily have a moral interest. This latter delight must be distinguished from the feelings of pleasure and pain which refer only to the harmonious disposition of our mental powers and which express the disinterestedness of the subject. In distinction from logical judgments, the predicate "beautiful" does not indicate any properties of the object of taste; rather it denotes the feelings that arise in the subject of this judgment. Judgments of taste are thus subjective; they refer the presentation of the object to the subject and its feeling of life. "Here the subject feels himself, [namely,] how he is affected by the presentation" (ibid., 44/204).

possible from the subjectivity of affective reaction. Kant understands the aesthetic moment as freeing itself from these interests and expressing the subject's reaction to the object as it is given to intuition. "We can easily see that, in order for me to say that an object is *beautiful*, and to prove that I have taste, what matters is what I do with this presentation *within myself*, and not the [respect] in which I depend on the object's existence."[47]

Kant argues that although aesthetic judgments differ in their subjectivity from moral and scientific judgments, they share their universal communicability and thus differ from judgments that pronounce an object agreeable but can require no universal assent. The difference lies in the disinterestedness of aesthetic judgment. When we declare an object agreeable to our senses, we refer to certain sensible qualities of the object. Aesthetic judgment, on the other hand, refers only to the form of the object and relates it to the feelings of the subject.

> When [something determines the feeling of pleasure or displeasure and this] determination of that feeling is called sensation, this term means something quite different from what it means when I apply it to the presentation of a thing (through the senses, a receptivity that belongs to the cognitive power). For in the second case the presentation is referred to the object, but in the first it is referred solely to the subject and is not used for cognition at all, not even for that by which the subject *cognizes* himself.[48]

I think that here Kant challenges the sensualistic theory of cognition. Kant claims that he is able to identify a mode of sensation that does not contribute to our knowledge of properties of the object, but instead refers exclusively to the subject and denotes a special constitution of its mental powers. Aesthetic judgments are about subjective sensations; they are not intended to convey knowledge of the object of taste, not even a knowledge of its sensible qualities.[49]

---

[47]Ibid., 46/205; second emphasis mine.
[48]Ibid., 47/206.
[49]See, for example, ibid., 48/207.

4.B.3. Subjective Universality

The disinterestedness of taste provides Kant with a basis for inferring the second moment of aesthetic judgment: its subjective universality. Since the subject has no interest in the existence of the object of taste, aesthetic judgment is not grounded in particular circumstances; it is therefore a universal judgment.

> This explication of the beautiful can be inferred from the preceding explication of it as object of a liking devoid of all interest. For if someone likes something and is conscious that he himself does so without any interest, then he cannot help judging that it must contain a basis for being liked [that holds] for everyone. He must believe that he is justified in requiring a similar liking from everyone because he cannot discover, underlying this liking, any private conditions, on which only he might be dependent, so that he must regard it as based on what he can presuppose in everyone else as well.[50]

As we shall see shortly, this presupposition turns out to be the free play of the mental powers.

Before proceeding I wish to reemphasize the importance of the discussion of the universality of aesthetic judgments. This discussion marks a change in Kant's understanding of the role of feeling in the economy of consciousness—a change that is crucial for Kant's attempt to establish unity—and it provides a necessary background for interpreting Otto's theory of religion. Otto's definition of religious feeling as universally communicable can be understood properly only if we realize that it is rooted in Kant's analysis of the universality of judgments of taste. Kant himself emphasizes the importance of this discussion; he says that the subjective universality of the aesthetic judgment is "a remarkable feature"[51] and is therefore of special interest for the transcendental philosopher. Its discovery is worth the effort of overcoming the major difficulties that stand in the way.

---

[50]Ibid., 53–54/211.
[51]Ibid., 57/213.

4.B.4. Immediacy of Aesthetic Experience

Up to this point in his transcendental philosophy Kant held that universality is necessarily objective. His analysis of taste discovers a property of our cognitive faculties that would otherwise have remained unknown. In the Introduction to the *Critique of Judgment* Kant asserts the existence of a priori necessary subjective principles of reflection. Kant asks now how a purely subjective judgment, namely, the aesthetic judgment, can claim universal validity. This discussion has an added significance because it highlights the immediacy that is the prerequisite of judgments of taste, an immediacy that is also an essential feature of religious moments in the theories of Otto and Tillich. Kant seeks the transcendental conditions of subjective universality; he inquires after the grounds of the conviction of the subject of aesthetic taste that there are objects that everyone ought to judge beautiful.

The inquiry is complicated by the fact that, as regards their "logical quantity," all judgments of taste are singular. An aesthetic judgment is concerned solely with the individual object that it judges. While logical judgment compares and contrasts several objects by means of a concept, in order to judge an object aesthetically we need to intuit an object immediately and to represent it to our feelings without using any concept.[52] "In their logical quantity all judgments of taste are *singular* judgments. For since I must hold the object directly up to my feeling of pleasure and displeasure, but without using concepts, these judgments cannot have the quantity that judgments with objective general validity have."[53]

The problem is made even more complex by the fact that to form an aesthetic judgment we must ourselves experience the aesthetic object without being able to rely on general rules:

---

[52]For discussion of logical versus aesthetic judgments, see ibid., 148/285, 150–51/286–87.

[53]Ibid., 59/215. Kant argues (p. 51/209) that "a judgment of taste, (on the other hand,) is merely *contemplative* (*bloß kontemplativ*), i.e., it is a judgment that is indifferent to the existence of the object; it [considers] the character of the object only by holding it up to our feeling of pleasure and displeasure."

> If we judge objects merely in terms of concepts, then we lose all
> presentation of beauty. This is why there can be no rule by
> which someone could be compelled to acknowledge that some-
> thing is beautiful. No one can use reason or principles to talk us
> into a judgment on whether some garment, house, or flower is
> beautiful. We need to submit the object to our own eyes, just as
> if our liking of it depended on that sensation.[54]

Kant asserts that in order to judge an object beautiful we need to
take personal pleasure in it and cannot rely therefore on concepts and
rules. Nevertheless, although the aesthetic judgment does not rely on
rules and concepts, we demand universal assent to our judgments of
taste. Kant maintains that since the universality of judgment of taste
cannot be grounded in objective concepts and rules, other potential
grounds of universality have to be explored. This exploration brings
Kant to analyze the relations between the feeling of life—in its mode
of pleasure and pain—and the judgment of taste.

4.B.5. The "Common Sense"

Kant must defend his assertion that the state of mind, which accompanies a presentation of an object we judge beautiful, can be
universally communicated; in other words, he has to demonstrate that
feeling can be determined a priori.[55] Kant holds that judgments of
taste are a priori and universal and that this universality is not grounded

---

[54]Ibid., 59/215. Kant's comments here on the immediacy of aesthetic contemplation and the singularity of the aesthetic object are extremely important.
I think that they inspired much of the later discussion of theologians like Otto
and Tillich in the analyses of religious experience. It is along these lines, for
instance, that we must understand Otto's methodology of sympathy, which is
designed to awaken in the subject a numinous consciousness since it is impossible to do so by means of objective concepts. In just the same way, the
religious feeling arises in the immediacy achieved as theoretical and moral
interests are transcended. Like Kant, Otto claims universality and communicability to the subjective religious moment, and like Kant he grounds this
claim in an a priori determination of feeling.

[55]In fact, Kant has to show not only that feeling can be determined a priori,
as he has shown with regard to moral feeling, but that aesthetic feeling has
cognitive status.

in determinate concepts of the Understanding.[56] In establishing the universality of judgments of taste Kant argues analogically. He compares the necessary conditions that must exist when we confer objectivity on scientific judgments employing a representation to those that must exist when we claim universality for judgments of taste.[57]

Kant reiterates the theory of the *First Critique*. He tells us that the mind possesses two sources of cognition: the Imagination, which apprehends the manifold of given intuitions, and the Understanding with whose concepts the Imagination determines this manifold. In logical judgments our Imagination and our Understanding stand in a definite relation, and this relation of the cognitive faculties will be common to everyone who performs such judgments. In declaring an object beautiful, the Imagination collects the impressions and unites them into a presentation and thereby accomplishes the innermost interest of the Understanding, that of imposing order on the manifold of given impressions. Thus, even if in perceiving a beautiful object the Imagi-

[56]We can comment here that Kant commits himself to saying that when both of us are looking at a beautiful picture or a beautiful flower, we shall both entertain feelings that are identical in character. Although we are both assumed to entertain identical feelings while judging an object beautiful, we cannot describe our feelings definitively. To do this we need objective concepts, but our analysis of the features of aesthetic judgment precluded this possibility. We cannot therefore describe the states of mind that underlie judgments of taste with objective concepts, and we cannot reason with each other and specify why we both ought to perform the same judgments. All that aesthetic judgment postulates therefore is a kind of "universal voice," a liking that, although not mediated by concepts, aspires to universality. Later we shall see that Otto characterizes religious judgments, along the lines of Kant's aesthetics, as subjective, utilizing concepts neither of the Understanding nor of Practical Reason, and therefore given to symbolic reference alone. Thus Otto's "ideograms," like Kant's aesthetic descriptions are not rule-governed, yet are universally communicable (see part two, section 6.D.1.b below).

[57]Kant obviously refers here to the conclusions of the Aesthetic of the *Critique of Pure Reason*. The source of universality has to be sought in the spontaneity of Reason. When we want to find the universality of aesthetic judgment regarding a given object (an object that Reason does not produce), we need to turn to the two mental faculties that the *First Critique* explored, namely, Understanding and Imagination.

nation does not rely on any definite concept of the Understanding, it can be said that the Imagination and the Understanding cooperate in perfect harmony. "A presentation that, though singular and not compared with others, yet harmonizes with the conditions of the universality that is the business of the understanding in general, brings the cognitive powers into that proportioned attunement which we require for all cognition and which, therefore, we also consider valid for everyone who is so constituted as to judge by means of understanding and the senses in combination (in other words, for all human beings)."[58]

This discussion is one of the most obscure in the book. We must however try to understand it both for the sake of understanding Kant and for understanding subsequent theories of religious feeling that presuppose it. We must therefore interpret Kant's assertion that the pleasure we feel in contemplating a beautiful object results from the harmonious interplay between our cognitive powers and is a means of awareness of them.

Kant claims that when we judge an object beautiful, we find in it some unifying principle of order. In becoming aware of the unity of the beautiful object we feel that the faculty of imagination, which apprehends the given manifold, harmonizes in some indefinite manner with the Understanding whose task is to provide unifying concepts. We comprehend that the manifold intuited by the imagination is regulated by a rule, but we do not know by what kind of rule, nor are we bothered by this ignorance. Our disposition is not that of a search for knowledge, rather we are attuned to ourselves;[59] we find within us a harmony between Imagination and Understanding. To us this is a welcome, though unexpected, surprise. We find ourselves projecting a unity upon a manifold, a unity which it is the interest of the Understanding to impose, without being able to account for this unity in terms of any specific objective concept of the Understanding. The apprehension of such regularity and unity is therefore doubly gratify-

---

[58]Kant, *Critique of Judgment*, 63–64/219.

[59]Of the judgments of taste Kant says, "Any reference of presentation. . . designates nothing whatsoever in the object, but here the subject feels himself, [namely], how he is affected by the presentation" (ibid., 44/204).

ing. Kant concludes that the universality of judgments of taste is due to a certain state of mind the result of which is the pleasure we feel while judging an object beautiful.[60]

In sum, Kant argues that although judgments of taste are singular and involve no determinate concepts, they do not express merely private and contingent pleasures, but claim universal validity. It is important for Kant that the pleasure we feel in contemplating beautiful objects is a result of the harmonious attunement of our mental faculties, which he calls a "common sense," and is a means of awareness of it.

> Now this merely subjective (aesthetic) judging of the object, or of the presentation by which it is given, precedes the pleasure in the object and is the basis of this pleasure, [a pleasure] in the harmony of the cognitive powers. But the universal subjective validity of this liking, the liking we connect with the presentation of the object we call beautiful, is based solely on the mentioned universality of the subjective conditions for judging objects.[61]

Kant concludes that in order to enjoy subjective universality, judgments of taste "must have a subjective principle, which determines only by feeling rather than by concepts, though nonetheless with universal validity, what is liked or disliked. Such a principle, however, could only be regarded as a *common sense. . .* (by which, how-

---

[60]The pleasure we entertain in judging an object beautiful is universally communicable because it is grounded in a state of consciousness which all humans share. If concepts cannot ground the universality of judgments of taste, it must be the state of mind that necessarily underlies such judgments. "This basis can be nothing other than the mental state that we find in the relation between the presentational powers [Imagination and Understanding] insofar as they refer a given presentation to *cognition in general*" (ibid., 61–62/217; emphasis mine). Kant culminates his search for the ground for the universality of the judgment of taste in the claim that the necessary condition of the universality of aesthetic judgment is the state of harmony between Imagination and Understanding. As we shall see later in our discussion, Kant eventually says that the idea of the supersensible is the principle that guarantees the universal necessity of aesthetic judgments.

[61]Ibid., 62/218.

ever, we [also] do not mean an outer sense, but mean the effect arising from the free play of our cognitive powers)."[62] The judgment that an object is beautiful must therefore precede our pleasure in it. All of us, in representing beautiful objects to ourselves, should become aware of the harmony of the cognitive powers and as a result of this awareness should feel the specific kind of pleasure that Kant also calls the feeling of life.

Before proceeding with my interpretation of Kant's argument I want to emphasize that this discussion of feeling and its relation to judgment is extremely important for our understanding of Otto. If we do not fully appreciate that for Kant the feeling of life is determined a priori and is not therefore contingent and merely subjective, but a reflection upon and a means of awareness of a universal state of consciousness, then we cannot understand why Otto regards the numinous feeling as universal and as universally communicable. Commentators who see in Otto's discussion of feeling a deviation from his Kantian methodology—an indication that for him religion departs from reason—could not have been aware of Kant's discussion of the feeling of life in the *Third Critique*. This discussion enables us to refute Paton's influential and uncharitable reading of Otto that accuses Otto of misunderstanding the nature of feelings. Paton, as I shall argue in due course (see part 2, section 6.B.2 below), must have relied exclusively on the discussion of feelings in the first two *Critiques*, without attending to Kant's revolutionary ideas regarding feelings and their a priori determinability in the *Third Critique*.

4.B.6. The Quest for Harmony

Having suggested the existence of a common sense, which secures the universality of aesthetic judgment, Kant suddenly retreats. He asks:

---

[62]Ibid., 87/238. Kant's attempted proof of the necessity of assuming the common sense is not important for this volume, and I shall not examine it. This is because, as we shall see, Kant himself questions the necessity of this assumption and provides an alternative transcendental ground for the universal claim of judgments of taste. This alternative is of utmost importance in the quest for unity, and we shall examine it at some length.

That we do actually presuppose this indeterminate standard of a common sense is proved by the fact that we presume to make judgments of taste. But is there in fact such a common sense, as a constitutive principle of the possibility of experience, or is there *a still higher principle of Reason* that makes it only a regulative principle for us, [in order to] bring forth in us, *for higher purposes*, a common sense in the first place?[63]

Until now Kant has argued analogically for the existence of a common sense. He compared the conditions necessary for universality in scientific judgment to those conditions that must be supposed to exist in order for aesthetic judgments to be universally communicable. Since no objective concept of the Understanding can account for the internal design we find in the beautiful object, and since, in any case, we cannot rely on any objective concept or rule in judging aesthetically but rather must expose ourselves to the singularity and immediacy of the situation, Kant is forced to investigate deeper dimensions of the cognitive faculties to account for the universality claim of aesthetic judgments.[64] He argues that the fact of the harmonious camaraderie of the Imagination and the Understanding entitles us to claim universal communicability for our judgment of taste. We assume, as we do in critical examination of the universality of scientific judgments, that these cognitive faculties are common to all humans and that therefore these faculties will cooperate similarly for everyone in similar situations. Kant consequently inferred the existence of a "common sense" and attributed to it the universal claim of aesthetic judgments.

Kant seems to have some second thoughts; he asks now whether the "common sense" should really be postulated as the constitutive

---

[63]Ibid., 89–90/240. Emphasis mine.

[64]To recapitulate, we assume that the general interest of the Understanding, namely, the imposition of unity, rather than particular concepts, is at work when we judge aesthetically. The Imagination collects the impressions and gathers them into a presentation, thus achieving the deepest interest of the Understanding. Both cognitive powers work together harmoniously to produce the presentation.

element of the aesthetic experience, or whether it is merely a front for a deeper transcendental ground.

> But is there in fact such a common sense, as a constitutive principle of the possibility of experience, or is there *a still higher principle of reason* that makes it only a regulative principle for us, [in order] to bring forth in us *for higher purposes*, a common sense in the first place? In other words, is taste an original and natural ability, or is taste only the idea of an ability yet to be acquired and [therefore] artificial, so that a judgment of taste with its requirement for universal assent is in fact only a demand of reason to produce such agreement in the way we sense?[65]

Kant asks whether we really need to commit ourselves to asserting the existence of the common sense as the transcendental condition of the universality of judgments of taste. He suggests the possibility that the idea of this common sense functions to regulate our aesthetic discourse in service of yet a higher interest of reason. He says that the study of aesthetic judgment does not permit us to specify what such a higher purpose of Reason might be. This would only be made possible by the conclusions of the *Critique of Judgment* as a whole. Anticipating the establishment of this principle through the discussion of purposiveness in nature, however, Kant alerts us to the fact that we have not yet found the ultimate transcendental condition of judgments of taste.

Kant's comment must be understood as anticipating the final results of all three parts of the *Critique of Judgment*. From this anticipated point of view it will become clear that the discussion of the aesthetic cannot culminate in the postulation of the common sense. The universal communicability of judgments of taste—judgments about

---

[65]Ibid., 90/240. Emphasis mine. This question echoes Kant's confession in the Preface to the *Third Critique* that his genuine motive for embarking on a critique of taste is not really his wish to help us form and cultivate taste, but the interests of his Critical project. (see ibid., 7/170). Kant seems to be saying here that nature provided us with an aesthetic taste not so much in order to enable us to enjoy beautiful objects, but because this propensity serves higher cognitive interests.

internal design and harmony in objects of nature—is a prerequisite of our recognition of the higher principle the content of which can be indicated only at the conclusion of the philosophy of biology. Kant therefore suggests now that we are entitled to speak in terms of a common sense because this enables us to recognize judgments of taste as universal, and for the time being he does not want to elaborate further on this topic. Kant announces that "these questions we neither wish to nor can investigate."[66] In section forty-two of the *Critique of Judgment*, however, which he entitles "On Intellectual Interest in the Beautiful," Kant begins to provide some explanation for this abrupt and curious turn of his argument. Section forty-two introduces a provocative theory; it suggests that aesthetic judgment ultimately serves the interest of Reason in finding unity between freedom and nature.

4.B.7. The Supersensible Substrate of Reality

In a rather obscure and neglected chapter, which examines the differences in our response to natural beauty and to artifacts, we find hidden a discussion that relates the critique of aesthetic taste to the overall interest of the *Third Critique*, that is, to the search for unity.[67] In examining our reaction to natural beauty Kant asserts that although an interest in the existence of beautiful objects cannot be the determinative ground of aesthetic judgment, once we come to judge a natural object beautiful we have an interest in its existence. Analysis of this discussion is a worthwhile detour for us because in it we find Kant's most intriguing assertions regarding the transcendental condition of aesthetic taste and the relations of aesthetic taste to the fundamental search for a principle that bridges the gap between nature and freedom.

---

[66]Ibid., 90/240.

[67]This particular chapter attracted minimal attention at most. It seems to me that only an awareness of the overall interest of the *Critique of Judgment* can enable Kant's readers to appreciate the explosive nature of his assertions in this chapter. Lack of such awareness is responsible, I presume, for the relative neglect of this chapter in commentaries on the *Third Critique*.

Rather peculiarly Kant calls our interest in natural beauty "moral"; he states that very few people actually have such an interest. In justifying his calling this interest moral, Kant draws parallels between our aesthetic ability to discern harmony in nature and our interest in finding a ground for harmony between the lawfulness of nature and the purposiveness of reason. The conclusions of this discussion strengthen our argument that the critique of taste should be interpreted as an integral part of the analysis of Reflective Judgment and that this analysis, in turn, strives to find a principle of unity. Although Kant calls this a "moral interest," it cannot be understood in the strict sense as a practical interest; it is an interest of morality that can only be achieved reflectively in terms of a "moral teleology."[68] It is an interest that, I shall argue, should more properly be called religious.[69]

Kant has argued consistently until now that an essential characteristic of judgments of taste is that "our judgment is not based on an interest and also gives rise to none."[70] The claim for the universality of aesthetic judgments rests neither on concepts of the Understanding nor on concepts of Practical Reason; rather it refers the presentation to the harmonious interplay of the mental faculties. In comparing judgments of taste to ethical judgments Kant claims that the latter share significant characteristics with the former, but also differ from them in a significant respect.

Kant's ethics abstracts from the content of a maxim and examines its form in light of the moral law. As such, the moral decision is not derived from any ulterior motives. Once the will is determined by the moral law, however, the moral agent has an interest in the realization

[68]I shall discuss Kant's notion of a "moral teleology" in my analysis of the Dialectic of Teleological Judgment (see section 4.F).

[69]For extensive discussion of the distinctions mentioned here, see my discussion of the Introduction to the *Critique of Judgment* (section 4.A.1). It is interesting to note that Fries, whose influence on Otto will be discussed below, refers to this interest as "religious." See Jakob Fries, *Knowledge, Belief, and Aesthetic Sense* (ed. Frederick Gregory; trans. Kent Richter; Geschichte der Wissenschaftsphilosophie; Cologne: Dinter-Verlag für Philosophie, 1989) 117, 226–44.

[70]Kant, *Critique of Judgment*, 167/300.

of the decision. This interest gives rise to a satisfaction in the realization of moral goals, a satisfaction Kant calls "a liking" ("wohlgefallen").

> We also have an intellectual power of judgment, i.e., an ability
> for determining a priori with regard to mere forms of practical
> maxims (insofar as such maxims qualify of themselves for giving universal law) a *liking* that we make a law for everyone; this
> judgment [too] is not based on any interest, *yet it gives rise to
> one.*[71]

In commenting on the introduction to the *Third Critique* we noted that the interest of the moral agent in the execution of her act is a part of a more comprehensive interest, that of being able to judge spatio-temporal events as realizations of moral purposes. To be able to recognize spatio-temporal events as moral acts, we need an ability to contemplate nature in terms of final causes. We need, in other words, to establish a point of view from which we can "think of nature as being such that the lawfulness in its form will harmonize with at least the possibility of [achieving] the purposes that we are to achieve in nature according to laws of freedom."[72] Kant repeats the same idea here and argues that

> Reason also has an interest in the objective reality of the ideas
> (for which, in moral feeling, it brings about a direct interest),
> i.e., an interest that nature should at least show a trace or give
> a hint that it contains some basis or other for us to assume in
> its products a lawful harmony with that liking of ours which is
> independent of all interest (a liking we recognize a priori as a
> law for everyone, though we cannot base this law on proofs).[73]

[71]Ibid. First emphasis mine.

[72]Ibid., 15/176.

[73]Ibid., 167/300. My interpretation of this passage differs from that of Paul Guyer (*Kant and the Claims of Taste* [Cambridge, MA: Harvard University Press, 1979] 369–70). Unlike most interpreters Guyer does not ignore this passage, but he too misses its systematic significance. This omission

Our basic question was why Kant characterizes the interest in beautiful objects as "moral." His initial answer is that there is an affinity between the aesthetic propensity, which contemplates harmony in nature, and morality, which strives to recognize moral purposiveness in spatio-temporal events. The further question that we must address is how the moral interest in discerning purposiveness in nature and the aesthetic interest in purposiveness might be related. Are the two quests for harmony to be understood as similar but unrelated quests, or might there be some common ground to both of them? Is it at all possible that the one may provide a transcendental ground for the other?

All interpreters of the *Third Critique* who read the book as a series of loosely related discussions will find these questions superfluous. They will therefore be unable to appreciate Kant's answer to them. In fact, Kant's discussion of these issues demonstrates that the critique of aesthetic taste should be read as an integral part of the analysis of teleological judgment, that Kant's analysis of the transcendental conditions of judgments of taste is actually concluded only in the study of organisms.

Kant's preliminary answer to the question regarding the relation between moral interest and the interest in natural beauty obscures more than it clarifies. Kant speaks of resemblance between the interests, a resemblance that somehow justifies characterizing the interest in the beautiful as moral.

---

probably results from Guyer's decision to discuss Kant's analysis of taste in isolation from the rest of the *Critique of Judgment*. Only from the point of view of the systematic unity of the work can the significance of Kant's remarks be appreciated. Guyer interprets the delight of which Kant writes as aesthetic, whereas I believe that Kant must have referred to moral feeling. Guyer accordingly presents the guiding interest of Reason not in establishing the possibility of harmonious reconciliation of nature and freedom, but in developing good moral character. I cannot see how the text can support Guyer's interpretation, especially not when the passage is read in light of the overarching interest of the *Third Critique*. The following quotation from p. 168/301—a passage that Guyer ignores—will provide further support for my interpretation.

> Hence reason must take an interest in any manifestation in na-
> ture of a harmony that resembles the mentioned [kind of] har-
> mony, and hence the mind cannot meditate about the beauty of
> *nature* without at the same time finding its interest aroused. But
> in terms of its kinship this interest is moral, and whoever takes
> such an interest in the beautiful in nature can do so only to the
> extent that he has beforehand already solidly established an in-
> terest in the morally good.[74]

Kant anticipates criticism that his architectonic linkage of the beautiful and the moral will appear forced and unjustified. He proceeds
therefore to support the kinship argument with another argument. Even
as I write these lines I am intimidated by the boldness of the suggestion that I find implicit in Kant's words. Kant now maintains that
people with a well-developed interest in the problems of morality do
not require additional arguments to understand his intention. The strong
analogy between the interest in the objects of pure judgments of taste
and the interest in the object of moral judgments, he says, is self
explanatory. I shall analyze his argument step by step. Kant proceeds
to say:

> Consider, in addition, how we admire nature, which in its beau-
> tiful products displays itself as art, [i.e., as acting] not merely
> by chance but, as it were, intentionally, in terms of a lawful
> arrangement and as a purposiveness without a purpose.[75]

So far Kant is consistent with his previous assertions regarding the
nature of aesthetic judgment. There is nothing new or unusual in this
characterization of our contemplation of beautiful objects as internally
designed, as displaying purposiveness without purpose. Kant proceeds
to say that "since we do not find this purpose anywhere outside us,
we naturally look for it in ourselves."[76]

---

[74]Kant, *Critique of Judgment*, 167/300.
[75]Ibid., 168/301.
[76]Ibid.

So far Kant is still consistent with his analysis of judgments of taste. Although we perceive beautiful objects as purposive, we do not really attribute their existence to any external purpose; rather the purposiveness is subjective. In his previous discussions Kant taught us that this purposiveness refers the presentation to our representational powers, to the harmonious interplay of our cognitive powers. Even though Kant's previous analysis throughout the Analytic of Judgment of Taste leads us to anticipate such an explanation here, Kant introduces an explosive difference. Instead of explaining the claim of universality of aesthetic taste in terms of a common sense, Kant surprisingly states that "since we do not find this purpose anywhere outside us, we naturally look for it in ourselves, namely, in what constitutes the ultimate purpose of our existence; our moral vocation."[77] This surprising conclusion forces us to reflect on Kant's second thoughts regarding the postulation of the common sense in section twenty-two.[78] There he maintained that it could be the case that the regulative idea of a common sense acts as a front for another, higher purpose of reason. It seems that now Kant indicates more explicitly what the nature of this interest is. The higher principle, the interests of which the aesthetic propensity serves, is the ability, required by morality, to see nature as purposive. We shall realize shortly that in his discussion of organisms Kant calls such purposiveness a "technic of nature." The transcendental condition of judgments of taste is the teleological principle that enables us to see purposiveness in nature. We need to be able at least to contemplate such purposiveness if we are to unite nature and freedom, to find internal reconciliation between our cognitive faculties. For the time being, in the context of the analysis of judgments of taste, Kant cannot define the unifying principle. The content of this purposiveness has yet to be examined and established, and Kant promises to undertake this task in his analysis of organic beings. In concluding his argument here, Kant writes, "the

[77]Ibid.
[78]Ibid., 90/240.

inquiry into the basis that makes such a natural purposiveness possible will, however, first come up in the teleology."[79]

4.B.8. A Higher Principle of Unity

While in this discussion Kant's reference to the higher principle of Reason for which the regulative idea of a "common sense" serves as a front is still indecisive, in the Dialectic of Aesthetic Judgment he restates the idea forcefully. Kant reexamines the claim of universality of judgments of taste and asserts that "a judgment of taste must refer to some concept or other, for otherwise it could not possibly lay claim to necessary validity for everyone."[80] Here Kant explicitly identifies such a concept as the "transcendental concept of the supersensible underlying all [that] intuition," and as "reason's pure concept of the supersensible underlying the object (as well as underlying the judging subject) as an object of sense and hence as appearance."[81] Kant argues that

> a judgment of taste is based on a concept (the concept of a general basis of nature's subjective purposiveness for our power of judgment), but this concept does not allow us to cognize and prove anything concerning the object because it is intrinsically indeterminable and inadequate for cognition; and yet this same concept does make the judgment of taste valid for everyone, because (though each person's judgment is singular and directly accompanies his intuition) the basis that determines the judgment lies, *perhaps*, in the concept of what may be considered the supersensible substrate of humanity.[82]

Kant is very cautious in introducing this concept. He is quick to remind us that it is an indeterminate and indeterminable concept and that therefore judgment of taste remains subjective. Kant, however,

[79]Ibid., 168/301.
[80]Ibid., 212/339.
[81]Ibid.
[82]Ibid., 213/340. Emphasis mine.

also states that the reference to this concept is the key to the aesthetic propensity:

> As for the subjective principle—i.e., the indeterminate idea of the supersensible in us—as the sole key for solving the mystery of this ability [i.e., taste] concealed from us even as to its sources, we can do no more than point to it; but there is nothing we can do that would allow us to grasp it any further.[83]

Although Kant proceeds very carefully in his discussion of the concept of the supersensible, at times even qualifying his assertions by saying that it is only *perhaps* the basis of judgment of taste, and although he alerts us to the fact that we can say very little about this principle since it is undetermined, Kant is willing to say one more thing about this concept. When we examine his additional comment from the perspective of our pursuit after the unity of freedom and nature, we begin to grasp how the discussion of taste relates to this quest. Kant says:

> Hence the subjective standard for that aesthetic but uncondi-tioned purposiveness in fine art that is to lay rightful claim to everyone's necessary liking cannot be supplied by any rule or percept, but can be supplied only by that which is merely nature in the subject but which cannot be encompassed by rules or concepts—namely, the supersensible substrate (unattainable by any concept of the Understanding) of all his powers; and hence the mentioned standard can be supplied only by [means of] that by reference to which we are to make all our cognitive powers harmonize, [doing] *which is the ultimate purpose given us by the intelligible [element] of our nature.* It is in this way alone, too, that this purposiveness, for which we cannot prescribe an objective principle, can be based a priori on a principle that is subjective and yet universally valid.[84]

---

[83]Ibid, 213–14/341.

[84]Ibid., 217/344. Emphasis mine. Earlier Kant referred to the supersensible, arguing that it is the point "[where] all our a priori powers are reconciled since that is the only alternative left to us for *bringing reason into harmony with itself*" (214/341; emphasis mine).

From the perspective of the quest for unity, these last sentences are of utmost importance. They prove that for Kant this quest is a serious problem and not just a passing interest. The need to find a solution to the problem of unity brings him to examine the power of Reflective Judgment. He thinks that the analysis of judgments of taste established the concept of the supersensible as the transcendental condition of the universality of aesthetic judgments.

It is important to reiterate that Kant discusses here a principle, a concept, and not the supersensible itself. It is *our thought* about the supersensible that is the transcendental ground of aesthetic judgment and not the supersensible itself. Kant does not overstep the limits of the critical method and does not discuss things in themselves. It is in the idea of the supersensible that Kant finds the solution to the problem of unity and not in the supersensible itself. In this context Kant cannot develop this thought any further. He will do this in his discussion of organisms. Anticipating this discussion I can say that Kant will identify the content of this principle as the idea of the Highest Good. This is the basis that enables the moral agent to identify spatio-temporal events as moral acts.

4.B.9. Summary and Conclusions

Kant is led to assert that judgments of taste imply reference to the supersensible substrate in which nature and freedom are one, because, according to his analysis, judgments of taste are shown to involve both a givenness and a purposiveness. The givenness of the beautiful is an immediacy of intuition; it apprehends the spatio-temporal object as beautiful. Apprehension of an object as beautiful is shown to be an identification of a purposiveness exemplified in the object. In aesthetic judgment this is an undetermined purposiveness, a purposiveness without a purpose. Aesthetic judgment is therefore shown to be an intuitive apprehension of purposiveness. Thus, the challenge of the fact of taste is to account for the possibility of the givenness of purposiveness. This givenness conflicts with the critical conclusions of the analyses of empirical experience and practical valuation that have shown that the Understanding does not recognize a teleology and that Reason, which generates ends and purposes, cannot affect intuitions.

In the judgment of taste we have an immediate unity of intuition and purposiveness. This is an immediacy for which we cannot account in terms of empirical intuitions, which are governed by the categories of the Understanding, for these were shown to exclude final causes. Nor can this immediacy be accounted for by the legislative powers of Reason, which set up ends and values, for it has been shown that the ends of Reason cannot determine the content of intuition of spatio-temporal objects. The fact of taste implies a unity of givenness and purposiveness that cannot be accounted for by the powers of the Understanding and Reason in themselves, but only in terms of a unity between them. The judgment of taste identifies a unity of givenness and purposiveness that transcends the constructions of Theoretical and Practical Reason and points beyond them to the source of all appearances, to things in themselves.

Just as the givenness of appearances in empirical intuition implies a transcendent source in a mind-independent substrate, in the thing in itself, so does the givenness of an intuition of purposiveness point beyond itself to a possible point of unity of purposiveness and givenness, in the supersensible substrate of reality. To be sure, the implications of taste are merely subjective and do not justify postulation of the existence of a supersensible; nor do we gain knowledge of the nature of the purposiveness that allegedly resides there. What the critique of taste does achieve is to show that the feelings of pleasure in the beautiful object commit us to *thinking* about a possible supersensible substrate in which the unity of givenness and purposiveness reside. Since a point of unity between givenness and purposiveness is sought after by the powers of Reason, as Reason seeks to reconcile the conflict between its powers, and since a point of such unity is *felt* to exist in judgments of taste, these feelings involve a possibility for an ultimate reconciliation of nature and freedom.

Feelings of taste therefore acquire an important place in the economy of our mental faculties. Feelings of taste imply that the constructs of Theoretical Reason on the one hand and of Practical Reason on the other are not merely constructs but may reflect the structure of reality in itself. This point was developed further by Jakob Fries who wanted to rescue Kant's *Critique* from the skeptical criticism that his philosophy is "philosophizing as if," by showing that Kant is committed to a special type of judgment that implies that the construction of a world of appearances, as a world of science, reflects somehow the structure of reality itself.[85] Fries developed this theme in his study of the special judgment that Kant identified in the judgment of taste. Fries presented his conclusions in his theory of "Ahndung" and this theory was taken over by Rudolf Otto as the foundation of his philosophy of religion. Otto's theory of "divination," which claims that religious feeling is a capacity to judge that an ideal of Reason is exemplified in empirical appearance (what Otto calls "seeing the infinite in the finite"), is ultimately based on the special notion of feeling that Kant identified in the *Critique of Judgment* (see part two, section 6.D.4., below).

Having found the transcendental ground of judgment of taste in the idea of the purposiveness of nature we now look back and examine the judgment of taste in light of these conclusions. Judgments of taste involve necessarily the thought about a possible supersensible unity of reason and nature. This thought which is implied in the judgment of taste, as its supreme transcendental ground, establishes in our thought a consideration of the possible unity of the faculties of reason. Insofar as the judgment of taste alone is concerned this unity is at its most minimal; a demand that it be possible that a purposiveness be united with an empirical intuition. The purposiveness, however, is merely formal, it has no content—a purposiveness without purpose. This is the first stage in the critique of Judgment beyond which the critique will advance by providing more elaborate determinations of the content of the purposiveness that the faculty of judgment recognizes.

Analysis of the purposiveness involved in the identification of organisms in a philosophy of biology will define this purposiveness as the moral person, considered as the end of nature. Moral teleology, which concerns itself with a possible purpose of the universe as a whole, will further define this purposiveness in terms of the Highest Good. As such, the three successive stages of analysis—each preparing the way for the one that follows upon it, while each successive

[85]Fries developed these ideas in *Knowledge, Belief, and Aesthetic Sense*.

stage reinterprets its predecessor in its own terms as its transcendental ground—amount to a systematic attempt to find a final answer to the question, "What may I hope for?" In raising the question of rational hope and in attempting to answer this question in terms of reflection on the teleological unity of the universe, the *Critique of Judgment* takes upon itself to settle, on critical rational grounds, the perennial religious question about the meaning of the universe and, within it, the meaning of human life. In undertaking this task the *Critique of Judgment* transforms itself into a philosophical theology. It is in this light that I believe, the *Critique* was read by followers of Kant like Fries, Leonard Nelson, Otto, and Tillich, and against the background of this understanding they sought to develop their philosophies of religion.

■ 4.C. The Argument from the Unity of the Laws of Nature

4.C.1. The Unity of Empirical Laws of Nature

In order to show that it is possible for us to think of a unity of nature and freedom Kant must first show that our idea of nature requires us in some way to think of nature teleologically. He does so by raising the question whether Reflective Judgment has a principle of its own. His answer is that Reflective Judgment has such a principle and that it is the principle of purposiveness. Kant established taste as a subjective yet universally communicable principle of reflection. Kant pointed out that the ability of taste to satisfy the Understanding's need to unify, beyond the ability of concepts of the Understanding to account for such unity, is gratifying for us. In this, taste resembles another mode of reflection about nature, the teleological judgment regarding the unity of the empirical laws of nature. We shall now consider briefly Kant's argument that scientific thought embodies reflection on nature in teleological terms.

Kant's discussion of scientific thought in the *Critique of Judgment* takes off where the *Critique of Pure Reason* ended. We have already learned that experience embodies relations of necessity which make possible awareness of objects and causes. The existence of such relations in the structure of experience makes possible a natural science that accounts for these necessities in terms of natural laws. The structure of appearance is made possible by the Understanding which legislates to it through its categories. This legislation, however, accounts only for the most general structure of experience. It does not determine the specific laws under which nature is ordered. These we must *discover* a posteriori.

To follow the logic of Kant's argument from this point on, it is important to keep in mind that the whole project of scientific explanation is for him an attempt to account, in the most general terms possible, for the necessary structures that we find in our experience. Science strives therefore to derive specific empirical laws from ever more general laws, to construct a deductive system of nature. The *possibility* of empirical necessity is established a priori by the categories of reason. The specific laws we find operating in nature, however, are merely a posteriori; they do not share the a priori necessity of the categories and the principles of the Understanding. Consequently, the empirical laws of nature are merely contingent. It is conceivable that they could be otherwise and that they can change. Explanation of natural phenomena according to contingent laws cannot, however, account for the necessity they have in our experience. If such an account is to be achieved, the empirical laws themselves must be necessary.

4.C.2. Subjective Principle of Reflection

4.C.2.a.

When we discover in our experience such elements as objects and causes, we know that we can attribute them to nature because they are determined a priori by the categories. When, however, we find a much higher unity in our experience, the unity of empirical laws that science discovers, we cannot account for the necessity they have through an a priori categorical source. The categories of the Understanding determine only the general structure of experience; they do not determine the specific laws under which it actually functions. As far as the categories are concerned nature could have many different forms. Yet we do consider the higher laws of nature as sustaining the necessity of more specific laws and ultimately the necessity of the causal relations we find in our experience. We are committed to thinking of the laws of nature as necessary, yet we cannot account for the source of this necessity in terms of the concepts of the Understanding and the higher principles that derive from them. Since we cannot establish the necessity of the laws of nature and are yet committed to their necessity, this necessity cannot be a matter of knowledge for us, but is at best a matter of reflective judgment.[86]

4.C.2.b.

What is involved in judging a system of nature to be necessary, and is such judgment justified by the practice of science? The answer to this question is at the heart of Kant's project. What is involved, Kant asks, in discovering that a certain law is a law of nature? We discover a regularity in experience, but the regularity itself cannot support a general causal law that will describe it. Observing the relation between the perceived regularity and the suggested explanation

[86]A subtle distinction is needed here between reflective consciousness and regulative ideas. The two are alike in that reflective conclusions can function regulatively. Kant believes that organic conceptions will direct the biological sciences in their quest for mechanical explanations. It would be an error, I believe, to think for that reason that reflective and regulative reasons are identical. Consider the regulative idea of "nature." In speaking of laws of nature we exhibit, according to Kant's analysis in the *First Critique*, an a priori presupposition that there is such a thing as nature which we can study scientifically. Kant emphasizes that this is an absolutely formal idea of a systematic unity which must be presupposed by science and which science can never establish (*Critique of Pure Reason*, 559–60/A686=B714). Since theoretical judgment is primarily interested in the existence of its object, it must assume a stance of "as-if" when it admits an idea of nature as such. The admission is justified by its theoretical usefulness. Reflective conclusions are different. A contemplative conception of nature follows our recognition that the empirical laws of nature that we discover through scientific efforts are unified in a way that requires explanation, and we find this explanation in the idea of the purposive unity of nature. It is not, therefore, an idea that must be presupposed if science is to be possible, but a contemplative thought which follows reflection on the conclusions of science. While the regulative idea of the *First Critique* was purely formal, the contemplative idea assumes extensive theoretical knowledge and goes beyond it.

in terms of a causal law, we find that we have two options. Either we can think of the regularity as a coincidence on which we successfully imposed a description in terms of causal relations, or we can think of the regularity as necessary and of the causal description as a discovery of a truth independent of the legislative capacity of the Understanding. Choosing the first option would negate the necessity of the laws of nature and, according to Kant, would render impossible a world of unified experience. If we are to account for the necessity we find in scientific explanation we must adopt the second option.

4.C.2.c.

How is it possible for us to think of an empirical regularity as necessary if it is not grounded in the powers of our legislation a priori? Kant suggests that the only way we can do so is by thinking of empirical structures as if they were grounded in an understanding unlike ours, an understanding that can determine the content of experience. This assumption amounts to a notion of a prestructured world of experience. But the idea of a prestructured world is not enough. Such a world could in principle be opaque to our cognitive powers, and if it were so our scientific description of it would be mere imposition. If we are to be able to think of science as describing the way things really are and accounting for the necessities that govern them, then we must think of the world not only as prestructured but as prestructured in such a way that our cognitive powers can understand it.

4.C.2.d.

It helps to think of Kant's argument in analogy to the thought processes in deciphering a code. First we must assume that a sequence of signs is indeed a code; we must further assume that the encoded text is in principle possible for us to understand. Without these assumptions the very idea of interpreting these signs is ridiculous. It is likewise with the scientific project of "reading the book of nature." In order to think of scientific achievements as discoveries we must think of nature as ordered according to laws that we can understand. In a sense, we must think of the book of nature as a letter addressed to us, or at least as a letter that we can intercept and read.

The basic assumption, which is inherent to these thoughts, is that the world is structured in order to be intelligible. Without this assumption our attempt to understand the world is absurd, but with it we are committed to attributing an aim to nature, namely, the aim to be understandable. Kant sees in this attribution an attribution of purposiveness that is the supreme condition that makes it possible for us to think of the empirical laws of nature as necessary.

Since it is only in reflection on the practice of science and its achievements that we come to think of the world as intelligibly prestructured, the judgment that it is so prestructured is a judgment of reflection. Furthermore, it is a judgment of reflection that is based on the attribution of a purposiveness to nature. It is in this attribution of purposiveness that Kant finds the principle of reflective judgment for which he searched. It is also a notion of purposiveness that begins to lay the foundation for bridging the gap between the givenness of nature and the purposiveness of reason; it is a foundation on which Kant will gradually build the edifice of the critique of Judgment.

4.C.3. The Subjectivity of the Principle

As we saw, Kant holds that the legislation of the Understanding accounts only for the most general structure of experience. It does not determine the specific laws under which nature is ordered. These we must *discover* a posteriori. Kant argues that when we find a systematic unity among empirical laws we rejoice in our success. "When we discover that two or more heterogeneous empirical laws of nature can be unified under one principle that comprises them both, the discovery does give rise to a quite noticeable pleasure, frequently even admiration, even an admiration that does not cease when we have become fairly familiar with its object."[87]

In the scientific exploration of nature, judgment appears to be in a unique position. It realizes in fact the innermost interest of the Understanding—a projection of unity on the manifold of given experience— without relying on the Understanding. It does so guided by its own reflective principle of purposiveness. Now "the attainment of an aim is always connected with the feeling of pleasure; and if the condition

---

[87]Kant, *Critique of Judgment*, 27/187.

of reaching the aim is an a priori presentation—as, in this case, it is a principle for reflective judgment as such—then [there is] a basis that *determines the feeling of pleasure a priori and validly for everyone.*"[88] Kant acknowledges that very few people enjoy the particular perspective that scientists can have, a perspective that enables them to attribute purposiveness to nature. Kant, however, thinks that his theory of the a priori determinability of feeling is reinforced by his previous study of the more common aesthetic judgment which also demonstrates an a priori determinability of feeling.

4.C.4. Conclusions

When we examine Kant's progress in his quest for unity, we realize that his achievement is limited. All he has established thus far is a subjective principle of purposiveness. In accounting for the higher principle of the unity of empirical laws Kant argues analogically. All he can say is that

> this principle can only be the following: since universal natural laws have their basis in our understanding, which prescribes them to nature (though only according to the universal concept of it as nature), the particular empirical laws must, as regards what the universal laws have left undetermined in them, be viewed in terms of such a unity as [they would have] if they too had been given by an understanding (even though not ours) *to assist our cognitive powers* by making possible a system of experience in terms of particular natural laws.[89]

It is important to emphasize that Kant insists that science does not presuppose the *existence* of God. The principle required by science is reflective: "In using this principle judgment gives a law only to itself not to nature."[90] He reemphasizes this point in saying, "Hence judgment, which with respect to things under possible (yet to be discovered) empirical laws is merely reflective, must think of nature with

[88]Ibid.
[89]Ibid., 19/180. Emphasis mine.
[90]Ibid., 20/180.

regard to these laws according to a *principle of purposiveness for our cognitive power.*"[91]

Kant does think, however, that this principle of a prearranged harmony between nature and our cognitive faculties is the prerequisite of any scientific search for a unified system. This point in Kant's argument links the current study to the study of organic purposiveness. We perceive organisms as organized systems that necessarily imply a prior idea that accounts for their internal interconnectedness and interrelatedness. They seem to require an explanation in terms of an intelligent cause.[92] Kant hopes that the study of organic nature will further his search for a unifying principle by providing a principle of objective purpose. We now turn to discuss Kant's philosophy of biology which strives to establish objective purposiveness in nature.

■ 4.D. The Argument from Organic Nature

4.D.1. In Search of Objective Purposiveness

We defined Kant's initial challenge as the establishment of a perspective from which spatio-temporal events can be identified as moral. The *First Critique* demonstrated that we know phenomenal occurrences through the prism of natural causality. The *Second Critique* established the autonomy of a will free from natural causality. The *Third Critique* tries to bridge natural necessity and freedom by justifying a teleological contemplation of natural events. Up to now Kant was able only to establish the existence of the principle of subjective purposiveness. Both aesthetic judgment and teleological judgment regarding the unity of empirical laws of nature disclose an adaptation of their objects to *our cognitive faculties.* Kant has not yet been able to establish a perspective from which we can discern an objective purposiveness in nature. To do so Kant needs to demonstrate that there are cases where explanations of natural phenomena in terms of mechanistic causality must be supplemented by inquiries into their

[91]Ibid., 23/184.
[92]Pre-Darwinian biology is assumed; see note 31 above.

functions or purposes.[93] He turns to analysis of biological method to establish this point.

Striving toward a principle of mediation between nature and freedom, Kant wants to establish a perspective from which culture and history can be seen as progressing toward the accomplishment of the moral end of the Highest Good. Kant thus strives to establish a perspective from which spatio-temporal events can be judged as purposive. But how can we possibly explain one and the same event through two mutually exclusive perspectives? In the Antinomy of Judgment Kant acknowledges that "as applied to one and the same natural thing, we cannot link or reconcile the mechanical and the teleological principle."[94] Confronting this problem, Kant argues that we must posit a higher principle that reconciles mechanical and teleological principles. "Now it is true that the principle of the mechanism of nature and the principle of nature's causality in terms of purposes, as both are applied to one and the same natural product, must be linked in a single higher principle and flow from it together, since otherwise we could not consistently use both in considering nature."[95]

4.D.2. Reconciliation of Mechanism and Teleology

Kant's proof of the unity of mechanism and teleology builds on his previous discussions of the limitations of human understanding. He attributes the antinomy between mechanism and teleology to the restrictions of discursive understanding and argues that such antinomy need not arise for an intuitive understanding. Contrasting discursive

[93]Judgments regarding functions and purposes differ significantly from aesthetic judgments. In the latter we are not interested in knowing properties of objects. Knowledge is not the point. Aesthetic judgments refer to the harmonious interplay of the faculties of the subject. In biology it is the properties of the objects that are at issue.

[94]Ibid., 296/411.

[95]Ibid., 297/412. Notice how closely this sentence resembles Kant's words in the *Second Critique* regarding the "expectation of bringing some day into view the unity of the entire pure rational faculty (both theoretical and practical) and of *being able to derive everything from one principle*" (Kant, *Critique of Practical Reason*, 94/91. Emphasis mine).

understanding with archetypal, or supersensible, understanding, Kant argues that we are entitled to think that the latter, if it were to exist, could somehow reconcile the mechanical and the teleological explanations of nature in one higher principle. Kant believes that this possibility justifies our use of both types of explanation in explaining phenomena. Kant adorns this simple argument with complicated comparisons of the two types of understanding. In what follows I will provide a concise account of the gist of this comparison.

In searching for the reconciling principle Kant alludes to the *First Critique* which disclosed that discursive understanding depends on the passivity of sensations and knows only the phenomenal world.[96] Kant maintains that the mere awareness of these limits already involves an idea of an intuitive understanding. To characterize the limits of discursive understanding we construct the idea of an intuitive intellect that is not so limited, an intellect that determines the particulars as it contemplates them and is thus pure spontaneity for which there is no conflict between what is and what ought to be. Such an intellect recognizes details as determined by the idea of the whole and is thus free from the endless human striving to bring its experiences under ever higher unity.[97]

In the *Critique of Judgment* Kant maintains that a discursive intellect compensates for its inability to intuit the unity of the whole, since it cannot derive the necessity of empirical laws of nature a

[96]Discursive understanding acquires its knowledge from experience as it moves from one experience to another, recognizing causal links between experiences, links which render experience a systematic whole, and has knowledge of a totality only as it knows its parts.

[97]Kant, *Critique of Judgment*, 286–87/403–404. Kant reiterates and expounds upon the theory of the *First Critique*, which holds that the distinctions between the possible, the actual, and the necessary are not ontological distinctions applicable to things in themselves, but are *epistemological distinctions*. An intuitive intellect could move directly from having a concept to intuiting its existence. For such an intellect, explanations in terms of efficient causes and explanations in terms of final causes would be identical. Unlike it, human beings realize their purposes (cause their existence) through bodily movements in the natural realm and understand them in terms of mechanical causality.

priori, by representing the idea of this unity as purposeful design. Involved in this presentation, inherently, is a thought of an archetypal intellect that determines the laws of nature according to its design of the whole. Such an intellect does not, of course, resort to reflective teleological judgments; from its point of view a purposive structure is nothing but the realization of its creative thought. For this intuitive understanding the laws of nature are necessarily interrelated in one intelligible system. It does not need to regard the unity of empirical laws as if they were designed by an intellectual designer.[98] Due to the nature of our understanding we are compelled to complement our limited knowledge with a reflective judgment of purposiveness. We recognize, however, as we do so that this supplementation is not necessary in itself. We can think of a nondiscursive intellect that sees in unity, as a concrete realization of its purpose, what we see in two distinct intellectual modes: a system of effective causes and an idea of a final cause.[99]

By forming a concept of a nondiscursive understanding we realize that explanations of nature in terms of purposes and mechanical cau-

---

[98]This can be seen as Kant's reformulation of the traditional theological idea that God's thinking the world is identical with God's creating it.

[99]It is important to reemphasize that we do not need to *prove* the *existence* of such an understanding. All we need is to show that a thought of such an understanding is inherent to reflection on the limits of discursive understanding and that the idea of such an understanding is not self-contradictory. "And [to make this point] we do not have to prove that such an intellectus archetypus is possible. Rather, we must prove only that the contrast [between such an intellect and] our discursive understanding—an understanding which requires images (it is an intellectus ectypus)—and the contingency of its having this character lead us to that idea (of an intellectus archetypus), and we must prove that this idea does not involve a contradiction" (Kant, *Critique of Judgment*, 292–93/408). This understanding, had it existed, would understand organisms as the result of a higher principle of causality, which, in a mysterious way, unites both mechanical and teleological principles. Since neither teleology nor mechanism apply to things in themselves but are rather principles of discursive understanding that knows only the phenomena, it is not impossible to think that these two principles are ultimately united in the thought of an archetypal intellect. Since this union takes place in the noumenal realm of which we can know nothing, Kant is excused from the need to explain the mechanism of this reunion.

sation do not really contradict each other. They would if they were determinative principles of a world of things in themselves. A discursive understanding, however, applies only to the phenomenal world that ultimately refers to a noumenal realm. A discursive understanding compensates for its shortcomings by combining mechanical and teleological methods in its study of the phenomenal world, but this phenomenal world may in fact be the reflection of its supernatural substrate which would only be known to an archetypal intellect.

For us teleology and mechanism remain conflicting methods. In the study of natural phenomena, however—which we cannot help but regard as products of design and for the study of which we require teleological guidance—we are entitled to subordinate mechanism to teleology and think of the mechanism of nature as the means for achieving moral purposes.[100] We do so as we think of them as if they had a common ground in the supersensible substrate. This common ground is neither design nor mechanism, and our limited intellect cannot but point to it without grasping its nature.[101]

4.D.3. The Theological Implications of Teleology

From the discussion above Kant concludes that "teleology cannot find final answers to its inquiries except in a theology."[102] We must notice immediately, however, that this is a very special theology. Kant emphasizes time and again that "physical-teleology" entitles us only to think the *idea* or a *principle* of a supersensible substrate. We

---

[100]Ibid., 333–34/444–45. Kant argues that mechanistic causality provides the only explanation of organisms which we can understand, but we know that it cannot provide a completely satisfactory explanation. The principle of teleology provides no explanation but it is indispensable in guiding our search for explanations. This is only a subjective principle and not a determinative judgment, hence it provides no knowledge in the strict sense of the term (pp. 295/410, 298–99/413). In studying organisms we need to find mechanical explanations of the functions of an organ, but we must guide this search by thoughts of the purpose an organ serves. We cannot find mechanical explanations unless we are guided by the teleological quest. We should not be satisfied, however, with an explanation that stops with a statement of the purpose. Thus there is a division of labor, but not a conflict, between the two.

[101]See ibid., 298/412–13.

[102]Ibid., 281/399.

are in no way permitted to assert the existence of an intellectual intuition that reconciles the differences between teleology and mechanism. In suggesting this perspective Kant remains faithful to the critical method. We resort to thinking of the supersensible basis because of the limitations of our cognitive faculties. "Physical-teleology" does not permit us to form any concept of the supersensible realm, and we cannot grasp the working of an intellectual intuition. All we can say is that we must think of the world as if it were the product of an intelligent cause. We must think so because of the limitations of our cognitive powers. But these limitations certainly do not permit us to assert the existence of God. Kant refuses to resurrect the "proof from design" of the existence of God.[103] Having clarified this issue we can proceed to follow Kant in his attempt to discover the principle that governs the archetypal legislation, the idea of which is presupposed by the recognition of the unity of the empirical laws of nature.

▉ 4.E. The Argument from Humanity as an End

The discussion of the unity of empirical laws disclosed that in pursuing the scientific goal we regard the empirical laws of nature as if they were systematized by a rational designer to conform to the requirements of our cognitive faculties. Accordingly, we employ a reflective principle of purpose in guiding our investigation of nature. Our aim in such inquiries, however, is to discover mechanistic explanations, the only kind of explanation that counts as real knowledge of nature. Kant warns time and again that we must remember the difference between reflection guided by the principle of the intelligible unity of nature and assertion that nature *is* a teleological system.[104] To bridge nature and freedom Kant cannot acquiesce in establishing the principle of purposiveness as a subjective principle of reflection.

---

[103]Ibid., 281–82/399–400.

[104]Our discussion thus far does not permit us to assert that we must understand nature as a teleological system the possibility of which must be explained by a reference to a designer who works purposively. In other words, Kant refuses to resurrect the "argument from design" for God's existence. We are not allowed to infer the existence of a designer who works according to a preconceived effect and adopts means to secure it.

He needs to establish purposiveness also as a principle that indicates the objective determination of things, that is, to establish it not just as formal and subjective, but as material and objective.

To be able to establish the purposive principle as objective, Kant needs to demonstrate the existence of a thing, which existence cannot be (causally) explained other than on the supposition that the idea of the effect is already present in the cause. In other words, he needs to show that we must regard certain natural phenomena as if their existence is, at least in part, due to the design of some intelligent being. Kant maintains that living organisms are the only example of such natural purposiveness.[105] In the study of organisms we cannot be satisfied with causal explanations of how certain events take place; we need to supplement this inquiry with teleological questions that ask why, for what purpose, certain things exist. To understand Kant's argument we need to make a brief detour through his discussion of biological methodology.

Kant introduces the concept of an *organized whole* as a regulative concept of reflective judgment that guides Reason, in its manifestation as Judgment, in its search for the efficient causes of organisms. Kant defines organisms as living beings whose parts reciprocally produce and maintain each other, each part being both a means and an end for the other parts of the same whole.[106] In studying organisms

---

[105]Ibid., 253/373.

[106]In section sixty-five, "Things [Considered] as Natural Purposes Are Organized Beings," Kant distinguishes between two kinds of causal connections: a causal connection in terms of efficient causes and a causal connection in terms of final causes. The understanding can identify only causal connections of the first kind. Such connections constitute a descending series of causes and effects wherein the effects which depend for their existence on preceding causes are not, in their turn, the causes of their own causes. In addition to efficient causality Kant defines a final causality in which causes and effects reciprocally condition each other. Objects which exhibit such causality are called natural purposes. "In order for us to judge a body as being, in itself and in its inner possibility, a natural purpose, what is needed is that all its parts, through their own causality, produce one another as regards both their form and combination, and that in this way they produce a whole whose concept ([if present] in a being possessing the causality in terms of concepts that would be adequate for such a product) could, conversely, be

we need to refer the parts to their function in maintaining the whole. Kant maintains that the fact that causal explanations fail to account fully for organisms necessitates and justifies the resort to teleological explanation.[107]

---

the cause of this body according to a principle, so that the connection of *efficient causes* could at the same time be judged to be a *causation through final causes*" (ibid., 252–53/373).

[107]In section sixty-three, "On Relative, as Distinguished from Intrinsic, Purposiveness of Nature," Kant says, "Only in one case does experience lead our power of judgment to the concept of a purposiveness that is both objective and material [or real], i.e., to the concept of a purpose of nature—namely, when we have to judge a relation of cause to effect which is such that we can see it as law-governed only if we regard the cause's action as based on the idea of the effect, with this idea as the underlying condition under which the cause itself can produce that effect" (ibid., 244/367).

In section sixty-four, "On the Character Peculiar to Things [Considered] as Natural Purposes," Kant argues that in order to justify our resort to explanation of natural phenomena in terms of purposes we need to show the existence of natural phenomena whose form cannot be understood by the understanding guided by its principles of mechanistic causality. "To say that a thing is possible only as a purpose is to say that the causality that gave rise to it must be sought, not in the mechanism of nature, but in a cause whose ability to act is determined by concepts. And seeing that a thing is possible only as a purpose requires that the thing's form could not have arisen according to mere natural laws, laws we can cognize by the understanding alone as applied to objects of sense, but requires that even empirical cognition of this form in terms of its cause and effect presupposes concepts of reason. . . that very contingency of the thing's form is a basis for regarding the product as if it had come about through a causality that only reason can have. Such a causality would be the ability to act according to purposes (i.e., a will), and in presenting an object as possible only through such an ability we would be presenting it as possible only through a purpose" (p. 248/370).

Kant argues then that if we can indicate the existence of natural phenomena, the acquisition of empirical knowledge of which (in terms of causes and effects) requires the assumption of purposiveness, of a rational will at work; we are entitled to subordinate the mechanistic understanding to a teleological explanation. When natural phenomena seem to owe their specific form to mere chance, when studied by the Understanding alone; Reason, which must recognize the necessity of that form, if only to understand the conditions connected with the production of the object, must regard the causality of the object as if it were possible only through an intelligible cause. In such cases,

Kant defines two kinds of purposiveness: extrinsic and intrinsic. He distinguishes accordingly between natural purposes and purposes of nature. When we regard a thing as an end we need to understand the function of its parts as if they were designed to maintain its existence. We examine it with the principle of intrinsic purposiveness and regard it as an intrinsic purpose of nature. A thing can also be regarded a means for sustaining something that is an end in itself. In this case we attribute to it extrinsic purposiveness and regard it as a natural purpose. Kant argues that in order to represent nature as a whole as natural purpose, to attribute extrinsic purposiveness to natural phenomena, we must first demonstrate the existence of intrinsic purposes of nature.[108] Once this is achieved, Kant believes, we will finally be able to bridge the gap between causal and teleological explanations of nature.

Kant observes that organisms are only a small part of nature. He asks whether, having recognized particular phenomena as organized wholes that require teleological explanations, we can view nature as a whole as purposive.[109] To answer in the affirmative Kant needs to

---

Kant argues, the teleological explanation is as vital as the mechanical one. "Indeed they [the scientists] can no more give up that teleological principle than they can this universal physical principle. For just as abandoning this physical principle would leave them without any experience whatsoever, so would abandoning that teleological principle leave them without anything for guidance on observing the kind of natural things that have once been thought teleologically, under the concept of natural purposes" (p. 256/376).

[108]Kant seems to argue that when we find a system of nature within which one element is known to be an intrinsic purpose, this intrinsic purpose becomes the purpose of the system as a whole: "Extrinsic purposiveness (a thing's being beneficial to others) can be regarded as an extrinsic natural purpose only under the condition that the existence of what it benefits proximately or remotely is a purpose of nature in its own right" (ibid., 246/368).

[109]Kant thinks that if we use teleological explanations of organisms when the causal explanation of the Understanding fails to satisfy us, we can go further and judge "products as belonging to a system of purposes even if they (or the relation between them, though [perhaps] purposive) do not require us, [so as to account] for their possibility, to look for a different principle beyond the mechanism of blind efficient causes" (ibid., 260–61/380–81). The purpo-

find a natural phenomenon that possesses an intrinsic value; an end that accordingly can be regarded as the (intrinsic) purpose of nature. Only if we demonstrate the existence of a purpose of nature can we look backward from it and contemplate nature as an organized purposive whole. Kant thinks that as long as we confine ourselves to physical teleology, to a study of nature and of ourselves as parts of it, we cannot identify any such end.[110] Moral philosophy, however, has shown

---

siveness of certain parts of nature, organisms, suggests to us that nature as a whole could be purposive. "Once we have adopted such a guide for studying nature and found that it works, we must at least try this maxim of judgment on the whole of nature too, since this maxim may well allow us to discover many further laws of nature that would otherwise remain hidden to us since our insight into the inner [nature] of its mechanism is so limited" (p. 280/ 398). This assertion could be a rather sensitive point in Kant's argument if it were examined merely from the narrow perspective of the philosophy of biology. Kant could say at most that such transition is permissible, but he could not say that the transition to the study of nature as a whole as a teleological system is as inevitable as it is in study of organisms. I do not think, however, that Kant intended his philosophy of biology to be read in isolation from the general argument of the *Third Critique* which is devoted to the quest for a viewpoint that enables us to see spacio-temporal events as purposive.

Analysis of the unity of nature (the unity of empirical laws) necessitates the employment of the teleological principle which allows us to regard nature as a teleological system organized by an intuitive intelligence to suit the capacities of our cognitive faculties. This provides only a principle of subjective purposiveness. The study of organisms allows us to attribute objective purposiveness to natural phenomena. The natural following step in a search for a principle of unity for nature and freedom is to try and see if the perspective of objective purposiveness which the study of organisms provides can be extended to nature as a whole. Kant thus asks whether nature can be seen as purposive.

[110]Kant argues that "this, however, we can never tell by merely examining nature; and hence it follows that, although relative purposiveness points hypothetically to natural purpose, it does not justify any absolute teleological judgment" (ibid., 246/369). As long as we examine nature as a mechanical system we cannot find purposes in it. Reason, however, has other functions beside the Understanding. In its practical capacity Reason functions as legislator of ends and is thus qualified to supply the required teleological perspective.

that the moral agent is an end in itself.[111] Since all things can be regarded merely as means and only moral agency as an end in itself, we can thus regard the moral agent as the ultimate purpose of nature. Having found an end in itself, an intrinsic purpose of nature, we can contemplate nature as a whole through the concept of extrinsic purpose, as a means designed to benefit moral agency.

> Therefore, if we find in the world arrangements in terms of purposes, and we follow reason's inevitable demand to subordinate these merely conditioned purposes to a supreme unconditioned one, i.e., a final purpose, then, to begin with, we are obviously not concerned with a purpose of (i.e., within) nature, so far as nature [already] exists, but with the purpose of the [very] existence of nature and all its arrangements. In other words, we are then concerned with the ultimate *purpose of creation*, and actually, within that purpose, with the supreme condition under which alone there can be a final purpose (where this final purpose is the basis that determines a supreme understanding to produce the beings of the world). Therefore, it is only as a moral being that we acknowledge man to be the purpose of creation. Thus we now have, in the first place, a basis, or at least the primary condition, for regarding the world as a whole that coheres in terms of purposes, and as a *system* of final causes. But above all, in referring natural purposes to an intelligent world cause, as the character of our reason forces us to do, we now have a *principle* that allows us to conceive of the nature and properties of this first cause, i.e., the supreme basis of the kingdom of purposes, and hence allows us to give determination to the concept of this cause.[112]

[111]This argument repeats and strengthens Kant's words in the Introduction: "The understanding, inasmuch as it can give laws to nature a priori, proves that we cognize nature only as appearance, and hence at the same time points to a supersensible substrate of nature; but it leaves this substrate wholly *undetermined.* Judgment, through its a priori principle of judging nature in terms of possible particular laws of nature, provides nature's supersensible substrate (within as well as outside us) with *determinability by the intellectual power.* But reason, through its a priori practical laws, gives this same substrate *determination.* Thus judgment makes possible the transition from the domain of the concept of nature to that of the concept of freedom" (ibid., 37/196).

[112]Ibid., 332–33/443–44.

We should note that Kant is careful not to suggest that the human race is the purpose of creation. He distinguishes here, as he does in his ethical writings, between human beings as merely natural creatures and humanity which he identifies with moral agency. It is not, therefore, human beings with their contingent desires that he proposes as the end of nature but moral agency. The idea of humanity as the crown of creation is a traditional idea that can be used to justify the exploitation of nature for human needs. In Kant's formulation of this idea our use of nature is subordinated to the moral law. Once we recognize moral agency as the only thing that can be an end in itself, according to Kant, we acquire a point of view from which all things that are mere objects can acquire purpose and become means. Thus the history of nature can be interpreted as a means to produce moral agency. In his writing on history Kant clarifies this idea further. It is not every creature or object in the world that should be interpreted narrowly through its serviceability to humankind; rather nature as a whole can be seen as a training ground in which moral character is forged.[113]

■ 4.F. The Argument from the Highest Good

4.F.1. The Highest Good as the Principle of Unity

Kant's discussion of the Highest Good in the *Critique of Judgment* is disjointed, and the logical relations between its parts are unexplained. It is in truth not quite a discussion but a series of suggestive hints that I find too important to ignore. The discussion in the follow-

---

[113]Since in his discussion of biology Kant does not speak of "feelings," it might be asked whether he is still discussing a faculty of judgment or resorts back to the regulative ideas of the *First Critique*. Since I read the *Critique of Judgment* as a unified book I do not accept a reading of the philosophy of biology in isolation. Discussions of biology come after the analysis of aesthetic judgment, which identified a capacity to identify harmonious wholes in nature, and after analysis of the unity of the empirical laws of nature. Philosophy of biology assumes this capacity in its claim that we are capable of identifying organisms. The task of the philosophy of biology, after the analysis of judgments of taste, is to show the objectivity of the judgment, namely, that certain types of objects require teleological explanations.

ing sections is an attempt to reconstruct Kant's view from his various statements. While Kant does not lead us by the hand through what I have called "the argument from the Highest Good," my reconstruction finds support in the fact that in *Religion within the Limits of Reason Alone* Kant draws the conclusion that follows from his argument as I present it here.[114]

Kant argues that a cooperation of what he calls "physical teleology" and "moral teleology" provides, for the first time, a content for the principle of purposiveness that reflection on the unity of the laws of nature presupposes.[115] The search for the unifying principle of nature and freedom culminates when moral teleology supplements physical teleology with a concept of an intrinsic purpose that establishes a perspective from which nature as a whole can be regarded as a system of purposes. As moral agents we are the only natural object that can be considered an intrinsic purpose.

Having established the moral agent as the purpose of nature, Kant is able to move on to the final stage of his argument. He does so with the aid of "moral teleology." Its first task was to establish the moral agent as an end of nature. Now, reflection on morality—a reflection that Kant had already conducted in the *Second Critique* and repeats here—indicates that morality itself has a final end that it sets for itself: the rational idea of the Highest Good.

> The moral law is reason's formal condition for the use of our freedom and hence obligates us all by itself, independently of any purpose whatever as material condition. But it also determines for us, and a priori, a final purpose, and makes it obligatory for us to strive toward [achieving] it; and that purpose is the *highest good* in the world that we can achieve through freedom.[116]

[114]For discussion of these conclusions see chapter five of this part.
[115]Kant, *Critique of Judgment*, 347/456.
[116]Ibid., 339/450. Note "that we can achieve," not "that God can bring about." See additional discussion of the Highest Good in the *Critique of Judgment* (pp. 323/435, 333/444).

Having learned that moral agency is the final purpose of nature, we are now reminded that moral agency too has an end, the realization of the Highest Good. Our teleological conclusion with regard to the purpose of nature is therefore extended; we can now recognize the Highest Good as the purpose of nature. Thus, in the final analysis, it is the moral agent who strives to realize the ideal of the Highest Good who provides the content for the teleological principle.

4.F.1.a. Implications of the Proposed Solution

The proposal that the Highest Good is the teleological principle through which the problem of unity is to be solved seems to me to involve the two following questions. (1) What justifies our attribution of the principle of the Highest Good to the intellectual intuition that supposedly designed the world? (2) Why does such attribution not imply historical necessity which realizes the Highest Good irrespective of particular moral decisions by human agents?

Kant, I believe, thinks about these issues as follows. When I reflect on the universe as a teleological structure and recognize the human striving to realize the moral law as the end of nature, I think of the universe as created in order that in it humanity will act morally.[117] These considerations are closely tied to an independent speculation concerning the possible goals of an intuitive intellect if such an intellect creates a world. When we think of the universe as the creation of an intellectual intuition, we think of the universe as created by a Pure Reason. Thinking of the way in which a Pure Reason, a Reason that has no material interests, might decide to create, we must further envision an end that would motivate its creative thought. What is it, we ask, that an Intuitive Reason could possibly strive to achieve? Whatever this end might be it would have to be an end that arises out of Pure Reason itself, as an ideal of Reason. Having come thus far in our contemplation, we readily recognize that we already have a concept of the one ideal of Practical Reason, an ideal that we recognize

---

[117]I think that Kant's reasoning is that a moral end cannot be an accidental purpose of nature; thinking of something as moral involves thinking of it as legislated by a rational will.

as an ideal of Pure Reason. In the *Critique of Practical Reason* we learned that Reason recognizes one supreme ideal a priori, the rational ideal of the Highest Good. The Highest Good, we must remember, is a purely formal ideal that represents the demand of justice that a perfect world be such that happiness accords with virtue. As a purely formal ideal of Pure Reason, the Highest Good is the only candidate we have for the ideal that might motivate a pure intuitive intellect in creating a world. Our contemplation leads us then to reflect on the universe as created in order to realize the Highest Good.

The idea of the Highest Good as the end of nature opens up a frightening possibility that a philosophy of history might be implied according to which the Highest Good will be realized in history irrespective of the moral decisions of human agents. If this possibility were to be verified, Reflective Judgment would force us to see all moral effort as insignificant. Whereas previously we might have feared that moral effort was futile because we could not guarantee that the ends of Reason can be accomplished in nature, it now seems that the ends of Reason will be accomplished in nature of necessity and that moral agents are mere puppets in the hands of the cunning of Reason. The way from this speculation to the idea of the world spirit working out its self-realization through our lives is short indeed. It is important to see that this cannot be Kant's view.

The suggestion that the Highest Good might be realized in history of necessity contradicts the notion of the Highest Good. The Highest Good is a requirement that nature be responsive to virtue, but virtue is nothing but the autonomous decision of the moral agent to act out of respect for the moral law. A world in which human beings would act according to the moral law out of the automatism of their nature would be a world in which the Highest Good could not possibly be realized. The ideal of the Highest Good as the supreme principle of Creation demands that autonomous rational agents be the end of nature, so that through their moral decisions the Highest Good will be realized. The philosophy of history that is implied by these considerations is a conception of history as the arena in which the realization of the Highest Good is possible, but the possibility is one that might never be realized if human beings do not rise to the occasion and act morally. This is a conception of history in which the realization of the ends of Reason is promised as an inherent possibility, but it is not an eschatology. It is important to emphasize that for Kant the moral law does not develop in history, although our awareness of its demands does. Since the moral law is a "fact of Reason," the possibility of the realization of the Highest Good requires no development in Reason. The Categorical Imperative, which is the ground of virtue, is transparent to the human mind *ab initio*. It is the tragedy of human history that we realize the possibility of moral action, which is inherent to our nature as rational beings, only after an endless series of moral failures.

4.F.2. From Teleology to Religion

Summarizing the findings of the *Critique of Judgment*, Kant argues that Reflective Judgment becomes the foundation of theology and religion.[118] The cooperation of physical teleology and moral teleology provide the reflective principle of an intelligent legislator of nature who is also the legislator of a moral kingdom of purposes. Kant goes even so far as to assert that this process of thought results in construction of the predicates we attribute to such a designer:

> Determining the principle of the causality of the original being in this way has the following consequences: We shall have to think of this being not merely as an intelligence and as legislating to nature, but also as the legislating sovereign in a moral kingdom of purposes. In reference to the *highest good*—possible solely under the reign of this being—namely, the existence of rational beings under moral laws, we shall think of this original being as *omniscient*, so that even our inmost attitudes (in which the proper moral value of the acts of rational world beings [*Weltwesen*] consists) will not be hidden from it. We shall think of it as *omnipotent*, so that it can make all of nature accord with that highest purpose. We shall think of it as *omnibenevolent* as well as just, because these two properties (which together constitute *wisdom*) are the conditions under which a supreme cause

118Ibid., 376/481.

of the world can be the cause of the world [taken] as the highest good under moral laws. And we shall similarly have to think of this being as having all the remaining transcendental properties (for goodness and justice are moral properties), such as *eternity*, *omnipresence*, etc., which [achieving] such a final purpose presupposes.[119]

Reviewing these conclusions, Kant asserts that "from that moral teleology and its relation to physical teleology reason advances to *theology*."[120]

Having said this, Kant is quick to emphasize that the only benefit nature is designed to provide moral agents is the means of cultivating their faculties. Nature provides moral agents with opportunities for acquiring and perfecting their technical and intellectual skills in their effort to establish a moral history. Anticipating Hegel,[121] Kant suggests the idea of the cunning of nature—an idea which he develops in his essays on history—and maintains that moral agents need to struggle with the difficulties nature poses before them in order to transform it into what he will call in *Religion within the Limits of Reason Alone* "the Kingdom of God."

We should be aware that the train of thought that Kant follows in his attempt to discover the principle of unity culminates in a very sensitive point. Kant asserts that the principle that governs the design of nature by the archetypal intellect—a designer of whom we must think in considering natural purposes, beautiful objects, and the unity of the empirical laws of nature—is the Highest Good. Such a conclusion, if misunderstood, could present Kant as reviving the "proof from design" for the existence of God. Aware of this danger, Kant feels obliged to prevent this misconception which also thwarts the autonomy of morality. As he did in the *Second Critique*, Kant quickly empha-

---

[119]Ibid., 333/444.

[120]Ibid., 337/448.

[121]Kant anticipates Hegel in raising the notion of the cunning of nature. However, as I shall explain later, he also differs significantly from Hegel in the context in which this notion takes place.

sizes that thought about such a designer is not determinative and therefore the autonomy of moral deliberation must remain intact.

Immediately following his assertions that teleology culminates in theology and religion, Kant repetitively cautions us to protect the autonomy of moral deliberation from the possible intrusion of religion. Kant warns us against attributing determinative status to our contemplation of the moral designer of the universe. He argues that we need to contemplate the existence of a moral designer "only for [the use of] judgment in accordance with the concepts of Practical Reason, and hence for reflective rather than determinative judgment."[122] We refer the purposiveness of nature to an external designer because of the limitations of a discursive understanding. This principle, however, provides us only with a reflective means for contemplating the unity of the lawfulness of the world and the purposiveness of freedom. We are allowed, and in fact need, to regard ourselves as living in a world designed by an archetypal intellect who designs according to the principle of the Highest Good. This contemplation, however, does not allow us to assert that such a designer actually exists or that we know its attributes.

In spite of these restrictions we must emphasize that the principle of the Highest Good is indispensable even in its restricted reflective status. It provides moral agents a principle from which they can contemplate spatio-temporal events as purposive; it makes it possible for them to believe that "the ideas that pure practical reason supplies may find incidental confirmation in natural purposes."[123] Armed with the reflective principle, moral agents have a means to judge whether and to what extent history progresses toward realization of the Kingdom of God on earth.[124]

In his attempt to emphasize the reflective status of the teleological principle, a principle that allows us to think of the archetypal intellect which governs in light of the principle of the Highest Good, Kant manifests his deep bias against organized religion. It seems that reli-

---

[122]Ibid., 346/455.
[123]Ibid., 334/445
[124]Kant develops this idea in *Religion within the Limits of Reason Alone*.

gion for him—by this term I think he refers primarily to "historical" or "positive" religion—is the greatest possible threat to the autonomy of morality and, by implication, to the cultural progress of humanity. Kant warns that in using the concept of the moral designer of the universe determinately we risk anthropomorphism.[125] Forgetting the reflective status of the idea of the moral designer of the universe, we will fall pray to demonology ("which is an anthropomorphic way of conceiving the supreme being"), and we will reduce religion either into theurgy ("a fanatical delusion that we can receive a feeling from, and in turn influence, other supersensible beings") or into idolatry ("a superstitious delusion that we can make ourselves pleasing to the supreme being by means other than a moral attitude").[126]

Kant's discussion of religion remains ambivalent. On the one hand he admits that teleology leads to theology, but on the other he is terrified of his own conclusions. As a true child of the Enlightenment it is important for him to qualify every mention of religion in order to avoid the danger of fanaticism. For this reason, even if his own thought leads him to recognize the reflective concept of an archetypal intellect—a designer of the world according to the principle of the Highest Good—as important and legitimate, Kant dares not conclude that religion is worthy of a separate Critique.

Thus Kant does not infer from his analysis the conclusions that Otto and Tillich developed in their theories of religion. Refusing to attribute intrinsic significance to positive religion, Kant saw in historical religion only a means that should ultimately be superseded by secular culture.[127] The ambiguity in Kant's thought about religion left room for thinkers like Otto and Tillich—who, together with Kant, acknowledged the indispensability of the unifying principle—to conduct an independent critique of religion.

---

[125]Kant, *Critique of Judgment*, 348/457.

[126]Ibid., 351/459. Kant repeats these warnings in *Religion within the Limits of Reason Alone*, 162–63.

[127]See Kant, *Religion within the limits of Reason Alone*, 79, 86, 88–89, 92, 94, 96, 100–106, 112, 143, 182–83.

5

RELIGION BEYOND THE LIMITS
OF PRACTICAL REASON

▪ 5.A. The Gradual Unfolding of Kant's Argument

I set out to show that the critique of the Faculty of Judgment is a
systematic inquiry into the unity of the faculties of moral Reason
and scientific Understanding and into the unity of the realms of nature and of freedom. I have demonstrated that the solution to the
problem that was introduced in the *Critique of Practical Reason* unfolds itself gradually in the *Critique of Judgment* through an examination of various employments of the principle of purposiveness. Kant
leads us through analysis of the aesthetic experience, of the scientific
recognition of the unity of empirical laws, and of biological method.
His study culminates in an analysis of the implications of the commitment of moral agents to realize the moral good in history. At the end
of this intricate inquiry Kant identifies a unifying principle that holds
Understanding and Reason together without reducing one to the other
and without preferring the interests of one over the other. Kant claims
that the critique of the faculty of reflective judgment uncovers a prin-

ciple that mediates between Understanding and Reason and functions as the supreme principle of the unity of "the entire pure rational faculty" from which the principles of both theory and praxis can be derived. Before turning to examine the implications of Kant's argument, let us reconstruct and integrate its gradual unfolding. My purpose here is exegetical rather than evaluative; I wish to consolidate the various arguments we studied above into one sustained argument. I shall focus therefore on the unified structure of the argument rather than on the validity of its various stages.

Kant began with an analysis of aesthetic taste. He argued that the highest transcendental condition of our ability to discern harmonious interconnectedness in natural objects is the thought of the supersensible will who designed nature in a way to which the harmonious interplay of our cognitive faculty responds—an interplay of which we become aware through the feelings of pleasure. From the point of view of Kant's ultimate goal—the establishment of harmony between nature and freedom—this analysis is a limited achievement, but a very significant one. It purports to show that in contemplating beautiful objects in nature we gain an awareness of something beyond it.

In the next stage of the argument Kant examined the scientific awareness of the unity of empirical laws. The Understanding discovers, through Criticism of its functions, that its supreme principles determine the conditions under which laws of nature may exist. They do not determine what these laws are or how they should be interrelated. The Understanding discovers this through a critical analysis of the structure of its experience. In scientific reasoning, however, the Understanding discovers a further fact of its experience. It discovers that the laws of nature are interrelated in a systematic unity of ascending magnitude, so that not only does experience reflect lawlike uniformity but the laws of nature themselves exhibit a higher order of unity. Critical evaluation of this higher unity, which the Understanding discovers, must explain what the origin of this unity is. Since the transcendental unity of apperception supplies only a formal unity of experience, the higher unity that reflects the content of the laws of nature and the relations between them must be assumed to originate elsewhere. Furthermore, since, as shown in the Copernican turn of the *First Critique*, this unity cannot be found in the givenness of intuition, and since it cannot be supplied by a discursive Understanding, it can only be attributed to a Reason unlike ours, that is, to an Intuitive Reason.[1] Thus the scientific endeavor, an *endeavor of the Understanding*, to discover the highest laws of nature presupposes a belief in the existence of an intelligible order of nature that the Understanding *discovers*.

This argument advances us beyond the conclusions from aesthetic experience. While the latter showed that judgment of beauty in natural objects presupposes a thought of an intellectual designer of nature, the analysis of the unity of nature discovered by science shows that insofar as the Understanding is aware of this unity it must understand itself, reflectively, as discovering an intelligible structure of reality. The Understanding becomes aware of itself as *discovering*, not as legislating. In discovering the unity, of which it thinks as imparted on nature by an Archetypal Reason, the Understanding discovers a harmony between Reason and itself. It now becomes possible to ask according to what principle Reason determines the laws of nature that the Understanding discovers. It is at least logically possible that this principle is a moral one, and if it were found to be so the possibility of a unity of freedom and nature could be established. The analysis of biological method strives to show that this logical possibility can be real.

The argument from the existence of biological organisms, interconnected wholes in which all parts function both as efficient and final causes, strives to move beyond the conclusions of the argument from the unity of nature. It strives to show that the rational unity of a natural entity can be teleological. In order to show that this further conclusion is logically possible Kant had to overcome the dichotomy between "is" and "ought." In doing so he strove to show that a judgment concerning a final cause can be a valid "is" (factual) statement, that statements like "the heart contracts in order to supply blood to the body" can be valid factual claims, and that a description of the

---

[1]This claim should alert us to a possible challenge to the autonomy of Reason. We shall see, as we proceed, that Paul Tillich addressed this question and gave it a central place in his theology. I shall say no more here, because the issue will be discussed extensively later on (see part two, section 7.D.7.a.).

heart that fails to include its purposiveness will not describe it adequately.

Since the argument follows upon the conclusion of the argument from the unity of nature, Kant's discussion of the relations between the "is" and the "ought" must refer not to a discursive but to an Intuitive Reason. Since it is assumed, as shown in the previous analysis, that Intuitive Reason supplies the unifying principle of nature, including biological nature, it becomes evident that the "is"/"ought" dichotomy dissolves, for an Intuitive Reason knows no gap between the ideal and the real, between what ought to be and what is. For us, there is inevitably a gap between the real and the ideal, but Kant's speculation suggests that we can think of a perspective from which this gap would disappear.

The logical possibility that there be no dichotomy between "is" and "ought" should already follow from the analysis of the uniformity of the empirical laws of nature. What biological method adds is an example of natural entities that actually require teleological explanations that allow us to claim that there are functions that a biological entity ought to perform. In this way "ought" statements are reintroduced into our scientific accounts. In judging that something has organic unity, we recognize that an account in terms of efficient causes must be supplemented by an account in terms of final causes. Insofar as the unifying principle of biological nature, as well as of nature as a whole, is thought of as a principle of an Intuitive Reason, it is possible for that principle to be a judgment concerning what ought to be. The argument has shown that a unifying principle of nature can be teleological and that at least with regard to biological entities it must be, but it does not tell us what the content of this teleological principle might be.

In order to establish the unity of Reason and the Understanding Kant must show not only that the unifying principle can be teleological but that it must be moral. Kant needs to show that there is a unifying teleological principle to nature as a whole and that this principle is moral. This is what Kant tries to do in his further argument on the basis of the doctrines of humanity as a final end and of the Highest Good as an ideal of Reason.

Is there a perspective available to us from which nature can be thought to have a function? Of course, if there were a God who created the universe, God's purpose would have provided a perspective for ascription of teleology, but this perspective would not be available to us. Kant thinks that there is a human perspective from which nature can be seen as teleological; this perspective is the status of the rational agent as an end in itself. Rational agency is the source of all value, apart from which all things are mere objects. It is rational agency that sets itself ends and ascribes values to things as means to them. Knowing ourselves to be both natural beings and ends-in-ourselves we already recognize an end of nature, the end that we have, to achieve moral perfection.

As rational agents human beings must see themselves as determining the value of all that participates in their quest to achieve the ends that they determine to be valuable. Every part of nature is susceptible to such valuation which endows it with a function in the achievement of a rational moral end (except other rational agents who must also be recognized as ends in themselves). As rational agents, we are committed to the pursuit of those ends that we contingently adopt, but not only to them. According to Kant, rational agency recognizes the synthetic a priori necessity of valuing the Highest Good. The rational ideal of the Highest Good demands that the universe be brought to a state in which virtue is realized and rewarded with happiness. The Highest Good requires that nature not be, in Kant's words, a "niggardly stepmother" alien to our values but attentive and responsive. While there is precious little that we can do to make nature morally attentive, we must nevertheless recognize that this is the supreme end of nature.

It is important for me to emphasize here that the supreme end of nature, in light of the ideal of the Highest Good, is not a deliberative end, and is, as such, beyond the legislation of Practical Reason which is concerned with what we ought to do.[2] Even though the Highest Good is not a deliberative end, it remains a rational ideal and as such

---

[2] I elaborate on this point in the next section.

constitutes an Archimedean point from which the ends of nature can be determined. Pursuit of the Highest Good in our moral life requires, according to Kant, a belief in its eventual realization, a belief that necessitates a further belief that nature is indeed so constituted as to be responsive to virtue. This amounts to a belief that the Intuitive Reason to which the unity of the empirical laws of nature was ascribed is also a moral will.

■ 5.B. The Highest Good as a Reflective Principle

In this interpretation of Kant's discussion of various forms of purposiveness in the previous sections and in the reconstruction in the last pages of what I believe is his central argument, we encountered once again the concept of the Highest Good which had played a central role in Kant's "official" philosophy of religion. We must notice, however, that the *Third Critique* provides a perspective for understanding the concept of the Highest Good that differs from that of the *Second Critique*. At the end of the final argument of chapter three of this part I concluded that religion, based on the Highest Good as a principle of Practical Reason cannot establish the unity of Reason. It is now the time to explain why the Highest Good can be regarded the unifying principle of Reason when it is considered a reflective principle rather than a Practical ideal.

In the *Critique of Practical Reason* the Highest Good is seen from the perspective of the deliberating agent. From that perspective the agent, who wishes not to decide absurdly, must be able to believe that his or her decision to act virtuously will result in happiness. Knowledge that a virtuous act will lead to happiness, however, thwarts morality altogether. Knowing that my act will in fact lead to happiness makes my lawful choice one of prudence rather than of respect for the moral law.[3]

Let us examine the point of view of the agent, the point of view of Practical Reason. Having a contingently given set of desires the satisfaction of which is the incentive of happiness in a given decision

---

[3]See Kant, *Critique of Judgment*, 352/460, 376–77/481–82; 380–81/485. This is because the happiness involved here is my own happiness, not the happiness of others (pursuit of which is an imperfect duty of mine).

situation, the agent can act according to the counsels of prudence or the maxims of skill and do whatever is needed to secure the desired end. Alternatively, the agent can evaluate the situation morally and decide to do what is right. In this situation, in which both the empirical counsel of happiness and duty are known to the agent, the introduction of belief in the Highest Good is disastrous. Insofar as the Highest Good promises that virtue leads to happiness, virtue becomes the counsel of prudence. At this level of practical thought, where duty and desire are both clearly set before the will, the Highest Good serves to bridge the gap between them. As it bridges the gap, the guarantee given by the Highest Good nullifies the sublimity of morality.

From the perspective of reflective Reason, however, the Highest Good undergoes significant change. Insofar as it is a guarantee, it is merely a general belief that moral actions are not in vain even as they seem futile in the world we know. It is an important promise that a moral act does ultimately have worthy consequences. Since this promise is only available reflectively it does not affect moral deliberation. The moment of reflection is not a moment of deliberation. The subject of reflection is not a moral agent to whom both desire and duty present themselves as motivating forces between which the agent must decide. Reflective Judgment allows the subject to believe that whatever moral acts the agent did, or will do, will ultimately be rewarded, but no incentive exists to give content to the ideal of happiness called to mind by the notion of reward. Thus, the reflective Highest Good does not bridge the gap between duty and any specific desire and cannot therefore render any duty a mere counsel of prudence.[4]

[4]However favorably we interpret the doctrine of the Highest Good in the *Second Critique*, even when we read it as an anticipation of the *Third Critique*, there remains a difference between the two books regarding the status of the Highest Good vis-à-vis morality. In the *Second Critique* the Highest Good is brought in to solve a problem within morality. It addresses the moral agent with the promise that through divine intervention the Highest Good will be realized. (This is a claim that most commentators understand as an outright promise of future reward, but now we are trying a more charitable reading.) In the *Third Critique* the Highest Good is introduced through a discussion of physical teleology which leads to an idea of a designer of the universe. In the *Third Critique* the idea of the Highest Good does not serve to prove the

From the point of view of an Intuitive Reason, the Highest Good is the end of both the moral law and the rational order of nature, and it is the end of both without rendering the moral law merely consequentialist. To see that this is so we need only consider the difference between a discursive and an intuitive reason. From our discursive point of view, knowing what will happen in the future has a devastating effect on our ability to decide morally. We deliberate morally as finite knowers who must do what is right because they cannot know what will ultimately be good. This consideration does not hold for an intuitive Reason for which what it decides becomes reality. Such a Reason cannot possibly decide according to what it knows will be, because what it decides ought to be determines what will be. The only principle available to such a Reason must then be the purely formal principle of rational decision that the moral law represents. Having no independent incentive to counteract the moral law—being therefore a holy will—intuitive Reason must determine nature to realize the rational ideal of the Highest Good, which at this level of abstraction (given no particular incentive) can only be purely formal. Armed with this reflective belief, a moral agent cannot know that a given desire that the agent has will be realized if he or she acts morally. What does become possible for the moral agent is to interpret his or her personal history in terms of moral reward or retribution and to identify, after the fact, the worthy results of moral action.

■ 5.C. The Kantian Foundation of Modern Religious Thought

In this discussion of the Highest Good I find justification for my claim that the *Third Critique* embodies Kant's most profound religious thought. In these considerations Kant transforms the idea of the Highest Good which arose from the considerations of the *Critique of Practical Reason* as a problematic belief in moral reward. The idea of the Highest Good has become the governing principle of a philosophy

---

existence of God. It is introduced as a possible principle of creation. Once the idea of the Highest Good is introduced in this way, as a contemplative idea, it does indeed shed light on the significance of morality and its role in history. It does not, however, enter into moral deliberation.

of history within which moral commitment is of paramount importance. The idea of the Highest Good is further depicted as the governing principle of creation in which Reason and nature are reconciled. It is to this notion of the Highest Good that we must look when we approach Kant's discussion of religion within the limits of Reason alone.

We must deduce from these considerations something that Kant himself never explicitly claimed. It seems to follow from the reflective necessity to think of the world as created by a designer who had the Highest Good as a regulative idea that the thought of the world as so designed must accompany our reflection on our scientific and moral activities. The idea of the Highest Good, as the constitutive ideal of creation, becomes therefore the highest point of transcendental unity of the powers of reason. Just as the "I think" of the transcendental deduction of the *First Critique* functions as the principle of the transcendental unity of apperception, and just as the principle of autonomy functions as the unifying principle of our affective life in the *Second Critique*, so does the Highest Good of the *Third Critique* function as the principle of the transcendental unity of Reason and Understanding, as the unifying principle of the domains of nature and freedom.[5] This conclusion, for which Kant had laid the ground but had never explicitly drawn, became the cornerstone of the theological thought of such pivotal figures as Otto and Tillich. Tillich's enigmatic theory of theonomy and of the import of meaning is inexplicable without this Kantian idea. Otto's theory of divination as the ability to judge that an Idea of Reason is manifested in a finite event is understandable only as a development of Kant's theory that the faculty of judgment allows us to see in nature a realization of rational ideals. As I shall explain in my chapter on Otto, Kant's view of our reflective ability to contemplate nature as the creation of a moral designer was picked up first by Jakob Fries and then by Leonard Nelson, and became in their hands the founding insight of a theory of *Ahndung*, a theory

[5]Once the idea of the Highest Good is established as the supreme principle of creation, the mechanical laws of nature can be seen as serving the purposes of freedom. This allows Kant to claim that the two distinct perspectives of interpretation, that of nature and that of freedom, interpret the same reality.

of our ability to perceive the reflection of the infinite in the finite. This ability became for them the corner stone of a philosophy of religion that Otto sought to bring to completion in his *The Idea of the Holy*.

■ 5.D. Contemplative Hope

In arguing for my integrative interpretation of the overarching quest of the *Third Critique* for a principle of unity, I need to confront, for the last time, the rival theory according to which the "primacy of Practical Reason" secures the unity of Reason. The most profound insight that a theory of the primacy of Practical Reason offers is to be found in its claim that the metaphysical aspirations of Reason, which could not be realized theoretically, find their satisfaction in moral action.[6] It is in moral action that the agent knows him or herself as a free noumenal being and ascertains the meaning of human existence in the realization of the rational ends that Practical Reason legislates a priori. It becomes clear from Kant's discussion of the Highest Good in the *Third Critique* that this insight is not available to Practical Reason.[7] As Kierkegaard noted, and as Kant had readily admitted, Practical Reason sets the standard by which actions are measured if they are to be moral. Practical Reason, however, has no ability whatsoever to determine, in any case, that a moral act was empirically performed. It cannot do so because Practical Reason has no empirical intuition, and because it demands that an act be performed out of pure motivation but cannot ascertain that any act has been so performed. Our conscience, informed by the Categorical Imperative, is a judge that can only condemn but never justify. It is impossible therefore for Practical Reason to satisfy the aspirations of Reason and to find the meaning of human existence in the moral act

---

[6]This is the conclusion of such commentators as Caird, Yovel, and Kroner. See my discussion of the doctrine of the primacy of Practical Reason in part one, section 3.C.1.a above.

[7]My discussion of the primacy of Practical Reason shows that, unlike other commentators, I do not think this insight is available to Practical Reason even in the *Second Critique*, but the *Third Critique* clarifies the issue further.

and its place in a moral history. This can only be done by a Reflective Judgment that the legislation of Practical Reason is indeed exemplified in an historical event. It is therefore only in Reflective Judgment that the aspirations of Reason are satisfied. Kant, somewhat reluctantly, admits that the reflective contemplation in which this is achieved is the basis of a rational theology.

A question that must, for the time being, remain unanswered, since Kant does not address it, is whether the reflective unity of Reason, which the Highest Good secures, can also resolve the specific conflicts that arise from the clash of the interests of Reason in its functions as theoretical and practical. We may tentatively suggest here that with the contemplative solution the context of the problem is shifted; science and morality no longer understand themselves as self-sufficient but as partners in service of an interest that is common to them and as such is beyond each of them. Science no longer understands itself as simply striving to know all that is possible, but as discovering the causal structure through which the end of nature is realized. Morality no longer sees itself as legislating to noumenal ideality, but as directing the will to implement the moral history which is the end of nature. It remains to be pondered how this altered self-understanding of the scientist and the moralist affects the arena of possible clashes. It is this issue, I believe, that is the focal point of Tillich's theory of theonomy.

■ 5.E. Concluding Remarks

5.E.1. On the Reflective Status of the Highest Good

Before I could bring myself to accord serious consideration to Kant's allusion to the ideas of God, Intuitive Reason, the Supersensible, and the Highest Good in the *Critique of Judgment*, I had to overcome a deep rooted suspicion that in these allusions Kant wildly overstepped the strict bounds he had set to philosophical discourse. This wariness reflects Heinrich Heine's jesting critique:

> After the tragedy comes the farce. . . . Kant relents and shows
> that he is not merely a great philosopher but also a good man. . .

As with a magician's wand, he revivifies deism, which theoretical reason has killed.[8]

Was it really necessary for Kant to bring ideas of God and of a
supersensible object into the discussion of the unity of nature and of
its purposiveness? In other words, should we take the argument of the
Third Critique so seriously as to see in it the outline of a philosophy
of religion beyond the doctrine of the postulates of Practical Reason?

Through repeated readings and rereadings of crucial points in the
text, I have come to appreciate the subtlety of Kant's argument and
its careful minimalism. It has become clear to me that nothing was
further from his mind than to postulate the existence of God as the
ground of the purposiveness of nature, which, in turn, accounts for a
unity of the worlds of nature and freedom beyond anything that Reason can establish. What he did try to achieve was a delineation of
certain points in which reflection on the creations of both Theoretical
and Practical Reason leads us, necessarily, to *thoughts* about an intuitive Reason that could have generated the laws of nature with a rational purpose in mind. At issue is a mere thought, not an intended
object. It is a thought considered regardless of whether or not it can
have an object. It is, however, a thought to which we are inexorably
led as Reason reflects on its theoretical and practical applications.

It was, I believe, Kant's intention to show that contemplation of
the reflective ideas, which are generated in the exercise of our faculty
of judgment, provides the final answer to the three great questions of
philosophy: What can I know? What ought I to do? and, What may
I hope for? Only with these ideas in mind can we understand the
empirical unity that our scientific activity discovers in nature, and
only thus can we conceive of the realization of our moral purposes.
Only the reflective possibility of the unity of nature and rational purpose enables us to pass moral judgment on historical events, an ability that, in turn, allows us to hope for an ultimate attainment of the
historical ideal of the Highest Good. While the activity of Reason in

---

[8]Heinrich Heine, *Religion and Philosophy in Germany* (trans. John Snodgrass;
Albany, NY: SUNY Press, 1986) 119.

scientific research or in moral deliberation is self-sufficient and independent in its determination of what is or of what ought to be, the interests of Reason, which motivate its functions as Theoretical and as Practical, can only be satisfied through contemplation of the worlds of nature and of freedom in light of the idea of a universe purposively ordered by a Reason that transcends our discursive limitations. The interests of Reason lead us then to contemplate the world as a divine creation embodying a moral purpose.[9]

Even in the *Third Critique* Kant does not allow us to claim any knowledge of God. All that we have is a contemplative thought about an Intuitive Reason as, for instance, the basis of the possibility of the unity of nature. It is clear then that Kant does not readmit knowledge that he denied us in his *First Critique*. The solution to the problem of the unity of Reason, which the *Critique of Judgment* attempts, is, accordingly, not a solution from God's point of view. It is a solution from the point of view of Reflective Judgment as it contemplates reality as it might be seen from the point of view of a Reason, which unlike ours, is intuitive. While the difference may be subtle it is crucial. The first would be a solution from a point of view we cannot inhabit. It would amount to a belief that in God's mind all may be well. The second is a solution from the point of view of reflective Reason as it contemplates the worlds of nature and of freedom and the possible relations between them. The contemplative idea of God, which underwrites the solution, implies no cognition of a supersensible entity: it is a pure construct of Reason in its function as a faculty of judgment.

5.E.2. On Kant's Theory of Positive Religion

Kant's last systematic work, *Religion within the Limits of Reason Alone*,[10] which is usually interpreted in light of the conclusions of the

---

[9]It is no accident that we can hear in these conclusions an anticipation of Schleiermacher's characterization of religion as a third counterpart of both theory and practice. See Friedrich Schleiermacher, *On Religion: Speeches to Its Cultural Despisers* (trans. John Oman; New York: Harper & Row, 1958) 38.

[10]Henceforth to be abbreviated as *Religion*.

Critique of Practical Reason, can be understood better and in a more nuanced way when it is read in light of the *Critique of Judgment*. While interpretation in light of the *Third Critique* may be more difficult, it is called for at least by the fact that Kant wrote his work on religion after the *Third Critique*, and cannot be thought to have forgotten what he wrote there. Kant's work in *Religion* is not intended to achieve any further development of the critique of reason. This becomes evident from even a cursory reading. Kant does not recognize positive religion as a product of a distinct faculty of reason, and *Religion* is not a critique of such a faculty. The work undertakes a study of the historical institution of religion, in order to see if and how it can fit into the domains of Reason that were mapped throughout the *Critiques*.

All reference to religion in this context will be to the historical institution of religion rather than to the reflective religious ideas that I illuminated in the discussion of the *Critique of Judgment*. Religion, according to Kant, finds a proper role for itself when it addresses a difficulty with which finite rational agents must grapple in their attempt to lead a moral life. Kant identifies this problem in his discussion of evil in *Religion*. The *Second Critique* and the *Grounding* sought to define the requirements of morality and the conditions for their possibility. They did not address themselves to the "mechanisms" of moral decisions, to the manner in which concrete persons in the fullness of rational and emotional life determine their will to follow the edicts of Reason rather than to abide by inclination.

In the systematic moral works the will was a rational will, a will capable of determining itself according to duty. It was, however, also a will capable of determining itself according to the maxims suggested by the inclinations. In terms of the discussion in *Religion*, the will can be moral but it can also be evil. In the systematic works this possibility was recognized and expressed in the metaphor that depicted the will at the crossroads between its a priori principle and its a posteriori incentive.[11] The systematic task was to show that the will

---

[11]Immanuel Kant, *Grounding for the Metaphysics of Morals* (trans. James W. Ellington; Indianapolis: Hackett, 1983) 13/400. For the German edition, see idem, *Grundlegung zur Metaphysic der Sitten* (1785; reprinted in *Kants Gesammelte Schriften*, vol. 5).

has an a priori principle and that the will can be determined by it. The question of how the choice at the crossroads is made had to be left unanswered. The reasons for this are perhaps simple; if there were in existence a mechanism, either natural or rational, through which the choice is made, the freedom of the will would have been compromised. This freedom of the will, the depiction of the will as a principle of radical choice, is discussed in *Religion* through the concept of *Wilkür*. While no mechanism can in principle be given for the operation of a principle of radical choice, it is just this principle through which the moral agent becomes good or evil. It is therefore of paramount importance for the agent to know if there is any way in which the scales of decision can be weighted toward a moral outcome. This is no longer a question of the critique of Practical Reason, which ascertains the grounds of obligation, but a question of moral education. The problem that moral education faces is, therefore, if and how it is possible to influence the outcome of the choice in the will without undermining its autonomy.

In *Religion* Kant sets out to cast religion in the role of a moral educator, through the influence of which the agent would be assisted in deciding morally. Religion is traditionally concerned with worthy actions, but in its attempt to encourage and secure worthy behavior religion is in constant danger of overstepping the bounds of Reason by falling into superstition or of undermining the autonomy of the will by resorting to "frightful representations as those of (divine) might and vengeance."[12] In the case of Christianity as an historical phenomenon, Kant is especially concerned with the moral danger of such ideas as the determination of the will by divine grace and by the notion of indulgence. In the positive parts of the discussion in *Religion*, Kant attempts to collect from the conclusions of his critical work ideas that may assist the moral agent in experiencing the compelling reality of moral duty, thereby counteracting the vivacity of the impressions of inclination. It is crucially important for him that these ideas, which he will introduce as the only possible genuine core of a rational religion, will have no implication for the ground of duty itself but should presuppose it and be totally subservient to it.

[12]Ibid., 47/443.

Utilizing the conclusions of his critical works Kant writes:

> It cannot be a matter of unconcern to morality as to whether or
> not it forms for itself the concept of a final end of all things
> (harmony with which, while not multiplying men's duties, yet
> provides them with a special point of focus for the unification
> of all ends); for only thereby can objective, practical reality be
> given to the union of the purposiveness arising from freedom
> with the purposiveness of nature, a union with which we cannot
> possibly dispense.[13]

Kant is trying to achieve two things here. On the one hand, he wants
to account for the traditional religious idea of an eschaton, an end of
history in which everything is as it should be. On the other hand,
Kant wants to show that such an idea as the ultimate realization of
the ideals of Reason is of concern to morality but of no danger to it.

The interest of morality in the eschatological idea is best understood in light of our previous comments regarding moral education.
The image of a concrete historical possibility, in which the ideals of
morality are realized, serves to overcome the impressions of a mere
ideality of moral concerns. Such impressions are characteristic of a
moral skepticism that recognizes duty, but cannot see how it is possible for duty to be realized and thus falls back upon the maxims of
prudence. If an idea of a realization of the ends of Reason as a
concrete historical possibility—which is perhaps more than a mere
possibility and rather an inherent goal of nature—could be rationally
justified yet not infringe on the grounds of duty, such an idea would
be a valuable asset to religion in its role as a moral educator.

The idea of an ideal of reason, an idea of the realization of "happiness proportioned to obedience to duty," arises in the *Critique of
Practical Reason*. This is not yet a belief in the realization of such an
ideal. Practical Reason generates, a priori, this ideal of the Highest
Good but cannot envision its realization other then by resort to a
postulation of "a higher, moral, most holy, and omnipotent Being

---

[13]Kant, *Religion within the Limits of Reason Alone*, 5.

which alone can unite the two elements of this highest good."[14] It is only through the conclusions of the *Critique of Judgment* that the moral agent can reflect on her duty and think of it as a contribution, indeed a participation, in the realization of the ultimate end of history which can only be realized through her actions and through the actions of other agents like her. The idea of this realization, from the reflective point of view, is no longer a mere possibility that might be realized if all human beings were miraculously to become moral. It can now be thought of as a certain achievement, underwritten by the very structure of nature, the purposiveness of the universe as a whole.

The conclusions of the *Third Critique* transform the status of the Highest Good from that of an ideal of Practical Reason, the realization of which can only be conceived of as a miraculous divine intervention in nature in order to bring nature to conformity with the ideals of morality, to the status of an end of creation of which we are aware, reflectively, as the unifying principle of nature and reason. It is through contemplation of this idea of the reflective Highest Good that the moral agent can transform the moment of moral choice from a mere momentary clash between the rational will and a temptation of inclination to participation in the cosmic drama of realization of the end of creation. It is as such that the idea of the Highest Good becomes the cornerstone of religion in its role as moral educator. Religion in this role, it will be observed, says nothing about the content of duty or about its ground. These remain secure in the hands of Practical Reason. Religion makes it possible for the moral agent to envision the concreteness of the realization of moral ideals in such a way that the incentives of inclination are seen as shadowy interruptions compared to it. It is in this way that religion can assist morality in determining the will to goodness.

It is in light of these considerations that Kant introduces a further development of an idea that he first presented in the *Grounding for the Metaphysics of Morals* as the Law of Nature formulation of the Categorical Imperative. In the *Grounding* Kant suggested that one of the ways in which a maxim can be evaluated is to envision it as a law of nature. Technically speaking, this is just a logical experiment in

[14]Ibid., 4–5.

universalization. A suggested maxim is universalized to test it for noncontradictoriness in a universal form. The idea of a law of nature, problematic though it may be in application as a principle of moral reasoning, embodies a moral vision that is important to Kant. The Law of Nature formulation, which is presented as equivalent to the Universal Law formulation, helps in fact to bring the idea of universalization closer to the concerns of morality.

Applying the Universal Law formulation, the deliberating agent is called upon to see herself as an embodiment of pure rationality, predicating the morality of a practical decision on logical consistency alone. The reformulation of the principle of universalization in the Law of Nature introduces an interesting shift in the perspective of the agent. Called upon to see herself as legislating to a system of nature, judging a maxim as if through her will the maxim were to become a Universal Law of nature, the agent is projected into the deliberative position of God and is called upon to undertake divine responsibilities. To be sure, at this stage the structure of deliberation is purely formal. The agent does not adopt divine purposes, indeed she cannot do so for she cannot intuit divine perfection and must derive ideas about divine purposes from requirements of duty, with the determination of which she is now involved. At this point the agent can only be concerned that a system of nature, which she envisions as created through her will, will be a viable system—a system the laws of which do not conflict. The dignity that the moral agent acquires in occupying the deliberative perspective of Law of Nature formulation is now utilized by Kant in the service of religion as a moral educator.

As the ideal of the moral agent as adopting a divine perspective is introduced into the discussion in *Religion*, it undergoes a transformation in light of the insights of the *Critique of Judgment*. The difference is twofold. The moral agent at this point is not in a deliberative situation; the recognition of what duty demands has already been secured. Knowing what ought to be done, the agent reflects on the duty itself. The situation of the agent is reflective, not practical. In addition, having traveled the path of the *Third Critique* the agent is aware of the purpose a divine being would have in creating a system of nature. The agent recognizes this purpose to be the Highest Good. In light of these transformations Kant writes:

Take a man who, honoring the moral law, allows the thought to occur to him (he can scarcely avoid doing so) of what sort of world he would create, under the guidance of Practical Reason, were such a thing in his power, a world into which, moreover, he would place himself as a member. He would not merely make the very choice which is determined by that moral idea of the highest good, were he vouchsafed solely the right to choose; he would also will that [such] a world should by all means come into existence (because the moral law demands that the highest good possible through our agency should be realized)[15] and he would so will even though, in accordance with this idea, he saw himself in danger of paying in his own person a heavy price in happiness—it being possible that he might not be adequate to the [moral] demands of the idea, demands which Reason lays down as conditioning happiness. Accordingly he would feel compelled by Reason to avow this judgment with complete impartiality, as though it were rendered by another and yet, at the same time, as his own; whereby man gives evidence of the need, morally effected in him, of also conceiving a final end for his duties, as their consequence.[16]

Institutional religion is the medium through which the agent strives to implement the ideal of the Highest Good as the principle of unity of nature and freedom. Kant describes this ideal in traditional religious terms as the historical striving to realize the kingdom of God on earth. Having shown that certain religious ideas are required by morality as it seeks to establish legitimate means to assist the will in determining itself toward duty and away from evil, Kant devotes the rest of the book to a condemnation of any suggestion that might imply a role to religion beyond what he had allowed.

---

[15]It should be noted that Kant's claim that the realization of the Highest Good is possible through *our agency*, is a development beyond his claim in the *Critique of Practical Reason* that Reason demands that the Highest Good be realized and must therefore postulate a God *through whose agency* the Highest Good will be realized. This development is made possible only by the discussion in the *Third Critique*. The *Critique of Judgment* makes it possible for us to contemplate history as the arena in which, through *our agency*, the Highest Good will be realized. This perspective is not available to Practical Reason.

[16]Kant, *Religion within the Limits of Reason Alone*, 5.

In interpreting *Religion* we need to ask what question that remains unanswered in the context of the Kantian system the book intends to solve. I maintain that *Religion* cannot be interpreted as providing an account of the historical evolution of Practical Reason which reaches full recognition of the moral law with the help and guidance of religious dogma and ritual. Kant could not have raised such an "evolutionist" theory of Practical Reason because for him the moral law is a fact of Reason. Throughout the *Grounding* and the *Critique of Practical Reason* Kant labors to exhibit this fundamental fact in order to establish the transcendental condition of moral decisions. The question, which the theory of the moral law as grounded in a fact of pure Practical Reason leaves unsolved, is the question of the determination of the will.[17]

The fact that we have in us an inborn capacity to recognize duty and to form a moral will does not guarantee that we shall indeed decide to accept the decree of morality as our principle of action. To establish the autonomy of morality, Kant portrays the will as a faculty that determines itself. Kant also points out that having formed a conception of duty, the will must decide whether to determine itself according to duty or to allow itself to be determined by incentives. Graphically speaking, *Willkür* resides at the heart of *Wille*. The temptation of incentives threatens constantly to incline the will, understood as the unprincipled *Willkür*, in their direction.

Once this is recognized the question arises as to what, if anything, can be done to assist the will in determining itself according to the duty it legislates to itself. Is it possible to find an expedient to help the will to realize its autonomy? Kant's answer is to be found in *Religion*. Historical religion is a nexus of dogma and ritual which provides the required expedients. It does so by portraying an eschatological picture of a world history. The religious story tells humans that the world is created and maintained by a divine governor who is ultimately responsible for the realization of the kingdom of God. It provides the moral agent a concrete image both of the realization of the ends of morality and of the real possibility of moral

---

[17]I understand Kant's discussion of radical evil not as an independent topic but as an aspect of his discussion of the determination of the will.

action. While the agent may be dimly aware of the requirements of duty and may find a shadowy voice of conscience within herself, these recognitions may be overwhelmed by the immediacy and the practicality of the objects of desire.

In depicting a world in which divine providence guarantees the final realization of ends, the ideals of Reason acquire concretization in the agent's mind and are no longer marginalized as mere idealizations that have little to do with real life. On the other hand, examples of saintly figures make undeniably manifest to the agent that it is humanly possible to be righteous. These religious symbols can be an aid to moral choice, but they can also corrupt it. They assist morality only insofar as they make morality real to the imagination of the agent;[18] they obstruct morality if and when they suggest additional or alternative duties. It is important to Kant that such aids to moral choice, with the danger that is inherent in them, can ultimately be discarded. As the human race marches through history and acquires a wide spectrum of moral examples, both in individual heroic figures and in historical moral achievements, the reality of the moral demand will impress itself upon us and will free us from dependence on the support of religion.

It is essential for this picture of the legitimate role of religion in the moral life that religion assists us in performing a duty of which we can already be aware without it. Religion is not the vehicle of the development of Reason through history. Kant does not relinquish his belief that our recognition of duty is grounded in a fact of Reason. The progress of culture from dependence on the aids of religion for moral choice to the awareness of the force of morality in human history depends on an ability to contemplate history as the arena in which moral ends are realized and in the ability to perceive particular events as moral. This ability, which is grounded in the principles of moral conduct legislated by Practical Reason, is not a practical ability; it becomes possible through the faculty of Judgment as Kant had

---

[18]It is interesting to note that in interpreting religious depictions of a visible kingdom of God, Kant writes: "All this may be interpreted as a symbolical representation intended merely to enliven hope and courage and to increase our endeavors to that end" (*Religion within the Limits of Reason Alone*, 125).

depicted it in the *Critique of Judgment*.[19] As is widely known, Kant asserted that morality inevitably leads to religion. As I hope my argument has shown, this claim cannot be understood as a direct transition from the *Critique of Practical Reason* to *Religion within the Limits of Reason Alone*. The transition is only intelligible as proceeding through the mediation of the *Critique of Judgment*.

This part of my study has presented and examined Kant's profound insights into the nature of religion as they appear in his Critique of the faculty of Judgment. I have explained why theologians and philosophers cannot rely on Kant's official theory of religion as practical faith in order to secure a proper place for religion in modern culture. I have also tried to show that the argument of the *Third Critique* provides a fertile ground for a philosophy of religion. While Kant himself did not develop these ideas beyond an embryonic stage, they were elaborated further in the writings of Rudolf Otto and Paul Tillich. We shall now turn to these writers to examine the two distinct ways they found to develop the Kantian ideas into comprehensive theories of religion.

I shall show that in his attempt to secure the rationality of religion Otto elaborated on Kant's analysis of aesthetic taste. In interpreting Otto I shall emphasize and attempt to clarify one major aspect of Otto's theory which I regard his most important contribution to current debates in the philosophy of science and in the scientific study of religion. I shall argue that Otto formulated a challenging conception of religious awareness that promises to overcome the problematic bifurcation of affectivity and cognitivity in the philosophy of religion.

---

[19]These comments of mine should be seen as a partial response to Yovel's argument in *Kant and the Philosophy of History*. Yovel argues that an interpretation of *Religion* such as the one I am proposing is impossible because it attributes to Kant a view that he rejected, the view that between the givenness of nature and the purposeful spontaneity of Reason there is only a difference in degree (see p. 281). Yovel's argument relies on Kant's radical distinction between nature and freedom, and his argument regarding the interpretation of *Religion* would have been valid had Kant not written a critique of Judgment that transcends the perspectives of the participating agent and of the Understanding and adopts the perspective of the spectator in whose reflective contemplation the abyss between nature and freedom is overcome.

In assessing Otto's contribution I shall point out that some aspects of Otto's defense of the rationality of religion could be developed further in directions which Otto himself would probably have not favored. His theory of the numinous consciousness could sustain a conception of religion as a realm that is not accountable to science and morality.

I shall further show that even though Tillich shared Otto's eagerness to secure the rationality of religion, he considered it vital to demonstrate that religion is not just an additional realm of culture alongside science and morality, but a depth dimension in all realms of culture. I shall argue that analysis of Tillich's theory of religion as theonomy sheds an important light on Kant's discussion of contemplative hope and clarifies an issue that Kant's own discussion left unresolved. Tillich's theory may help us understand how Kant's theory of the contemplative thought about God reflects on his theory of the autonomous will as the sole legislator of the moral law. Concluding my discussion of Otto and Tillich, I shall suggest that the complex relations between their theories reflect a tension that is internal to the phenomenon of religion. I shall also sketch the outline of a possible reconciliation.

Part Two

6 ⊠

THE NOETICITY OF RELIGIOUS FEELING: RUDOLF OTTO'S THEORY OF THE RELIGIOUS A PRIORI[1]

▣ 6.A. Introduction

My discussion of Otto in this chapter will interpret his work in light of Kant's *Critique of Judgment* in order to determine how he uses Kant's insights in developing his theory of religion and in rejecting Kant's subsumption of religion under ethics. Throughout I shall emphasize and attempt to clarify two aspects of Otto's theory in

---

[1]In using the word "noeticity" to signify that an experience is a state of knowledge, I follow William James's influential analysis of mystical states. In *The Varieties of Religious Experience* he says that mystical states have a "noetic quality" and explains that "they seem to those who experience them to be also states of knowledge. They are states of insight into depth of truth unplumbed by the discursive intellect" (Lecture 16).

which I see important contributions to current debates in the philosophy and scientific study of religion. I shall argue first that Otto formulated a challenging conception of religious awareness that promises to overcome the problematic bifurcation of affectivity and cognitivity in the philosophy of religion. A later part of the chapter will explain Otto's twofold conclusion regarding a science of religion: (1) that it cannot be purely historical, and (2) that the science of religion cannot be subsumed under any one of the social sciences or under any combination of them.

I shall explain that Otto attempted to implement the spirit of the critical enterprise in his own work and outlined a Kantian method in the study of religion as a normative science that requires the intimate cooperation of three disciplines: the philosophy of religion, the historical-comparative study of religion, and theology. Otto's integrative suggestion, which emphasizes the intrinsic interdependence of philosophy and empirical investigation of religion and presents theology as the third branch of the study of religion (conceived of as a normative realm), suggests a way in which the various disciplines involved in the study of religion may be integrated without compromise. This suggestion is of special importance today given the contemporary isolation of the philosophy of religion from the achievements and the concerns of the empirical study of religion, as well as the tendency of the empirical study toward an uncritical "toolbox" approach to theoretically ununified interdisciplinary studies.

Otto often writes in a sketchy and diffuse way, frequently neglecting to substantiate bold assertions and at times resorting to rhetoric when analysis and proof are needed. When he actually substantiates his fundamental assertions, he tends to rely on the Friesian and Nelsonian versions of neo-Kantianism that supplement the transcendental analysis of experience with a psychological introspection intended to uncover the synthetic a priori principles of experience in the spontaneity of reason. Some interpretation of their theories (which were relatively unknown at the time they were conceived and are virtually forgotten today) will be required if Otto's views are to be understood. In spite of its rather anachronistic character, I consider it important to analyze Otto's thought seriously and to reveal its philosophical foundations. Otto's insights can still prove valuable today, and a thorough analysis and reconstruction of his position is well worth our while.

6.A.1. From Kant to Otto

Kant's theory of contemplative hope acknowledges the need to reunite nature and freedom, but his solution to this problem, from a contemplative perspective, is limited to an intellectual elite. In his discussion of the intellectual interest in beauty, Kant admits that "this direct interest in the beautiful in nature is actually not common, but is peculiar to those whose way of thinking is either already trained to the good or exceptionally receptive to this training."[2] Likewise, an examination of his analysis of teleology discloses that only those who can follow the torturous path that leads from a recognition of the unity of the laws of nature, through the study of organic nature, to moral teleology, find contemplative hope. This chapter will argue that Otto strives to show that an insight into ultimate meaning in life is available at all levels of culture, from the primitive to the most so-phisticated. While Otto gladly concedes to Kant that higher religions are moral in character, he claims that religious awareness is to be found at all levels.

In spite of Kant's declaration that teleology leads to theology and religion, and although he conceded that positive religion is a moral congregation that aspires to realize the moral ideal of the kingdom of God in history, Kant's suspicion of historical religion prevented him from recognizing the cognitive significance of religious language and behavior. Wary of fanaticism and anthropomorphism, Kant was never able to develop a philosophy of religion that accounts critically for the intrinsic value of these religious phenomena. In the following pages I shall show that Otto undertook to redress this lacuna with his own Kantian philosophy of religion.

In order to appreciate Otto's contributions to a Kantian philosophy of religion, his work should be interpreted in its context, in light of

---

[2]Kant, *Critique of Judgment*, 168/301. I take Kant to be saying not that only intellectuals can appreciate beautiful objects, but that they have a direct interest in finding purposiveness in nature.

the rather obscure conceptions of the psychologistic neo-Kantianism of Jakob Fries. It will be incumbent upon us to avoid the pitfalls awaiting the unwary reader of Otto's cryptic writing. The precise significance of ideas central to Otto's thought, such as his conceptions of feeling, introspective verification, and sympathetic awareness, will be determined carefully. Throughout I shall point out what insights of Otto I find important for the philosophy and science of religion and for theology. It will become clear that I find in Otto the foundations for a philosophical interpretation of religion that goes beyond Kant, the basis of which is to be found in the interpretation of Kant to which I dedicated the first part of this study.

6.A.2. The Religious A Priori

6.A.2.a. Apprehension of the Infinite in the Finite

Building upon Kant's analysis of aesthetic judgment, Rudolf Otto offers a theory of religion as an ability to perceive the meaning of crucial moments of human experience—or, in his technical terminology, to perceive the infinite in the finite—in a form of judgment that, like Kant's aesthetic feeling, combines affective and cognitive moments. Otto characterizes the affective elements of this complex judgment as the different modes of what he calls "the numinous experience"— mysterium tremendum, fascinans, and creature-feeling[3]—and presents an indeterminate principle of religious judgment that he identifies as an a priori category of Reason. It is important to notice from the outset that, working with Kant's model of aesthetic judgment, Otto considers the "numinous feeling" an affective state that is not contingently empirical but is determined by an a priori principle: an indeterminate principle that Otto calls the "category of the numinous." Thus, as a state of feeling which is determined a priori, the numinous experience is presented as both an affective state and an awareness that the object of the experience satisfies the conditions of the principle.

---

[3]My enumeration of the moments of the "numinous experience" differs from standard references. For explanation see section 6.D.1.b. below.

6.A.2.b. The Immediate Reference of Feeling

Although he builds upon Kant's analysis of reflective judgment, Otto differs significantly from Kant in one fundamental respect. The implications of this divergence are momentous, and they determine the character of Otto's theory of religion and of his theology, for better or for worse. I shall have more to say about these as we proceed.

Otto argues that as important and instructive as Kant's analysis of Reason and its domains is, it overlooks the distinctive religious a priori. As we saw in Kant's discussion of Reflective Judgment, the appeal to the divine designer of the universe is always a reflection upon a prior cognition. In the realm of taste, the aesthetic feeling refers primarily to the internal design and harmony in the beautiful object. Only through a critical analysis of a judgment of taste do we learn that the transcendental principle of aesthetic judgment is the thought of a divine designer of the universe. Similarly with teleological judgments, it is through a transcendental investigation that we recognize the thought of a divine designer as a constitutive element of scientific thought. Using Kant's analysis of reflective thought in his own philosophy of religion, Otto goes a step further. He identifies a moment of consciousness, the numinous experience, in which the distinctive religious feeling has an immediate reference to a "numinous object."[4]

---

[4]In speaking of "numinous objects" Otto refers primarily to spatio-temporal objects and events in which persons of religious sensitivity can perceive an extrarational meaning which Otto identifies as "numinous." Such objects could be a statue of the Buddha, the Torah Scroll, etc. Otto's example of the most perfect numinous object is the person of Jesus in whom his disciples could see the Christ. Otto says that divination is an intuition by which "we recognize in Christ the portrayal and presentment of God. . . one whose being. . . repeats and reveals the divine nature in human fashion." See Rudolf Otto, *The Idea of the Holy: An Inquiry into the Non-Rational Factor in the Idea of the Divine and Its Relation to the Rational* (trans. John W. Harvey; London: Oxford University Press, 1958). For the German edition, see idem, *Das Heilige* (1917; reprinted Munich: Beck, 1987).

Just as a feeling of joy refers inherently to whatever occasions it—however vaguely the object may initially be identified—so is the numinous experience a feeling of terror of something that is simultaneously fascinating. This something, to which the numinous feeling refers, remains a mysterious X designated by the uninformative title "the numinous." The object, which remains mysterious to us, is identified by the distinctiveness of the numinous experience and its referential quality. Since the object to which the religious experience refers surpasses our understanding and cannot be referred to by determinate concepts, it can be recognized only through the state of feeling that identifies it—a state of feeling which, Otto claims, is determined a priori and can only be expressed symbolically by means of indeterminate concepts. As we shall see, Otto takes pains to explain that in the awareness of the numinous he does not mean a direct intuition of a mind-independent reality. It is an awareness of that which constitutes the highest a priori ground of our cognitive faculties—that which, following the language of introversive mysticism, Otto calls the "fundus anima." It is important for Otto to stress that his theory of the numinous consciousness remains strictly within the limits of a critical philosophy.

6.A.2.c Judgment versus Contemplation

As we learned from the *Third Critique*, by reflecting on the cognitions of various reflective judgments, we reach contemplative conclusions. We suggested that the contemplative idea of the Highest Good is the most important of them. We differentiate in Kant between reflective judgments and thought. A judgment of taste that finds an object beautiful is of the first type. The thought of a divine designer working in light of the idea of the Highest Good is of the second kind; it is a reflective thought about the significance of a reflective judgment. Otto is unwilling for religion to be only a second order contemplation. He strives to secure the cognitivity of religious experience by identifying a special religious a priori that is the constitutive element of reflective religious judgments. We should therefore see Otto as undertaking to complement Kant's delineation of Reason and its domains by identifying a reflective religious judgment, and by establishing its cognitivity through critical analysis.

This distinction that I draw between reflective judgment and thought, or between judgment and contemplation, explains a fundamental difference between the respective ways in which Otto and Kant understand religious life. If, as Kant seems to think, reflection on the divine designer is only a second order contemplation, this reflection cannot be determinative of a distinct realm of experience. It is a reflection that depends through and through on the first order reflective judgment. If, on the other hand, as I interpret Otto, religious experience is a reflective judgment of the first order, grounded in its own indeterminative a priori principle, it is possible to see how this principle—like the aesthetic—is constitutive of a distinct realm of experience. Demonstration of this is the major task of *The Idea of the Holy*, and the book cannot be properly understood unless we read it as an elaborate attempt to establish religion as a distinct realm of meaning which has to be understood and evaluated in its own terms.

6.A.3. Otto's Contribution to the Philosophy of Religion

6.A.3.a. Affectivity and Cognition

To convince his readers to acknowledge the veracity of religious experience, Otto follows the guidelines of the critical method as it was reformulated by Jakob Fries and Leonard Nelson. Otto first derives the religious principle through a metaphysical deduction that leads to the identification of the category of the numinous as the supreme transcendental ground of religious judgment. He then proceeds to justify the conclusions of the metaphysical deduction through an "anthropological deduction," that is, an introspective examination that substitutes for Kant's transcendental deduction in the Kantianism of Fries and Nelson. Brief words of explanation are in order here.

A Kantian critique, we recall, begins with sets of judgments that we precritically accept and strives to discover the conditions that are necessary for their validity. Having found such conditions, Kant seeks further to prove that the conditions hold and that the original judgments are valid. Instead of Kant's device of a transcendental deduction, which has always encountered objections, some Kantians, then and now, suggest that the conclusions of the metaphysical deduction are already as verified as they can ever be if upon reflection we find that we do indeed think as the deduction suggests we must. The discovery that certain principles or modes of thought function in our cognitive and evaluative life, is an empirical fact about us. Hence the name, "anthropological deduction." Being empirical, that is, a finding of introspective self-examination, this discovery is far from infallible; it should never be confused with classical claims to self-evidence or with intuition of a priori truths. The anthropological deduction should not be confused with attempts, made famous by Wittgenstein's scathing attack upon them, to verify inner experiences through introspection. Rather, we have here something more akin to appeals to basic intuitions in contemporary philosophical discussion and to Wittgenstein's discoveries, after lengthy investigations, that some procedures cannot be justified beyond an acceptance that flows from the recognition that they are simply characteristic of the way he thinks.

These neo-Kantian appeals to an introspective description of a moment of consciousness and to the confidence we must have in principles that we must already presuppose in any attempt to prove them are in interesting affinity to later Husserlian and Wittgensteinian ideas. Both elements play central roles in Otto's work. By identifying in consciousness the awareness of the numinous, Otto gains both the confirmation that the category of the numinous is part of the structure of consciousness, immediately endowed with a trust of reason in itself, and a principle through which a method of sympathy for understanding religious phenomena becomes possible.

While Otto's work cannot be understood other than in its neo-Kantian matrix, the validity of most of what I find important in Otto's work depends directly on Kant's theory of aesthetic judgment. This is true particularly of Otto's phenomenological analysis of the various moments of the religious experience as a unity of affectivity and cognition. Otto's identification of the essence of religion in an ability to perceive the infinite in the finite by means of the numinous awareness makes an important contribution to the philosophy of religion in suggesting a way of overcoming the bifurcation of cognition and affectivity in the philosophy of religion. As I shall explain, Otto sees in the numinous awareness a complex judgment that combines both the affective states of mysterium tremendum, fascinans, and creature-feeling and the awareness of the infinite as exhibited in the finite. It is essential to note that the affective states with which he is concerned cannot result from a prior recognition that the infinite is exhibited in the finite, rather it is only through these unique affective states that we become aware of the infinite in the finite.[5] This relation between the moments of the judgment is analogous to Kant's analysis of aesthetic states. As Kant taught us in the *Third Critique*, in aesthetic judgment we become aware of a purposiveness or a harmony in a particular object only through the particular aesthetic satisfaction that is a state of feeling that responds to the purposiveness or harmony in the aesthetic object. In my discussion of Kant I demonstrated that, according to him, the aesthetic feeling is not a contingent sensation; rather it is determined a priori by what Kant calls the "indeterminate principle of reflective judgment" the content of which, I argued, is the thought about a "supernatural substrate of reality" or, in other words, about the purposiveness guiding the divine designer of the universe. Likewise, in Otto's theory of religious feeling, it is in and through the numinous feeling that we become aware of the manifestation of the infinite in the object of religious experience. This delicate balance of affective and cognitive elements in a state of feeling[6] is of special importance for a philosophy of religion.

6.A.3.b. Beyond the Bifurcation

It is a perennial difficulty in philosophical interpretations of religion that they tend to separate the affective and the cognitive elements of religion, to emphasize one of them at the expense of the other, sometimes to the point of virtual disappearance. Examples of such imbalance abound in history. We can see it, for instance, in Kierkegaard's insistence that a person may know and believe all the

[5]In just the same way, according to Kant, we recognize the beauty of the aesthetic object through the pleasurable response of our "feeling of life." See my discussion in part one, section 4.B.1.

[6]Here and henceforth I use the term "feeling"—as in "states of feeling" and "judgment of feeling"—to translate the German term "*Gefühl*" in the special philosophic sense it is given in these Kantian writings, a sense which has already been elucidated in my discussion of Kant.

doctrines of Christianity yet fail to be a Christian, implying that being a Christian is a matter of one's affective state rather than of what one knows.[7] Other examples of emphasis on the affective range from Tertullian to Buber and find influential formulation in the Wittgensteinian school in the philosophy of religion.[8] The history of theology, on the other hand, abounds with examples of the view that religion cannot be understood as pure affectivity and must involve religious knowledge which then occupies most of the writer's attention.[9] The contemporary scene reflects the dichotomy between knowledge and affectivity in the competing Wittgensteinian and empiricist schools in the philosophy of religion, the former stressing affectivity to the exclusion of all claims to knowledge, and the latter stressing the factuality of religious beliefs.[10] In Otto's category of the numinous we find an important attempt to reunite cognition and affectivity in one

[7]This is the way Kierkegaard is commonly understood. Close scrutiny of his arguments would reveal, I believe, that even he acknowledged the importance of "objective" beliefs and practices and did not attribute religious importance to uninformed feelings.

[8]While many writers of differing philosophical persuasions claim to be followers of Wittgenstein, influential students of his remarks on religion radically dissociate the so-called depth grammar of religious language from the language of factual assertion and interpret its use as embodying a distinctly religious *attitude* that they are often hard pressed to characterize. For examples, see Peter Winch, "Meaning and Religious Language," in Stuart C. Brown, ed., *Reason and Religion* (Ithaca, NY: Cornell University Press, 1977) 193–221; and Norman Malcolm, "The Groundlessness of Belief," in Brown, *Reason and Religion*, 143–57; and D. Z. Phillips, "Faith, Skepticism and Religious Understanding," in idem, ed., *Religion and Understanding* (New York: Macmillan, 1967) 63–79.

[9]The great scholastic theologies exemplify this tendency.

[10]For recent examples of exclusive emphasis on propositional religious belief, see Alvin Plantinga, "On Taking Belief in God as Basic," in Joseph Runzo and Craig K. Ihara, eds., *Religious Experience and Religious Belief* (Lanham, MD: University Press of America, 1986); and George I. Mavrodes, *Revelation in Religious Belief* (Philadelphia: Temple University Press, 1988). For a perceptive historical analysis of the problem, see John E. Smith, "Faith, Belief, and the Problem of Rationality in Religion," in C. F. Delaney, ed., *Rationality and Religious Belief* (Notre Dame, IN: University of Notre Dame Press, 1979).

moment of awareness, thereby overcoming their problematic bifurcation. A thorough interpretation of Otto's sketchy arguments will serve to clarify his promising insight regarding the unity of thought and feeling in moments of religious awareness.

According to Otto, no awareness of a manifestation of the infinite in the finite is possible other than through a judgment of feeling. In so claiming, Otto closely follows Kant's delineation of the structure of reflective judgment. From Kant he learned of a reflective approach to reality in which affective and cognitive elements are combined, and in which we become cognizant of the ultimate meaning of natural events and moral actions, a truth that is disclosed only to reflection. Unlike Kant, who found disclosure of ultimate meaning only in rare reflective moments that are accessible to an aesthetic and scientific elite, Otto thought that such moments of awareness were possible to all people at all times and claimed that they are based on the a priori category of the numinous. He maintained that this category is an original constituent of Reason and is constitutive of the various systems of religious symbols that are the essence of religious life.

6.A.3.c. Kantian Dualism and Religious Insight

Otto accepted the sharp Kantian dualism of nature and freedom that corresponds to a distinction between phenomenal and noumenal being—a distinction he considered an essential religious insight, and on account of which he regarded Kant as an important successor to Luther. Having accepted this dualistic world view, Otto seems to have identified the "infinite" with the Ideas and the Ideals of Reason of Kant's Dialectics, and considered our empirical scientific and psychological experiences, especially our empirical self-awareness, as the realm of the "finite." Like Kant, Otto could find no way of bridging the abyss between the finite and the infinite, other than by a mode of reflective judgment in which the infinite is felt to be manifest in the finite. Following the example of Kant's analysis of aesthetic judgment, Otto sought to characterize the religious judgment as a state of feeling in which affectivity and cognition are one. Reflective judgment that combines affectivity and cognition is the only way to become aware of such manifestations, since Ideas of Reason are known conceptually only as ideals, never as realizations, and theoretical understanding has no knowledge of them.[11] This is what Otto learned from Kant, who taught that only an affective state that is determined by an a priori principle can disclose that an ideal is indeed exhibited by a particular object. In Kant's analysis of reflective judgment, the feeling is simultaneously an awareness of the subjective condition of the judgment (i.e., the harmonious interplay of the cognitive faculties and the indeterminate principle) and of the objective condition of judgment (i.e., the presentation of purposiveness in the object). Because of Kant's separation between intuitions, which are given only to the Understanding and Ideas, which are the property of Reason, only a feeling determined a priori can be cognizant of their unity. Otto learned from this that insofar as religious judgment is considered an awareness of the ultimate meaning of events and actions, religious judgment must be reflective.

6.A.4. The Kantian Foundation of Otto's Theory of the Holy

My attribution of an important insight into the nature of religious awareness to Otto depends heavily on my interpretation of his work in light of Kant's *Third Critique*. It is therefore one of my goals in this chapter to establish that in his striving to secure the veracity of religious convictions, Otto turned to Kant, in whose critiques of Reason and its domains he found methodological anchorage and in whose discussion of reflective purposiveness he found both an inspiration to and a confirmation of his theological insights.

Readers of Otto's most popular book, *The Idea of the Holy*, who were unaware of this Kantian background, systematically misunderstood Otto's theory of religion. What is most important, namely, his notion of feeling, was totally misinterpreted. This is due partly to the fact that in *The Idea of the Holy* Otto assumed the Kantian background to which we have dedicated the previous chapters; he did not undertake to restate, to explain, and to justify it, although he did do so in previous works to which he constantly refers. Accordingly, Otto's place in the Kantian tradition has not been duly appreciated. It is the

---

[11]Kant elaborates on this issue in his Introduction to the *Third Critique*. See my discussion in part one, section 4.A above.

task of this chapter, in part, to reappraise Otto's theory of religion in its true Kantian context.

In spite of his repeated warnings and protests, Otto was frequently considered an "emotionalist"; as identifying "religious feelings" with "emotions," conceived as contingent sensations completely separated from reason. Otto was presented as promoting a theory of religious intuition of a mind-independent reality and as a proponent of a separation between religion and Reason.[12] Otto was then accused of misconstruing his Kantian heritage. The common evaluation of Otto's enterprise is that "the most valuable part of Otto's study consists of his careful analysis of the feeling-states that constitute the numinous experience."[13] Various Otto scholars encourage us, accordingly, to focus on his phenomenology of religious feelings and to ignore his philosophical theory. I consider this an unfortunate mistake which we should carefully analyze so as not to repeat.

Reflecting on his understanding of other thinkers, Otto argues that "to understand a thinker in his more abstract style and to follow his more methodical exposition, it is often well to look at the subsoil on which his philosophy is built and shaped. . . no man's thought, no man's intellectual life, is in general a self-started machine."[14] In my

---

[12]Robert F. Davidson writes (*Rudolf Otto's Interpretation of Religion* [Princeton: Princeton University Press, 1947] 180) that Otto endeavors "to free religion from dependence upon reason." Philip C. Almond writes (*Rudolf Otto: An Introduction to his Philosophical Theology* [Studies in Religion at Chapel Hill: Chapel Hill/London: University of North Carolina Press, 1984] 68), "Otto may have adopted the phrase *wholly other* from Jakob Fries, but even so, he filled the term with a content much richer than did Fries, using it *against any attempt to confine religion within the web of human reason.*" Second emphasis mine.

[13]John Macquarrie, *Twentieth-Century Religious Thought: The Frontiers of Philosophy and Theology, 1900–1980* (2d ed.; London: SCM Press, 1981) 215. A similar assessment of *The Idea of the Holy* can be found in Davidson's commentary (*Rudolf Otto's Interpretation of Religion*, 109): "Actually his historical and psychological interpretation of religious intuition rather than his theory of religious knowledge is the more significant contribution."

[14]Rudolf Otto, *The Philosophy of Religion: Based on Kant and Fries* (trans. E. B. Dicker; London: Williams & Norgate, 1931) 30.

study of Otto I intend to follow this advice and to uncover the philosophical foundations of his theory of religion. This task is made easier
by the fact that Otto very generously indicates repeatedly throughout
his various writings what authors and texts influenced him.

Otto acknowledged his indebtedness to Schleiermacher's theory of
religion. He thought Schleiermacher was able to improve upon Kant's
theory of religion by discovering that "there is a third relationship to
the world: this is not the science of the world, neither is it action
upon the world; it is experience of this world in its profundity, the
realization of its eternal content by the feeling of a contemplative and
devout mind. . . . It is religion: the immediate appraisal of the universe as the one and the whole, transcending the mere parts which
science may grasp, and at the same time the profound spiritual experience of its underlying ideal essence."[15] Otto thought that Schleiermacher was able to see that what is not disclosed to the understanding
can be felt in contemplation. In religious feeling we can intuit the
inner meaning of the world. To the religious person the world becomes, so to speak, transparent; in contemplative feeling the eternal
shines through the temporal, the infinite, which neither space nor time
can comprehend, is revealed in the finite forms of time and space.[16]

Although he admired Schleiermacher's discovery, Otto accused him
of falling into the trap of subjectivism. Otto thought that Schleiermacher was not interested in establishing the noeticity of religious feeling and that consequently his theory of religion fell prey to the charge
of subjectivism.[17] Otto blamed Schleiermacher for making God only
an inference from self-consciousness rather than a direct reference of
religious feeling. In his attempt to correct this flaw in Schleiermacher's
theory of religion, Otto relied heavily on the philosophy of Jakob
Fries.

---

[15]Rudolf Otto, *Religious Essays: A Supplement to "The Idea of the Holy"*
(trans. Brian Lunn; The Oxford Bookshelf: Oxford: Oxford University Press,
1937) 75.

[16]Ibid., 76–77.

[17]I think that this charge is unfounded, but I shall not discuss the issue any
further here.

Otto came across the writings of Jakob Fries through the influence and the encouragement of Leonard Nelson. Reading Fries, Otto became convinced that Fries's philosophy of religion takes over where Schleiermacher left off and establishes the noeticity of the religious feeling. According to Otto, "In the teaching of Fries, philosophy's noblest task is to discover the real nature of belief, the ideal sphere of conviction, and to make their truth secure."[18] Examining Fries's theory of religious feeling, and particularly his theory of *Ahndung*, Otto claims that "the source of Fries' doctrine of 'Ahndung'—so far as it is not just the positive experience of the man himself—is the Kantian Criticism of Judgment. In this connection, whoever hears the word with discrimination and compares other utterances of Kant, some quite early ones, is bound to see that this important theory was already present as a companion of his theory of ideas."[19]

In reading Otto, then, we come back full circle to Kant's *Third Critique*. If we are to understand Otto's theory of religion we must read it against the background of Kant's discussion of the contemplation of purposiveness in nature. In interpreting Otto our task is to see where he takes over and what his distinct contribution to the study of religion is. As I shall show toward the end of this chapter, Otto criticized Fries for not paying enough attention to the history of religion. Like Kant, Fries directed his efforts to uncover Ideas and mental capacities. Both Kant and Fries failed to acknowledge that the essence of religious life is the incorporation of religious Ideas in religious history. Thus Otto dedicated his own work to complete the analysis of religion that began with Kant and Schleiermacher and continued with Fries. Interpreted against this background, Otto emerges as the thinker he really is: a scholar who searches for a reliable method for the historical and comparative study of religion, a philosopher who undertakes to correct the inadequacies of Kant's theory of religion, and a Christian theologian who aspires to establish the veracity of religious judgments, primarily those of his own tradition.

---

[18] Otto, *The Philosophy of Religion*, 24.
[19] Ibid., 23.

■ 6.B. In Search of a Method

6.B.1. "Sympathy"

In *The Idea of the Holy* Otto sets out to establish the distinctive nature and significance of religion. Arguing that the unique nature of various religious phenomena is often elusive and that therefore we usually confuse them with other things, Otto urges us to explore the depths of our consciousness and to detect a primary state of mind, which, he argues, is the constitutive element of religion.

> The reader is invited to direct his mind to a moment of deeply-felt religious experience, as little as possible qualified by other forms of consciousness. Whoever cannot do this, whoever knows no such moments in his experience, is requested to read no farther; for it is not easy to discuss questions of religious psychology with one who can recollect the emotions of his adolescence, the discomforts of indigestion, or say, social feelings, but cannot recall any intrinsically religious feelings. We do not blame such a one, when he tries for himself to advance as far as he can with the help of such principles of explanation as he knows, interpreting "aesthetics" in terms of sensuous pleasures, and "religion" as a function of the gregarious instinct and social standards, or as something more primitive still. But the artist, who for his part has an intimate personal knowledge of the distinctive element in the aesthetic experience, will decline his theories with thanks, and the religious man will reject them even more uncompromisingly.[20]

Striving to uncover the real nature of religion, Otto approaches the readers of *The Idea of the Holy* with an intriguing proposition: should they be willing to submit to his guidance and to follow his instructions, Otto will provide them the key to the hearts of other people. If they allow Otto to take them by the hand and to lead them in a long journey of exposure to the modes of worship, to myths, to religious artifacts, etc., of foreign traditions, Otto's readers will gradually find themselves responding to these phenomena as if they themselves were

[20]Otto, *The Idea of the Holy*, 8.

members of these different traditions. Otto thus asserts that in principle everyone has a recourse to the religious moods and feelings of other people, and he offers a method of "sympathy" as a vehicle of penetrating imaginatively into what passes in the minds of other people. Setting out to help his readers to comprehend the distinct religious state of mind, Otto claims that the reader must be

> guided and led on by consideration and discussion of the matter
> through the ways of his own mind, until he reaches the point at
> which "the numinous" in him perforce begins to stir, to start
> into life and into consciousness. We can cooperate in this process by bringing before his notice all that can be found in other
> regions of the mind, already known and familiar, to resemble, or
> again to afford some special contrast to, the particular experience we wish to elucidate. Then we must add: "This *X* of ours
> is not precisely *this* experience, but akin to this one and the
> opposite of that other. Cannot you now realize for yourself what
> it is?" In other words our *X* cannot, strictly speaking, be taught,
> it can only be evoked, awakened in the mind; as everything that
> comes "of the spirit" must be awakened.[21]

Otto is by no means the only proponent of "sympathy" as a method in the study of religion. In fact "sympathy" is one of the key terms used by various scholars of religion in their attempt to convince us that, somehow, we all can acquire the ability to "walk in the shoes" of other people and to see the world through their eyes. It is often assumed that a certain common denominator, the nature of which is not always explicitly defined, makes it possible for members of one tradition to understand the meaning of foreign religious phenomena.

It is characteristic of these proponents of sympathy that, as they recognize introspectively an element of their own experience, they claim that this recognition makes it possible for them to identify experiences of others and to form a genuine understanding of elements of foreign cultures which they study. It is important to point out that, since this type of sympathetic approach to the experience of others depends ultimately on the empirical results of introspection, it cannot

[21]Ibid., 7.

by itself achieve objective certainty; its results are necessarily tentative and contingent. There is always the possibility that another observer, or even I myself at another time or in different circumstances, might reach another interpretation. Proponents of this version of sympathy must therefore seek independent verification of their findings. One such method of verification that suggests itself is to endorse only such interpretations as are acceptable to a native of the culture under study.[22]

If we want to understand Otto's notion of sympathy accurately we must realize from the outset that it is *diametrically opposed* to the one I just outlined. Seeking to overcome the limited logical force of inquiries based on empirical induction, Otto strives to identify the a priori categories of reason on the basis of which alone religious experience is possible. He does this by following the Critical method in the study of Reason as it was established by Kant and developed further by both Jakob Fries and Otto's friend and mentor Leonard Nelson. Otto attempts to identify the necessary organizing principles of Reason, and his method of sympathy is based on his belief that

---

[22]The various writings of Wilfred Cantwell Smith exemplify this approach. In his *Towards a World Theology: Faith and the Comparative History of Religion* (Philadelphia: Westminster, 1981), Smith urges students of other traditions to use the method of sympathy. As an example he argues that "to appreciate the significance of that temple, we must get into the consciousness of those for whom it is a sacred space" (p. 66). His recommendation of this method is based on his view that "to be an historian, or, indeed, a rational student in any humane field, is to stand imaginatively in the shoes of others." Accounting for the sympathetic ability, Smith claims that "this is possible, in principle, because we are persons, and because they are persons, two of the fundamental qualities of humanity are the capacity to understand one another and to be understood" (p. 68). Discussing the validity of the results arrived at with this method Smith contrasts the study of religion with the study of natural phenomena and claims that the former, being part of the "humane studies" is much more complex: "Humane knowledge is much more complicated than is objective, of course; but here a verificationist principle is this: that no observer's statement about a group of persons is valid that cannot be appropriated by those persons. . . . No statement about Islamic faith is true that Muslims cannot accept" (p. 97).

everyone must presuppose precisely these ultimate principles and can presuppose only these.[23]

As we shall see shortly, Otto's "sympathy" is based on the assumption that in so far as others are rational beings like us, their experience reflects the same ultimate organizing principles. The study of the experience of others becomes therefore the attempt to see how this suprastructure of organizing principles is manifest in their experience. Being exposed to texts, stories, monuments, artifacts, etc., I reflect on my informed experience of them, seeking to interpret them as manifestations of the a priori form of experience which previous analysis had established.

Once an a priori element of reason is identified, it is a moot question whether we can find it in other people or in other cultures. If we accept a principle as an a priori principle of reason we necessarily accept it as a principle of every manifestation of reason. Our assumption that this principle exists in others is not merely a conclusion from our identification of them as rational beings or as humans, but a necessary condition of such identification. It follows from this that it is possible, in principle, for those whose experience we study, to follow our critical steps and to achieve a similar analysis of their experience, but the validity of our conclusion is independent of their ever doing so. The basic difference between the two notions of sympathy is, to recapitulate, that the former depends on the contingencies of empirical experience, whereas the latter relies on the a priori category that is their necessary condition.

6.B.2. Against the Charge of Emotionalism

Convinced that the true nature of religious phenomena often eludes us, Otto undertakes to develop a method that can help us discover the unique underivable nature of religion. Otto urges us to explore the depths of our consciousness and to detect a primary state of mind, which, like other elementary data, cannot be reduced to other moments of our mental life. He invites us to direct our attention in-

---

[23]See Leonard Nelson, *Socratic Method and Critical Philosophy: Selected Essays* (trans. Thomas K. Brown; New Haven: Yale University Press, 1949) 129.

wardly and to conduct an introspective examination of the states of our mind in moments of religious experiences. To those of us who can remember no such experiences Otto offers his services as the "Socratic midwife" who initiates a process of "anamnesis," in which analogous feelings call one another into consciousness.[24] Calling to mind certain feelings that were previously recognized, this process brings new feelings to the light of consciousness and awakens the ability to experience the religious feelings and, eventually, under Otto's skillful guidance, to recognize them for what they really are.

In Otto's invitation we find expression of the insight that what is essential in religion is neither assent to some propositions, nor the performance of some rituals, but a state of consciousness that he characterizes as "feeling." Otto calls the fundamental religious state of mind a "numinous feeling" which arises in our mind in the presence of an object perceived as qualitatively superior. Perceiving such an object as wholly other, we are both attracted to it and repelled by it. We consequently feel deficient. Otto characterizes this experience of deficiency as the feeling of creatures who are submerged and overwhelmed by their own nothingness in contrast to that which they conceive as supreme above all.

Otto argues that the religious feeling is a primary and unique property of the mind and as such can only be pointed out and discussed, but not strictly expressed or defined. He contends that the religious apprehension of the "wholly other" eludes logical proof and conceptual demonstration. It is rather a matter of inward and spontaneous awareness that issues from deep within our souls.

Such expressions, especially when they are taken out of their Kantian context, together with the fact that Otto calls the religious propensity "non-rational," may cause serious misunderstanding. As I noted above, Otto was indeed understood as a thinker who separated religious feeling from reason and developed a theory of religious emotions, a theory that takes emotion to be an immediate intuition of mind-independent objects. It is my position that such interpretations either overlook Otto's repeated warning against emotionalist and irra-

---

[24]Otto, *The Idea of the Holy*, 12, 65, 143–44.

tionalist interpretation of his theory or fail to understand the meaning of Otto's assertion that the nonrational is a pure a priori category, namely, an original capacity of Reason that underlies experience as its ultimate principle.[25]

Otto seems to have anticipated these objections, though his countermeasures obviously did not suffice. Otto goes out of his way to protect his book from the charge of "vague and arbitrary phraseology of an emotionalist irrationalism."[26] Already in his preface Otto explains:

> In this book I have ventured to write of that which may be called "non-rational" or "supra-rational" in the depths of the divine nature. I do not thereby want to promote in any way the tendency of our time towards an extravagant and fantastic "irrationalism". . . . The "irrational" is today a favorite theme of all who are too lazy to think or too ready to evade the arduous duty of clarifying their ideas and grounding their convictions on a basis of coherent thought. This book, recognizing the profound import of the non-rational of metaphysics, makes a serious attempt to analyze all the more exactly the *feeling* which remains where the *concept* fails, and to introduce a terminology which is not any the more loose or indeterminate for having necessarily to make use of *symbols*.[27]

Later on in the *The Idea of the Holy* Otto says:

> The words "non-rational" and "irrational" are to-day used almost at random. The non-rational is sought over the most widely different regions, and writers generally shirk the trouble of putting down precisely what they intend by the term, giving it often the most multifarious meanings or applying it with such vague generality that it admits of the most diverse interpretations. . . .

---

[25]I shall explain below how Otto proposes to substantiate his assertions. For the most part these will be charitable reconstructions based on Otto's all too sketchy "proofs." Otto's philosophical shortcomings should not prevent us from appreciating his more penetrating insights.

[26]Otto, *The Idea of the Holy*, 59.

[27]Ibid., xxi.

> Whoever makes use of the word "non-rational" today ought to say what he actually means by it. This we did in our introductory chapter. We began with the "rational" in the idea of God and the divine, meaning by the term that in it which is clearly to be grasped by our power of conceiving, and enters the domain of familiar and definable conceptions. We went on to maintain that beneath this sphere of clarity and lucidity lies a hidden depth, inaccessible to our conceptual thought, which we in so far call the "non-rational."[28]

Despite these warnings and explanations, Otto's view was misinterpreted exactly as he had feared. A typical example is the assessment of Otto and his work by Herbert James Paton, a prominent Kant scholar who influenced other interpreters of Otto. Paton claims that, in his attempt to characterize an emotion as an a priori constitutive ground of an experience of a transcendent object, Otto confused the spontaneity of emotions with the spontaneity of the categories of reason and committed a fallacy of equivocation. He suggests that Otto fails to see that emotions are themselves experiences and cannot be the self-reflective ground of experience.[29] It seems to me that Paton arrives at this conclusion because he interprets Otto's terminology in terms of the analytical part of Kant's *Critique of Pure Reason*. Paton fails to acknowledge Otto's repeated assertions that he uses the terms "Category," "Idea," and "Feeling" in the meaning that Fries has given them, in the light of Kant's *Critique of Judgment*. Failing to take account of this background, Paton can see only nonsense and confusion in Otto's philosophical argument and suggests that only his psychological insights are of value.

Against such assessments of Otto's work I argue that isolation of Otto's psychological introspection from its context in a systematic critique of Reason is dangerously misleading. Detached from its Critical context, the religious experience Otto characterizes is reduced to a merely contingent empirical datum. Otto's notion of sympathy, ac-

---

[28]Ibid., 57–58.

[29]Herbert James Paton, *The Modern Predicament: A Study in the Philosophy of Religion* (New York: Collier, 1962) 129–45.

cordingly, must be misunderstood as the first of the two notions of sympathy I characterized above.

■ 6.C. The A Priori Status of the Nonrational

6.C.1. Elements of the A Priori Category

Otto did not write his book *The Idea of the Holy* simply to describe the various affective moments that are involved in the religious experience, though such a description was certainly an important part of his project. Otto wrote this book to present religion as a distinct realm of meaning that must be understood and evaluated in its own terms. He intended to do this by introducing us to the distinct religious category of the "holy," a complex category with rational and nonrational elements—a category that he considered the constitutive element of religious judgments. Otto's indebtedness to Kant's *Third Critique* is manifest in the fact that already in introducing the "category of the holy" Otto refers us to the "beautiful." He says:

> "Holiness"—"the holy"—is a category of interpretation and valuation peculiar to the sphere of religion. It is, indeed, applied by transference to another sphere—that of ethics—but it is not itself derived from this. While it is complex, it contains a quite specific element or "moment," which sets it apart from "the rational". . . and which remains inexpressible—. . . an ἄρρητον or *ineffable*—in the sense that it completely eludes apprehension in terms of concepts. The same thing is true (to take a quite different region of experience) of the category of the beautiful.[30]

Otto thinks that when we examine religious language we usually focus mainly on what he considers its "rational" element. Doing so we fail to see that this element already embodies and translates a "non-rational" element. He undertakes to correct this mistake by introducing us to the nonrational element and by displaying its relation

---

[30]Otto, *The Idea of the Holy*, 5. We have to read this remark in light of Otto's further discussions (p. 124), which I shall analyze in part two, section 6.C.2.

to the rational. Otto's goal is to convince us that "not only the rational but also the non-rational elements of the complex category of 'holiness' are *a priori* elements and each in the same degree."[31] Even as he identifies the rational element as "moral," it is important for Otto to confront Kant's reductionist challenge by emphasizing that "religion is not in vassalage either to morality or teleology, *ethos* or *telos*, and does not draw its life from postulates; and its non-rational content has, no less than its rational, its own independent root in the hidden depths of the spirit itself."[32] Otto thus strives to prove that "the 'holy' in the fullest sense of the word is a combined, complex category, the combined elements being its rational and non-rational components. But in *both*—and the assertion must be strictly maintained against all sensationalism and naturalism[33]—it is a *purely a priori* category."[34]

Having claimed that both elements of the holy are a priori properties of Reason, Otto focuses primarily on the "non-rational" to which he assigns the name "numinous." It is important to note that even though Otto emphasizes the distinctness of the numinous consciousness, he argues persistently that the numinous is, like the categories of the understanding and the moral law, a property of Reason that must be approached along the lines of Kant's critique of Reason.

> The facts of the numinous consciousness point therefore—as likewise do also the "pure concepts of the understanding" of Kant and the ideas and value judgments of ethics and aesthetics—to a hidden substantive source, from which the religious ideas and feelings are formed, which lies in the mind independently of sense experience; a *"pure reason" in the profoundest sense*, which, because of the "surpassingness" of its content, must be distinguished from both the pure theoretical and the pure practical reason of Kant, as something yet higher or deeper than they.[35]

[31]Ibid., 136.
[32]Ibid.
[33]The German is *"Sensualismus und Evolutionismus."*
[34]Ibid., 112.
[35]Ibid., 113–14. Emphasis mine.

6.C.2. Introspection and Critique

In writing the *The Idea of the Holy* Otto undertakes to focus primarily on the numinous consciousness and to display its affective and cognitive dimensions. He says that he wishes to analyze both "the ideas of the numinous and the feelings that correspond to them."[36] Otto thinks that in order to characterize these ideas and their corresponding feelings and to establish their noetic status he must conduct a special kind of inquiry. Describing the method that guides him throughout the book and the reasons for undertaking it, Otto says:

> The numinous. . . issues from the deepest foundation of *cognitive apprehension* that the soul possesses, and, though it of course comes into being in and amid the sensory data and empirical material of the natural world and cannot anticipate or dispense with those, yet it does not arise *out of* them, but only *by their means.* They are all the incitements, the stimulus, and the "occasion" for the numinous experience to become astir, and, in so doing, to begin—at first with a naive immediacy of reaction—to be interfused and interwoven with the present world of sensuous experience, until, becoming gradually purer, it disengages itself from this and takes its stand in absolute contrast to it. The proof that in the numinous we have to deal with purely *a priori cognitive elements* is to be reached by *introspection and a critical examination of reason such as Kant instituted.*[37]

Regrettably, Otto does not take the readers of *The Idea of the Holy* by the hand and tell them exactly what he means by the terms "introspection" and "critical examination of reason." He does not explain the logical structure of these two movements of inquiry, nor does he state explicitly when he conducts them and how. This is a serious lacuna which may have contributed to the confusion in the interpretation of *The Idea of the Holy.* Otto assumes, it seems to me, that his readers are already familiar with his previous book, *The Philosophy of Religion*, which outlines the basic threads of the critical method—

[36]Ibid., 124.
[37]Ibid., 113; the last two emphases are mine.

the only method Otto considers appropriate for the study of religion. Otto actually refers readers of *The Idea of the Holy* to his previous book, and when we read *The Idea of the Holy* against the background of *The Philosophy of Religion* we realize that in his description of the relations between the rational and nonrational, Otto follows the critical method as he himself outlined it in *The Philosophy of Religion*:

> The work begins with the actual given kinds of knowledge, examines what suppositions underlie these, and if and how these in their turn have their foundation in the reasoning mind. When the "if" and the "how" are established, then we have the final justification for the particular starting-point. This is what[38] distinguishes the critical method from skeptical and dogmatic thought alike. . . . The analytical observation moves backwards from the given cognitions, tries to find their underlying assumptions, separates them according to the sources of the knowledge, and thus at last discovers what fundamental kinds of real knowledge Reason really possesses.[39]

We shall see momentarily that these outlines of the critical method express Otto's fundamental acceptance and appropriation of the Friesian and Nelsonian modification of Kant's critical method. In essence, Fries and Nelson criticized Kant's transcendental deduction for resulting in skepticism. Of the two movements of Kant's Transcendental Argument they retained the "Metaphysical Deduction," in which they saw the essence of the critical philosophy which distinguishes it from speculative idealism, and replaced the "Transcendental Deduction" with an introspective investigation which relies on "Reason's trust in itself."

---

[38]The translator wrote "that," but "what" seems more appropriate.

[39]Otto, *The Philosophy of Religion*, 47. When Otto says in *The Idea of the Holy* that "the proof that in the numinous we have to deal with purely *a priori cognitive elements* is to be reached by introspection and a critical examination of reason such as Kant instituted" (p. 113, my emphasis), his all too brief remarks should be understood as a concise restatement of his more elaborate discussion in *The Philosophy of Religion*.

6.C.3. A Normative Science

Otto's Kantianism is not limited to strictly philosophical issues; it extends itself to some of his most challenging ideas about a science of religion. Reflecting in *The Philosophy of Religion* on the situation of the science of religion, Otto argues that it cannot and should not avoid the issue of the veracity of religious convictions. The student of religion must also be able to confront "reductionist" approaches that do not acknowledge the intrinsic value of religious phenomena. Otto argues that only the critical method can perform this task:

> If the question is raised "how far is religious conviction valid?" there is only one method, the method of the individual ascertainment of the religious consciousness, i.e., nothing other than the investigation of its origin, immediate knowledge and how far it can be trusted. This method is. . . the critical demonstration that Ideas are founded in reason; how this arises; and what ideas are thus founded.[40]

Asserting that the study of religion cannot succeed as a true science as long as it does not assume a normative role, Otto turns to Reason to find the transcendental conditions of religious experience:

> In the sphere of the science of religion. . . we must go back to. . . the rational principles of religion in the human intellect. . . . To search for this principle in man's intellect, to discover it, and to bring it to light—such is clearly the first task of all real endeavor in the sphere of the philosophy of religion, and without it no research in the history of religion can have a firm foundation. In this sense a philosophy of religion is a very sober task. . . . In Kantian phrase, its business is a "Criticism of Reason"—that is to say, the analysis, the testing of the human intellect, with the aim of discovering if it possesses any such principles, and if it does, to ascertain their nature. Kant himself in his Theory of Ideas, the loftiest and most splendid achievement of his thought, laid the foundation for this.[41]

[40]Otto, *The Philosophy of Religion*, 94.
[41]Ibid., 16–17.

Otto argues that to avoid a haphazard wandering among events the comparative and historical study of religion must proceed according to preestablished principles of selection and evaluation of empirical data. Such principles cannot be derived inductively from the empirical data but require independent grounding.

> Of the history of religion there is no end. But how can it develop from a mere description of religion into a science of religion, if it is nothing but a history of religion. . . . And. . . how can there be a history of religion without the possession of some inward principle. . . according to which the historical subject-matter is selected—I will not say classified?[42]

> If the history of a subject is to be presented, one must first of all know what the subject is. It is necessary to have a conception of the matter before starting. For example, to write the history of agriculture one must know what is meant by agriculture. So it is with the history of religion. Its principle is the idea of religion, and that must be first possessed, or the history will be a haphazard wandering among events.[43]

To stand on a firm foundation, Otto believes, the historical and comparative study of religion needs to be supplemented by a Critical analysis of the a priori conditions of experience. This is the task of the philosophy of religion which must conduct a "Criticism of Reason" in order to discover if Reason possesses such principles, and if it does, to ascertain their nature. Proceeding from firmly established criteria, the student of religion necessarily undertakes the normative task of assessing the true nature of the material.

> Religious. . . conviction. . . cannot be "accidental truths". . . the ultimate validity of religious truth could not depend on author-

---

[42]Ibid., 17; compare Paul Tillich, *What is Religion?* (ed. James Luther Adams; New York: Harper & Row, 1973) 38.

[43]Otto, *The Philosophy of Religion*, 205. This very insight is echoed in Otto's admonition (*The Idea of the Holy*, 8) to the skeptic not to join the sympathetic journey.

ity, teaching, ecclesiastical tradition, the scriptures, the miracles, or historical actuality, but on a particular principle in man's inner self.[44]

Every inquiry into a priori knowledge means a searching after and a setting up of concepts, ideas, judgments which, independent of all experience, are founded on pure reason, which reason possesses in its own right, which are its own property, certain and indisputable. The discovery of this "a priori" in general was the great task of the Kantian Criticism of Reason.[45]

Confident that he chose the proper method, Otto writes *The Idea of the Holy* guided by the fundamental insights of Kant's criticism of Reason, albeit with a different conception of the structure of a critical argument. In the next section I shall explain the nature of the change and the reasons for it. A subsequent section will explain the critical method as Otto understands it.

6.C.4. Against Skeptical Idealism

In choosing the critical method, Otto accepts the fundamental Kantian insight that the categories of the understanding are constitutive elements of valid factual judgments. Nevertheless, Otto's critical method differs significantly from Kant's. Otto agrees with Kant that the Categories are "pure a priori conceptions." Following Fries and Nelson, he argues that as such, however, they themselves impart *real knowledge*. Once the categories have been brought to our awareness by means of a critical examination of the judgments that describe our empirical experience, we are able to see that the categories reflect something inherent to Reason itself. "In them," Otto writes, "we comprehend, quite independently of experience, from pure reason, purely of ourselves alone, what is the fundamental condition of all Being. We know beforehand that all that exists must correspond to them. In this sense we are prescribing laws for Being."[46]

[44]Ibid., 33–34.
[45]Ibid., 18.
[46]Ibid., 52. Although the language may suggest dogmatic idealism, the priority Otto has in mind is not temporal but transcendental. When dealing

Otto argues that Kant committed a dangerous error that opens the critical system to a charge of skeptical idealism, a charge that our experience is merely a collective projection of arbitrary forms. "In establishing the a priori types of knowledge," Otto writes, "Kant had at the same time made the *perilous affirmation* that their validity was merely subjective and that whatever was known through them was 'ideal.' Since these kinds of knowledge spring from pure reason and are not given to reason 'from without,' in Kant's opinion they have *no* claim to validity apart from our own presentation of them, no claim to a *corresponding external reality*."[47] Kant infers, Otto proceeds to say, that "since this knowledge is altogether a priori, it can only hold good for the subjective world of our conception, not for an objective world of Being-in-itself, independent of ourselves. *From the a priori nature of the Categories he concludes that they are ideal. . .* the Categories are to be subjective principles of form; they enable us to shape for ourselves a picture of the universe which has consequently no claim of objectivity."[48] Otto's language is imprecise and misleading, especially in its use of the term "subjective" in a way that seems to miss altogether Kant's definition of objectivity in terms of universality and necessity. I would suggest, though I find no textual basis for it, that Otto is critical of Kant for not according the Categories the status of a "fact of Reason."

Otto understands Kant's *First Critique* as claiming that the Categories of the Understanding are but arbitrary projections of Reason upon the material of sensation.[49] The world of experience, which the categories synthesize, may accordingly be considered skeptically as an ideal projection of Reason. In confronting this problem Otto turns to

---

with Fries it is sometimes difficult to ascertain whether he oversteps criticism into idealism, but Otto has been influenced by Nelson's more careful discussions.

[47]Ibid., 18. Emphasis mine.

[48]Ibid., 52. Emphasis mine.

[49]This interpretation is problematic though not uncommon. The philosophical picture of the imposition of categorical structure on the unstructured manifold of impressions is suggested by Kant's *Prolegomena*, but it does not represent the doctrine of the *Critique of Pure Reason* and is rejected by the argument of the transcendental deduction in its second edition.

Jakob Fries's theory of *Ahndung* or "divination." With this theory
Fries proposed to redeem Kant's transcendental philosophy from the
charge of skepticism by establishing the fundamental principles of the
Understanding and of Practical Reason as partial expressions of the
Ideas of Reason, and by presenting the latter as constituents of the
intelligible world that we ourselves, qua thinkers and deliberators,
inhabit.[50]

Although we have no intellectual intuition of things in themselves,
Fries argued, we can reflect introspectively on the schematized categories, which are revealed to us in Kant's metaphysical deduction,
and abstract them away from the limitations of space and time.[51]
Doing so, we can intuit in them a positive content which does not
lend itself to exact conceptual definition,[52] but which can be translated into certain ideas, foremost of which is the Idea of the Highest
Good, an Idea which we express conceptually with the concepts of
God, the world, and the immortality of the soul.[53] Fries argues that
although we cannot give any precise conceptual formulation to the
ideas we intuit in feeling, our Reason has a full trust in them,[54] and,
in fact, it is this self-trust of Reason in its Ideas which rescues our
understanding of the phenomenal world from skeptical idealism.[55] Some
of these ideas will be explained further in the following section.

---

[50]Fries developed these ideas systematically in his books *Knowledge, Belief,
and Aesthetic Sense* and *New Critique of Reason*. Only a brief summary of
their arguments is possible in this context. Fries discusses the introspective
method in *Knowledge, Belief, and Aesthetic Sense*, 74–75.

[51]Fries, *Knowledge, Belief, and Aesthetic Sense*, 21, 23, 74–77, 95–97,
99–100, 113, 127, 131–32, 154. Though Fries clearly goes here beyond Kant,
his procedure and his results are surprisingly similar to the ideas Kant himself
developed in the Dialectic.

[52]Ibid., 99, 151–53.

[53]Ibid., 46–49, 75, 87, 151–53.

[54]Ibid., 74–75.

[55]See ibid., 46–49, 74–77, 83, 87, 151–53. I think that Otto and Fries
should be understood as referring to a certain ambiguity in Kant's discussion
of the cognitive status of the unschematized categories. Concluding his discussion of the Deduction and of the Schematism, Kant states that since the
categories determine only objects of empirical experience, we could suspect

In his analysis of religion Otto claims to have adopted the main insights of Kant's criticism of Reason. However, in confronting the alleged danger of skepticism, Otto argues, echoing Fries and Nelson:

> The fact that we really *know* something in our sense-perception, i.e., that we conceive an object which really exists and conceive it according to its being, is solely based on Reason's natural self-confidence that it is capable of truth and knowledge, a confidence that no skepticism can really shake. This applies with no

---

that if we dispensed with the restricting conditions represented by the schema, the scope of the concepts, which was previously restricted, could be extended (*Critique of Pure Reason*, 186/B186=A146–47). But Kant dismisses this supposition and argues that the pure concepts of the understanding, considered apart from their schemata, have only a "logical" meaning. Kant reiterates his assertion that "thoughts without intuitions are empty" (p. 93/B75=A51). The unschematized categories are empty forms awaiting to be filled by the material of sensation. The empty forms themselves can be put to no use since they give us no indication as to how they are to be applied or to what (see p. 186/B186–87=A147; and also pp. 264/B303=A246–47 and pp. 485–86 /B595–96=A567–68). The unschematized categories are merely functions of the understanding; they convey no knowledge and are not determinate thoughts. They are merely empty abstractions and as such have no cognitive status. However, in the Dialectic of the *First Critique* Kant assigns cognitive significance to the regulative ideas while writing that the pure categories can be used in order to think about things in themselves. He develops this theory further in the *Second Critique* where he argues that he was able to give objects to the regulative but empty ideas of the understanding. In the previous chapter of this work, which dealt with the *Critique of Judgment*, we saw that in the *Third Critique* Kant portrays feeling as the mental apparatus that apprehends, in reflection, the indeterminate concept of the moral designer of the universe. Fries found in the *Third Critique*, and especially in Kant's discussion of aesthetic taste, an inspiration and a confirmation to his position regarding the cognitive value of the Ideas. (See *Knowledge, Belief, and Aesthetic Sense*, 114–18, 145–49, 156.) Fries argued against Kant that a transcendental deduction is superfluous and misleading, as are all attempts to prove primary principles. When it comes to such principles, Fries argued, all that is needed and all that can be had is a "self-confidence of Reason" (*Selbstvertrauen der Vernunft*) (pp. 31–34). We shall see, shortly, how the principle of the self confidence of Reason is brought into play in Otto's proof of the a priori status of the category of the numinous.

less force—rather, with more—to a priori kinds of real knowledge than to such as depend on sense perception.[56]

In writing *The Idea of the Holy* Otto puts the teachings of Fries
and Nelson to use. Together with Fries and Nelson, who proposed to
redeem the Kantian Critique by replacing the transcendental deduction with a psychological inquiry that acknowledges the cognitive
value of Reason's feeling of truth, Otto undertakes a twofold critical
inquiry: an analysis of judgments into "questions of fact" (*quid facti*)
and into "questions of legality" (*quid juris*). The first inquiry aims to
point out the logical conditions of our judgments; the second inquiry
is concerned with the validation of the factual claims. Whereas Kant
conducts the second inquiry as a transcendental deduction, Fries,
Nelson, and Otto substitute for it a psychological introspection. It is
an introspective inquiry of this kind that Otto conducts in his sympathetic exercise. In order to understand this exercise better we need to
sketch briefly the basic threads of the critical method as it was modi-
fied by Fries and Nelson.[57]

6.C.5. The Two Movements of the Critique

The revised Critical method, like Kant's, proceeds from judgments—
that certain events are causally related, that there are things that we
ought to do, that a scene is beautiful—to inquire under what conditions these judgments can be valid. Since judgment is an act of synthesis of concepts in various forms, Criticism seeks the conditions
that make such syntheses possible. As scrutiny of sense impression
reveals that the forms of synthesis—exemplified in concepts like Unity,
Cause, and Duty—cannot be derived from sense data, their only source
can be the structure of our thought. Proceeding regressively from the
judgments of common experience, Criticism discovers that *if* these

[56]Otto, *The Philosophy of Religion*, 53.

[57]The following is a brief summary of the main thrusts of the critical
method as it is presented by Leonard Nelson in his *Socratic Method and
Critical Philosophy*; by Jacob Fries in *Knowledge, Belief, and Aesthetic Taste*;
and by Rudolf Otto in *The Philosophy of Religion*.

judgments are to be valid, reason must be able to provide, out of itself, the principles of synthesis. The identification of the full set of principles, the set which constitutes the structure of reason, is the analytical task of Critical philosophy. In Kantian terms, this is the Metaphysical Deduction of the Categories of Reason.

The Metaphysical Deduction is a hypothetical reconstruction of what the structure of reason must be *if* our judgments are valid. The identification of the structure of reason remains a mere hypothesis unless it can be shown independently that its discovery is indeed the necessary condition of the possibility of our experience. But how can it be possible to prove that a supreme principle is indeed supreme? Being the ground of all possible judgment, it would have to be assumed by any attempt to prove it. Kant had argued that the Metaphysical Deduction can only be validated by a further Transcendental Deduction. Seeing in this deduction the danger of skepticism, Otto followed Jakob Fries and Leonard Nelson who had substituted for it a Psychological Deduction.

Proceeding from experience, the Metaphysical Deduction abstracts the necessary forms of synthesis. At this stage its findings are still tainted with traces of experience. We have not quite reached the pure elements which are the original endowment of Reason. From the final findings of the Deduction, however, Reason can proceed by itself to apprehend immediately the pure forms of Reason that the Deduction had pointed out, forms which are its own structure. As inherent to the structure of Reason, the pure forms of Reason are conceived as belonging to the world of things-in-themselves, as part of the structure of an intelligible world. It is important to emphasize that there is no claim here to intuitive or speculative knowledge of the pure forms. This is a crucial point in the Friesian-Nelsonian critique; it carefully tries to delineate an *awareness* that a category as it governs our experience is an aspect of something that we absolutely cannot know— a pure category of Reason. But even as we cannot know it, we do have an awareness of what the pure category must be, that in it we apprehend something real. Once the pure category that Metaphysical Deduction has revealed is apprehended, the category is no longer conceived as merely an analytical construct, but as an *immediate awareness of reason.*[58] This immediate awareness of reason gives rise to a *self-confidence of reason* in virtue of which whatever reason recognizes as its own structure is necessarily elevated beyond the possibility of doubt.[59]

Since the immediate awareness of reason is achieved at the culmination of a regression from judgments the validity of which was merely assumed, the possibility exists that these judgments are invalid and reason is led to put its trust in a pseudoprinciple. We can only ascertain that reason does not delude itself in having confidence in a pseudoprinciple by discovering if the alleged principle can be shown, independently, to be part of Reason. As the immediate awareness should be not only a logical construct but also a distinct moment of experience, it can and must be available to psychological introspection.[60] Whereas the Metaphysical Deduction begins with given judg-

[58]What I think this claim amounts to, as I suggested above, is that we come to accept the category as a fact of reason.

[59]It will become clear as our discussion proceeds that this self-confidence of reason, characterized by Nelson as a feeling of truth, as a feeling of unshakable trust, is not considered infallible. (It may prove interesting to compare these neo-Kantian observations on the feeling of truth with William James's analysis of the "sentiment of rationality.")

[60]The appeal to psychological introspection immediately raises the problem of self-deception. The prospect of self deception would most likely be devastating for any attempt to verify introspectively the claims of a closed system of philosophy. In essence, however, Kant's critical philosophy is not a closed system but a method for an open-ended examination of the products of a restless Reason. The open-endedness of the project is reflected clearly in Nelson's explanation that the introspective findings are philosophically significant only in conjunction with a regressive logical procedure which seeks to identify the highest principles. This procedure has no natural point of completion; it must be continuously applied to ever-evolving fields of human experience. The danger of self deception is minimized by the dialectical movement of the inquiry from the phenomena to principles (which are verified, tentatively, by introspection) and back to a scientific study of the ever-widening field of phenomena armed with the conclusions of the previous analysis which now serve as explanatory hypotheses. I shall soon argue that these ideas inform Otto's conception of the science of religion and that they are worthy of our serious consideration.

ments and *derives* principles as their logical conditions, an independent Psychological Deduction proceeds empirically, by introspection, in a process of association based on reciprocal attraction of analogous ideas to establish that the principles are indeed part of Reason and worthy of its trust. The two Deductions are mutually supportive. Introspection verifies that an alleged principle is indeed part of Reason, while analysis establishes that an element of introspective experience has the logical status of a principle.

The point at which the two movements of the deduction converge is of crucial importance, for, according to Fries, it is at this level of reason that the feelings of religion come into play. As we have seen, the apex of the Metaphysical Deduction is an awareness that manifests itself in a judgment that the formative principle of experience is a limited manifestation of an unknowable pure category. This judgment, usually referred to by Fries, Nelson, and Otto as "feeling,"[61] is necessarily preconceptual and thus nonrational, though it is of paramount cognitive significance. Being a judgment that the constitutive elements of experience are manifestations of the pure structure of Reason, this feeling is, ipso facto, a judgment that the content of our consciousness is an appearance of an unknowable noumenal world to which we ourselves belong as free rational agents, though the manner in which we are such beings must remain a total mystery for us. All that we can do is judge that elements of our finite experience are manifestation of an eternal reality. As we shall see later, following Fries, Otto called this ability of ours "a faculty of divination" (*Ahndung*). Otto claims that it is through *Ahndung* that we are able to perform religious judgments and that such performances provide the final proof that the numinous category is constitutive of a realm of experience. In turn, religious judgments, which become possible through *Ahndung*, are made the starting point of a Metaphysical analysis that will bring the category of the numinous to the light of consciousness—an analysis that will be confirmed by Otto's introspective examination.

---

[61]"Feeling" is used to translate the two German terms *Gefühl* and *Ahndung* (an archaic form of *ahnen*), both of which are given special philosophic meaning.

▨ 6.D. The Argument of *The Idea of the Holy*

Armed with his understanding of the Critical method Otto sets out to show that religion is a distinct realm of meaning which must be understood and evaluated in its own terms. Otto undertakes to guide his readers in a sympathetic process of anamnesis, or remembrance, to evoke in them the religious feeling and the trust in its noeticity. Here too, it seems to me, Otto follows Kant's insight regarding the nature of the beautiful. In his discussion of aesthetic taste Kant argued that in order to judge an object beautiful one must perform the judgment oneself; one must feel the unique aesthetic feeling which alone discloses the harmony in the beautiful object. One can be guided into this experience by exposure to examples, but one can be taught no rules of inference, as the aesthetic judgment is not founded on a determinative concept. The aesthetic judgment, according to Kant, is a matter of personal and immediate experience.[62] Fries and Nelson appropriated this insight in their discussions of the immediate awareness of the Ideas of Reason, and Otto followed them in his discussion of the category of the numinous.[63]

Guiding his readers through exposure to various manifestations of religious experience, Otto's primary goal is to establish the noeticity of religious feeling. Otto does so as he strives to give a meticulous phenomenological description of the unique and underivable nature of the religious feeling. To establish the cognitive value of religious feeling, Otto undertakes to establish both that the religious feeling has a direct and immediate reference to a religious object that is apprehended only in feeling and that the religious feeling is determined a priori by a distinct religious category. Concluding his discussion, Otto endeavors to demonstrate that the distinct religious category is constitutive of a distinct religious realm of meaning. In this discussion Otto goes beyond the teachings of his mentors and argues that the study of religion cannot be completed before we acknowledge the significance of the history of religion.

---

[62]See discussion in part one, section 4.B.4.

[63]This insight, I suggest, led Otto to issue his famous admonition to the skeptic not to go on reading *The Idea of the Holy*, 8.

Although he is utterly dissatisfied with what I call Kant's "official theory of religion," Otto finds in Kant's theory of aesthetic judgment a profound insight into the nature of religion. He finds in the *Third Critique* both a methodological inspiration for his own analysis of the numinous category and a confirmation to his theory of the nature of religion as the ability to experience the infinite in the midst of our finite reality. Otto argues that Kant followed Luther in discerning such an ability and that in discerning it both thinkers were able to give expression to human religiosity.[64]

6.D.1. The Noeticity of Religious Feeling

6.D.1.a. Introduction

In his phenomenology of the religious experience Otto strives to establish the noeticity of religious feeling. In one of the most important statements of the book Otto explains that a state of feeling in which the understanding is overwhelmed is still a noetic state; it is a state of knowledge in which we are aware of that which we do not understand.

> Something may be profoundly and intimately known in feeling for the bliss it brings or the agitation it produces, and yet the understanding may find no concept for it. To *know* and to *understand conceptually* are two different things, are often even mutually exclusive and contrasted. The mysterious obscurity of the numen is by no means tantamount to unknowableness.[65]

Building upon Kant's discussion of the "feeling of life" in the *Third Critique*, Otto aims to show that we identify the numinous

---

[64]Otto, *The Philosophy of Religion*, 40–42.

[65]Otto, *The Idea of the Holy*, 135. Otto is not careful enough in his choice of terminology. The term "to know" can cause confusion if understood as denoting scientific knowledge. It is obvious, however, that Otto wants to say, like Kant, that cognition is not limited to the realm of the understanding nor to the realms of determinative concepts. We explained this point extensively in our discussion of the *Third Critique*.

object through our feeling in just the same way as we discern the internal harmony of the aesthetic object through aesthetic feeling. He argues that in feeling we apprehend a positive content, a content that can be expressed only symbolically with "negative terms." On the basis of this analysis we can understand, Otto claims, that the negative language of mysticism refers to something positive that can be disclosed only to feeling. Although the understanding can give no direct conceptual definition to the cognition reached by feeling, the feeling provides a genuine cognition of the ultimate meaning and purpose of the world.

> It is through this positive feeling-content that the concepts of the "transcendent" and "supernatural" become forthwith designations for a unique "wholly other" reality and quality, something of whose special character we can *feel*, without being able to give it conceptual expression.[66]

Later in this discussion, describing various expressions of religious feeling, Otto says:

> All this teaches us the independence of the positive content of this experience from the implications of its overt conceptual expression, and how it can be firmly grasped, thoroughly understood, and profoundly appreciated, purely in, with, and from the feeling itself.[67]

In reading Otto's following claims—that religious feeling has a primary reference to an object that eludes conceptual apprehension, that our recognition of this object is not a reflex on our feeling but is disclosed in and through this feeling, and that we do not have any prior conceptual apprehension of the religious object—we must realize that Otto is building upon Kant's distinction between determinate and indeterminate judgments. Religious feeling, like Kant's aesthetic feeling, discloses to the mind an object that is not determined by the

[66]Otto, *The Idea of the Holy*, 30.
[67]Ibid., 34.

concepts of the understanding. We become cognizant of the essential characteristics of religious objects, as we become cognizant of purposeless purposiveness in judgments of taste, only in and through feeling. Religious ideas, like aesthetic ideas, can be expressed symbolically with concepts that allude to them but cannot exhaust their nature.[68]

Since he believes that religious feeling is the only access to the religious object, it is important for Otto to delineate meticulously the various elements of the religious experience. He explains that as we feel the presence of a "wholly other" object, the numen, we experience simultaneously feelings of attraction and repulsion and that we, at the same time, feel our deficiency before that which we perceive as qualitatively superior. Otto names the moment of repulsion "tremendum," and the moment of attraction "fascinans," and he names the feeling of submersion before the "wholly other" object—which he calls "mysterium"—as "creature-feeling." Otto's phenomenology of the religious experience is well known, and its importance is generally acknowledged. I shall focus therefore on its methodological and philosophical dimensions. My basic goal is to demonstrate that in his discussion of the various moments of religious feeling Otto claims persistently that religious feeling unites cognitive and affective moments. I shall point out Otto's philosophical comments and locate them, as Otto does, in the critical context of Kant's *Third Critique.*

6.D.1.a.(1). Postponement of Comparison to Kant's Sublime: I shall not be able to undertake here a comparison of the various moments of Otto's religious experience to Kant's characterization of both the feeling of respect for the moral law and the feeling of the sublime.[69] Otto's theory of religion depends partly on his ability to show that the religious feeling in and through which the "numinous object" is recognized, is distinct and unique, and that religious judgment dif-

---

[68]Though Otto does not say so explicitly, he clearly relies on Kant's discussion of the symbolic expression of aesthetic ideas. See Kant, *Critique of Judgment,* 182–83/314–15, 214–15/342, 225–28/351–53.

[69]See especially Kant's discussions in the *Critique of Judgment,* 114/257, 115/258, and *Critique of Practical Reason,* 75–76/73–74, 77/75, 81/79, 83–85/81–84, 89/87.

fers from theoretical, moral, and aesthetic judgments. The problem of the ambiguous relations between Otto's numinous consciousness and Kant's theory of the sublime is manifest in Otto's various references throughout the *The Idea of the Holy* to the similarity and difference between them. Though he admits that there is a significant similarity between the sublime and the numinous and even argues that "a proof that there exists a hidden kinship between the numinous and the sublime which is something more than a merely accidental analogy, and to which Kant's *Critique of Judgment* bears distant witness,"[70] Otto insists that the sublime is ultimately just a pale reflection of the numinous. Discussing the numinous feeling Otto says:

> In the category and feeling of the *sublime* we have a counterpart to it, though it is true it is but a pale reflexion, and moreover involves difficulties of analysis all its own. The analogies between the consciousness of the sublime and the numinous may be easily grasped. To begin with, "the sublime," like "the numinous," is in Kantian language an idea or concept "that cannot be unfolded" or explicated (*unauswickelbar*). Certainly we can tabulate some general "rational" signs that uniformly recur as soon as we call an object sublime; as, for instance, that it must approach, or threaten to overpass, the bounds of our understanding by some "dynamic" or "mathematical" greatness, by potent manifestations of force or magnitude in spatial extent. But these are obviously only conditions of, not the essence of, the impression of sublimity. A thing does not become sublime merely by being great. The concept itself remains unexplicated; it has in it something mysterious, and in this it is like that of the numinous. A second point of resemblance is that the sublime exhibits the same peculiar dual character as the numinous; it is at once daunting, and yet again singularly attracting, in its impress upon the mind. It humbles and at the same time exalts us, circumscribes and extends us beyond ourselves, on the one hand releasing in us a feeling analogous to fear, and on the other rejoicing us. So the idea of the sublime is closely similar to that of the numinous, and is well adapted to excite it and to be excited by it, while each tends to pass over into the other.[71]

---

[70]Otto, *The Idea of the Holy*, 63.
[71]Ibid., 41–42.

Otto's insistence notwithstanding, it is difficult to see how the two experiences can be differentiated in the way his theory requires. I would tentatively suggest that Otto may not have considered the Kantian sublime an independent experience. He seems to have thought that in his discussion of the sublime Kant had begun to see the aesthetic as a religious category. Otto suggested that Fries "elevated aesthetics into religion."[72] To compare Otto's phenomenology of religious feeling to Kant's characterization of the feelings of respect for the moral law and of the sublime and to see if Otto succeeded in distinguishing the religious feeling from these others will remain a task for a different study.

6.D.1.a.(2). *Rejection of Subjectivist Conceptions of Religion*: Through his phenomenology of the religious experience Otto tries to defend his views from the charge of subjectivism that is often directed against theories of religious feeling. Otto considers Schleiermacher's theory of "feeling of dependence" one of the reasons for this charge,[73] and his attack on Schleiermacher shows how he wants his own theory of religious feeling to be understood. Otto blames Schleiermacher for neglecting to establish the cognitivity of religious feeling and for making the cognition of the religious object an inference from a prior determination of feeling. He interprets Schleiermacher as taking "as basis and point of departure what is merely a secondary effect." He says that Schleiermacher "sets out to teach a consciousness of the religious object only by way of an inference from the shadow it casts upon *self*-consciousness."[74] Otto accuses Schleiermacher of arguing that the believer can come upon the very fact of God only as a result of an inference from the religious emotion which is a sort of self-consciousness that has no direct reference to an object other than to the self.

---

[72]Otto, *The Philosophy of Religion*, 133.

[73]Otto is one of many who see in Schleiermacher a proponent of subjectivist religion. There are, I believe, good reasons to think that this is an erroneous interpretation, but this is a matter I cannot pursue further in this context. For an alternative account, see Richard R. Niebuhr, *Schleiermacher on Christ and Religion*.

[74]Otto, *The Idea of the Holy*, 20.

The religious category discovered by him, by whose means he professes to determine the real content of the religious emotion, is merely a category of *self*-valuation, in the sense of self-depreciation. According to him the religious emotion would be directly and primarily a sort of *self*-consciousness, a feeling concerning oneself in a special, determined relation, viz. one's dependence. Thus, according to Schleiermacher, I can only come upon the very fact of God as the result of an inference, that is, by reasoning to a cause beyond myself to account for my "feeling of dependence." But this is entirely opposed to the psychological facts of the case.[75]

Contrary to this theory of religious feeling, which he ascribes to Schleiermacher, Otto argues:

Rather, the "creature-feeling" is itself a first subjective concomitant and effect of another feeling-element, which casts it like a shadow, but which in itself indubitably has immediate and primary reference to an object outside the self. Now this object is just what we have already spoken of as "the numinous." For the "creature feeling" and the sense of dependence to arise in the mind the "numen" must be experienced as present, a numen presence, as in the case of Abraham.[76]

In addition to this charge, Otto condemns Schleiermacher for neglecting to establish the veracity of religious judgment:

Schleiermacher only succeeds with difficulty, and always as if it were a task of minor importance, in establishing the connection between religious feeling and religious conviction: feeling without conviction should inevitably lack the support of principle and justice. Schleiermacher, at first, will not admit any validity as knowledge in such conviction. This is most prejudicial to religion, and is contrary to its most primary and essential nature.[77]

[75]Ibid., 10.
[76]Ibid., 11.
[77]Otto, *The Philosophy of Religion*, 23–24.

To counteract the damage he accuses Schleiermacher of causing and to establish the noeticity of religious feeling Otto strives to show: (1) that the religious feeling refers to an object, (2) that it is determined a priori by a distinct religious category, and (3) that it is therefore constitutive of a distinct realm of meaning. Although Otto does not present them as such, I consider these to be three distinct logical movements of an argument for the noeticity of religious feelings. I further maintain that these three movement define the literary structure and the philosophical argument of *The Idea of the Holy*. The first informs Otto's phenomenology of the experience, the second guides his epistemological discussion, and the third informs his conception of a history of religion and impels his sketch of the faculty of divination. In the following sections I shall highlight and explain many of Otto's more theoretical statements in these discussions in order to show that the argument for the noeticity of religious feeling is indeed the backbone of his book.

6.D.1.b. The Moment of Mysterium Tremendum

Otto discerns in the religious experience three distinct affective moments: mysterium tremendum, fascinans, and creature-feeling. My enumeration differs from the traditional account of Otto's phenomenology of the experience as an experience of mysterium, tremendum, and fascinans. As my ensuing analysis will show, Otto takes great care in his account to differentiate between the various affective moments of the experience and their objective reference. The three moments of tremendum, fascinans, and creature-feeling are depicted as elements of our characteristic affective response to our feeling-encounter with the object of the experience, with the mysterium. The experience combines two distinct poles, one of subjective affectivity and one of objective reference.[78] The subjective pole is a moment of self-consciousness in face of the numinous X. Otto differentiates in this pole three distinct moments of affectivity. The objective pole, which accounts for the cognitivity of the experience, is the apprehension of the numinous object that is given only to feeling.

---

[78]Kant's account of our experience of beauty is obviously a model for Otto's analysis.

My analysis of Otto's description of the affective moments will show that in all three of them Otto repeatedly emphasizes the noeticity of the feeling. He tries first to show systematically that religious feeling has a direct reference to an object. Having shown this, he proceeds to argue that the feeling is determined a priori by a distinct religious category. It is particularly important for Otto to show that the feeling is determined a priori because he holds that all three moments are effective only in a developed religious sensitivity. He wants to be in a position to claim that in other cases in which one of the moments is dominant and the others remain latent, the experience refers directly to the numinous object.

Though the numinous object eludes conceptual apprehension, in the numinous feeling, Otto argues, we apprehend something positive. In the feeling we observe a reference to the numinous object. In his phenomenological analysis of our feeling-encounter with the mystery of the numinous, Otto explains that it is not simply the limits of our possible knowledge that we come against; our experience appears as a confrontation with something we recognize as wholly other.

> The truly "mysterious" object is beyond our apprehension and comprehension, not only because our knowledge has certain ir-removable limits, but because in it we come upon something inherently "wholly other," whose kind and character are incommensurable with our own, and before which we therefore recoil in a wonder that strikes us chill and numb.[79]

This assertion must not be interpreted as affirming a cognition of transcendent beings. When taken out of context, this statement can be misconstrued in this manner. However, when it is read in its immediate context in which the employment of the numinous category is discussed, and against its theoretical background in Fries and Nelson, it is obvious that such an interpretation fails to comprehend the true meaning of Otto's argument. In *The Philosophy of Religion* Otto characterizes the feeling of mystery as the feeling that envelopes the awareness of the highest Ideas of Reason, which, as such, cannot be

[79]Otto, *The Idea of the Holy*, 28.

given a conceptual description. Following Fries, Otto insists that we can only express the content of this awareness in terms of a double negation.[80] Otto insists that our awareness of the highest Ideas is itself an awareness of mystery. It is an awareness of something that, being the highest Ideas of Reason, cannot in principle be known to the understanding. Otto says, there, that this "mystery awareness" is the fundamental mystery of religion. He warns against the prevailing mistake of advocates of "mysticism" who argue that this feeling can pass beyond the limits of Reason. Such positions, Otto argues, result from a misunderstanding of the nature of this mystery.[81]

We can return now to examine Otto's claim that in religious feeling we apprehend an object that eludes conceptual apprehension. Discussing the moment of "tremendum" Otto asserts that

> it is again evident at once that here too our attempted formulation by means of a concept is once more a merely *negative* one. Conceptually *mysterium* denotes merely that which is hidden and

[80]For discussion of double negation as a mode of rational expression, see my analysis of the stages of the critical method in part one, section 1.C.5. above.

[81]In *The Philosophy of Religion*, Otto argues that "through Faith knowledge is brought about, and that in 'double negation' i.e., in such a way that we do not obtain positive cognition-contents as to transcendental realities; rather do we conceive them by denying the limits of that knowledge which we possess. To predicate positively as to the real nature of eternal things is not given to us. No philosophy can penetrate behind the veil of space and time (except through the negation of both). And Faith can predicate absolutely nothing as to the *in se* of Deity, just as little can it predicate of the World as proceeding through God" (p. 100).

Following this line of thought Otto warns against the "soaring flights of speculation" which "tried to conceive in 'intellectual intuition' the proceeding of the many from the one, the transition from God to the Universe." Otto disengages his theory from "the passion for roving, the mania for building airy structures in the Transcendental" (p. 100). He insists that "for a *positive* affirmation on the Infinite, an 'intellectual intuition' of the kind that Fichte's school loved to describe, would be necessary. But no such intuition is granted to us. Our intuitive perception is wholly confined to the sensuous. It follows that a 'comprehending' knowledge, a knowledge of the Infinite in positive concepts, is not possible for us. The Infinite for us is still the Incomprehensible" (p. 100).

esoteric, that which is *beyond conception or understanding,* extraordinary and unfamiliar. The term does not define the object more *positively* in its qualitative character. But though what is enunciated in the word is *negative,* what is meant is something absolutely and intensely *positive.* This pure positive we can experience in feelings, feelings which our discussion can help to make clear to us, in so far as it arouses them actually in our hearts.[82]

Otto emphasizes here that the positive content is accessible only to feeling. He argues that this content can only be expressed symbolically by means of what Otto calls ideograms, or by negative concepts. In light of our previous discussions we realize that in speaking of negative concepts Otto alludes to the way our apprehension of the unschematized categories or the Ideas of Reason can be expressed according to Fries, and to the way the indeterminate principle of aesthetic taste is expressed according to Kant (see part one, section 4.B., note 32). Otto's position is that there is an object that we can cognize only through feeling. This seems to be what Otto means when he explains that

it is through this feeling-content that the concepts of the "transcendent" and the "supernatural" become forthwith designations for a unique "wholly other" reality and quality, something of whose special character we can *feel,* without being able to give it clear conceptual expression.[83]

6.D.1.c. The Moment of Fascinans

Otto's view that the religious feeling encompasses complex moments of consciousness, which involve both subjective affectivity and objective reference, finds similar expression in his description of the second moment of the experience—the fascinans. Whereas the moment of tremendum was discussed in ontological terms as our affec-

---

[82]Otto, *The Idea of the Holy,* 13; all emphases except "mysterium" are mine. It is noteworthy that Otto himself tries to arouse this feeling of mystery in the minds of his readers through his method of sympathy.

[83]Ibid., 30.

tive identification of a wholly other order of being, the fascinans is described as our response to a wholly other order of value. Every moment of the experience is to have, in Otto's analysis, both a subjective and an objective aspect.

> There will, then, in fact be two values to distinguish in the numen; its "fascination" (*fascinans*) will be that element in it whereby it is of *subjective* value (=beatitude) to man; but it is "august" (*augustum*) in so far as it is recognized as possessing in itself *objective* value that claims our homage.[84]

Reflecting on this assertion, Otto further elucidates his theory of the noeticity of feeling by drawing an illuminating comparison between feelings of joy and religious bliss. We shall see immediately that his discussion presupposes and alludes to Kant's theory of aesthetic judgment. Setting his comparison forth, Otto says:

> A deep joy may fill our mind without any clear realization upon our part of its source and the object to which it refers, though some such objective reference there must always be. But as attention is directed to it, the obscure object becomes clearly identified in precise conceptual terms. Such an object cannot, then, be called, in our sense of the word, "non-rational." But it is quite otherwise with the religious "bliss" and its essentially numinous aspect, the *fascinans*. Not the most concentrated attention can elucidate the object to which this state of mind refers, bringing it out of the impenetrable obscurity of feeling into the domain of conceptual understanding. It remains purely a felt experience, only to be indicated symbolically by "ideograms." That is what we mean by saying it is non-rational. And the same is true of all the moments of the numinous experience.[85]

The comparison between joy and bliss is instructive as it helps bring out Otto's meaning in speaking of a religious experience. We

---

[84]Ibid., 52.

[85]Ibid., 58–59. This quotation also makes it perfectly clear that in speaking of a nonrational, Otto refers not to the affective aspect of the feeling, as subjectivist interpretations of Otto assume, but to the object to which it refers.

often experience joyfulness without, at the same time, being aware of what it is that causes us joy. According to Otto's theory of the emotions—a theory of which we must be aware if we are to understand his notion of a religious experience—experiences like joyfulness are essentially referential. They refer to an object even when no awareness of the object is clearly present in our mind. Our ability to recognize an experience of joy allows us to proceed to identify that which brings us joy, but our recognition of the experience and our identification of the object are distinct cognitive moments. Religious bliss differs experientially from ordinary joy in ways which Otto so elegantly and perceptively describes. It also differs referentially in that its objective reference cannot be recognized other than in and through it.

It is clear that Otto works here in close analogy to Kant's theory of the beautiful. The subjective feeling of aesthetic satisfaction is identifiable and distinguished from other feelings of gratification and identifies a perfection in the object it considers "beautiful." This perfection to which we respond in aesthetic satisfaction, cannot be recognized other than in and through the aesthetic feeling. Just as Kant argued that the aesthetic feeling is determined a priori, so, as we shall see, Otto claims that the distinct religious feeling can be shown to be determined a priori by what he calls "the category of the numinous."

6.D.1.d. The Moment of Creature-Feeling

Otto returns to the bifacial character of the feeling again in his discussion of the self-reflective moment of the religious feeling that he calls "creature-feeling." This moment of feeling manifests itself as a self-devaluation that is triggered by the encounter with the wholly other order of being and value and identifies it:

> [T]his self-depreciation feeling is marked by an immediate, almost instinctive, spontaneity. It is not based on deliberation, nor does it follow any rule, but breaks, as it were, palpitant from the soul—like a direct reflex movement at the stimulation of the numinous. It does not spring from the consciousness of some committed transgression, but rather is *an immediate datum given with the feeling of the numen*: it proceeds to "disvalue" together

with the self the tribe to which the person belongs, and indeed, together with that, all existence in general. Now it is today pretty generally agreed that, all this being the case, these outbursts of feeling are not simply, and probably at first not at all, *moral* depreciations, but belong to a quite special category of valuation and appraisement. The feeling is beyond question not that of the transgression of the moral law, however evident it may be that such a transgression, where it has occurred, will involve it as a consequence: *it is a feeling of absolute "profaneness"*. . . the most uncompromising judgment of self-depreciation, a judgment passed, *not upon his character, because of individual "profane" actions of his, but upon his own very existence as a creature before that which is supreme above all creatures.*[86]

Two points here are important for our discussion. Otto stresses that the "creature feeling" is a *direct reflex movement* at the stimulation of the numinous and that it is distinctly a religious feeling and not a moral one.

Otto has earlier explained that our subjective response depends on the character of the mysterious wholly other. Reiterating this idea he explains that it is through the response that we become aware of its object:

All that this new term "creature-feeling," can express, is the note of submergence into nothingness before an over-powering, absolute might of some kind; whereas everything turns upon the *character* of this overpowering might, a character which cannot be expressed verbally, and can only be suggested indirectly through the tone and content of a man's feeling-response (Gefühls-reaktion) to it. And this response must be directly experienced in oneself to be understood.[87]

[86]Ibid., 50–51.

[87]Ibid., 10. Claims that something must be directly experienced in order to be understood may be suspect of being disingenuous attempts at making one's position invulnerable to criticism. While the suspicion may at times be justified, its critical force is rather limited. It seems rather unreasonable to deny that some things must be experienced in order to be understood (consider the two very different candidates: pain and Buddhist enlightenment). The pivotal issue is not the legitimacy of appeals to self-experience, but whether we are

It is important to remember that Otto attempts to characterize the religious feeling-response because he holds that we identify the numinous object only through this response. Otto emphasizes the fact that in feeling we have access to a cognitive content that eludes conceptual formulation. Lastly, he emphasizes that we must discern in the feeling two distinct elements: the subjective and the objective.

> The "creature-feeling" (Kreatur-gefühl) is itself a first *subjective* concomitant and effect of another feeling-element, which casts it like a shadow, but which in itself indubitably has *immediate and primary reference to an object outside of the self*.[88]

The objective reference of the religious feeling is obviously very important in Otto's view, for he immediately returns to it and asserts categorically that "the numinous is thus felt as objective and outside the self."[89]

Having argued that religious feeling refers to a numinous object, Otto undertakes to justify its referential claim. In order to prove the noeticity of the religious feelings he had described, Otto proceeds to claim that, like the aesthetic feeling Kant analyzed in the *Third Critique*, these religious feelings are determined a priori.

6.D.2. The A Priori Determination of the Numinous Consciousness

6.D.2.a. Rejection of Empiricist Accounts of Religion

In the preceding discussion I showed that Otto begins to establish the noeticity of religious feeling by presenting it as the only mental faculty that can apprehend the numinous object. Having argued persistently that religious feeling has an immediate and direct reference

---

given enough descriptive material to be able to identify the experience should we be inclined to attempt it. It is also important that sufficient explanation and analysis be supplied to capture our interest in the project. It seems to me that Otto goes a long way toward satisfying these requirements. We should remember that the model Otto has in mind is Kant's claim that an object must be experienced in order to be judged beautiful (see part one, section 4.B.4).

[88]Otto, *The Idea of the Holy*, 10. Emphasis mine.
[89]Ibid., 11.

to the religious object, Otto proceeds with the second stage of his argument. He strives to establish the universal communicability of religious judgments by demonstrating the a priori determination of religious feeling. Otto aims to distinguish the religious feeling, which he regards the core of religious judgment (the feeling that discerns the infinite in the finite), from mere contingent affectivity that reflects the sheer passivity of emotions. Doing so, Otto again should be understood as building upon Kant's discussion of taste which strove to distinguish the aesthetic feeling of pleasure and pain from the contingent feeling of the "liking of the agreeable."[90] Otto chooses to establish his position by attacking a sensualist view that regards the mind an empty slate upon which external objects inscribe their impressions and sees in feelings passing impressions devoid of cognitive import. In an instructive passage that discusses the ways in which he thinks that Jesus was perceived by his followers as a manifestation of the numinous, Otto argues:

> For this factor—the mind's own witness to the impression—is, it need hardly be said, an indispensable one. Without it all "impression" is without effect, or rather no impression could occur at all. Therefore, all doctrines of the "impression made by Christ" are inadequate if they do not pay regard to this second element, which indeed is nothing but the *mental predisposition necessary for the experience of holiness, to wit, the category of the holy, potentially present in the spirit as a dim or obscure a priori cognition.* "Impress" or "impression," that is, presupposes something capable of receiving impressions, and that is just what the mind is not, if in itself it is only a "tabula rasa." In that richer sense in which we use the word here, we do not in fact mean by "impression" merely the "impression" which, in the theory of the Sensationalist [sensualist] school, is the psychical result of sense-perception and is left behind as a psychical trace or vestige of the percept. To be "impressed" by some one, in the sense we use the term here, means rather to cognize or recognize in him a peculiar significance and to humble oneself before it. And we maintain that this is only possible by an *element of cognition*, comprehension and valuation in one's own inner conscious-

---

[90]See discussion in part one, section 4.B.2.a above.

ness, that goes out to meet the outward presented fact, i.e., by the "spirit within."[91]

An immediate analogy that comes to Otto's mind as he tries to demonstrate the a priori determinability of religious feeling is Kant's discussion of the beautiful. In his discussion of the feeling of dread, which is one of the manifestations of the moment of tremendum in the religious experience, Otto himself draws an interesting comparison between aesthetic cognition and the numinous consciousness:

> But it must be repeated that in its content even the first stirring of "demonic dread" is a purely *a priori* element. In this respect it may be compared from first to last with the aesthetic judgment and the category of the beautiful. Utterly different as my mental experiences are when I recognize an object as "beautiful" or as "horrible," yet both cases agree in this, that I ascribe to the object an attribute that professes to interpret it, which I do not and cannot get from sense-experience, but which I rather ascribe to it by a spontaneous judgment of my own. Intuitively I apprehend in the object only its sensuous qualities and its spatial form, nothing more. That the *meaning* I call "beautiful" fits the object, i.e., that these sense-data *mean* "beautiful," or even that there *is* any such meaning at all—these are facts which sensory elements can in no wise supply or tell me. I must have an obscure conception of the "beautiful itself," and, in addition,

---

[91]Otto, *The Idea of the Holy*, 160. Emphasis mine. Otto continues with an analogy from aesthetic judgment to illustrate his argument regarding the noeticity of religious judgment: "Music can only be understood by the musical person; none but he receives an 'impression' of it. . . Once again let us recall the example of the beautiful. A beautiful thing can only make an impression as such, i.e., as signifying beauty, if and in so far as a man possesses in himself *a priori* the potentiality of framing a special standard of valuation, viz. aesthetic valuation. Such a disposition can only be understood as an original, obscure awareness and appreciation of the value of 'beauty' itself. Because man has this in him, or better, because he is capable of realizing it by training, he is able to recognize beauty in the particular beautiful object that he encounters, to feel the correspondence of this object with the hidden 'standard of value' within him. And so, and only so, will he get an 'impression'" (pp. 160–66).

a principle of subsumption, by which I attribute it to the object,
else even the simplest experience of a beautiful thing is rendered impossible. And the analogy may be pursued farther. Joy
in the beautiful (*Freude-am-Schönen*), however analogous to mere
pleasure in the agreeable (*bloßen Lust-am-Angenehmen*), is yet
distinguishable from it by a plain difference in quality, and cannot
be derived from anything other than itself; and just such is the
relation of the specific religious awe to mere natural fear.[92]

Otto, then, wants us to recognize the special nature of religious
feeling. He urges us to discern both its affective and its cognitive
dimensions, to realize that the feeling has a direct referent in the
numinous object and that religious feeling is determined a priori by
the numinous category. He expresses this insight in the following
concise statement regarding the numinous consciousness:

There must be felt a something "numinous," something bearing
the character of a "numen," to which the mind turns spontaneously; or (*which is the same thing in other words*) these feelings
can only arise in the mind as accompanying emotions when the
category of "the numinous" is called into play.[93]

Otto is determined to make clear his view that religious feeling is
determined a priori by the numinous category, and he repeats this
claim adamantly throughout the book. Already at the beginning of
The Idea of the Holy Otto gives notice:

I shall speak then, of a unique "numinous category of value and
of a definitely "numinous" state of mind, which is always found
wherever the category is applied.[94]

[92]Ibid., 134. The German is Otto, *Das Heilige*, 162. Otto clearly refers
here to Kant's attempt in the *Third Critique* to distinguish the contingent
liking we feel toward the agreeable and the pleasing from the feeling of
aesthetic pleasure and pain (see Kant, *Critique of Judgment*, 47/206).
[93]Otto, *The Idea of the Holy*, 11. Emphasis mine.
[94]Ibid., 7.

6.D.2.b. The Self-Attestation of Religious Ideas

Following the lesson he learned from Fries and Nelson, Otto refuses to indulge in proving the conclusions of his analysis. He agrees with them that the Critical method should not address itself to the skeptic. All it can do, and all it aspires to achieve, is to disclose the constitutive grounds of judgments whose truth is tentatively assumed. Otto argues accordingly that "there can naturally be no defense of the worth and validity of such religious intuition of pure feeling that will convince a person who is not prepared to take the religious consciousness itself for granted."[95]

Like Fries and Nelson, who consider themselves followers of Kant's doctrine of aesthetic taste, Otto sees in "Reason's trust in itself" the only viable proof that the category of the numinous which religious judgments presuppose is indeed an a priori category. Otto hopes to bring us to share his conviction by guiding us along the sympathetic-introspective journey through which our religious potential may stir and attest to this truth. Expressing his conviction that only "Reason's trust in itself" can verify the a priori determination of feeling, Otto says:

> The justification of the "evolutionist" theory of today stands or falls with its claim to "explain" the phenomenon of religion. That is in truth the real task to the psychology of religion.[96] But in order to explain we must have the data from which an explanation may be forthcoming; out of nothing nothing can be explained. Nature can only be explained by an investigation into the ultimate fundamental forces of nature and their laws: it is meaningless to propose to go farther and explain these laws themselves, for in terms of what are they to be explained? But in the domain of the spirit the corresponding principle from which an explanation is derived is just the spirit itself, the reasonable spirit of man, with its predispositions, capacities and its own

---

[95]Ibid., 173.

[96]In German (Otto, *Das Heilige*, 139), *"Religionswissenschaft,"* i.e., science of religion.

inherent laws. This has to be presupposed: it cannot itself be explained.[97]

Otto reiterates his conviction regarding the self-attestation of Reason in the following passage:

> Naturalistic psychologists. . . ignore a fact which might be thought at least to have a psychological interest, and which they could notice in themselves by careful introspection, namely, the *self-attestation* of religious ideas in one's own mind. This is, to be sure, more certain in the case of the naive than in that of the more blase mind; but many people would identify it in their own consciousness if they would only recall deliberately and impartially their hours of preparation for the ceremony of Confirmation. But what the mind "attests" it can also under favorable circumstances evince and elicit from itself.[98]

Otto recommends that the skeptics undergo a process of remembrance if they wish to appreciate his discussion. There can ultimately be no other support to his theory regarding the noeticity of religious feeling, just as, Otto holds, there can be no other proof to the validity of the aesthetic judgment. Otto thinks, however, that if we cooperate with him willingly, our common journey of introspection will end in our realization that "all this points to the existence of *a priori* factors *universally and necessarily latent in the human spirit.*"[99] Otto thus ends the second stage of his discussion of the noeticity of religious feeling by asserting that the numinous consciousness is determined a priori by the distinct religious category of the numinous. From here he proceeds to the last stage of his argument for the noeticity of religious feeling. Now he wants to show that the numinous category is constitutive of a distinct realm of meaning; he wants to prove that

---

[97]Otto, *The Idea of the Holy*, 114–15. Otto seems to refer here both to Kant's discussion of the moral law as "the pure fact of Reason" and to the theory of reason's trust in itself developed by Nelson and Fries.

[98]Ibid., 130.

[99]Ibid., 140. Emphasis mine.

this category is our highest criterion of interpretation and evaluation of the history of religion.[100]

6.D.3. The History of Religion

So far Otto has led us in a sympathetic journey of introspection to identify the distinct religious feeling and to recognize the distinct religious a priori as its determining principle. Otto argues that the numinous ideas, however, are merely empty abstractions as long as they do not become an operative reality in the religious life. Therefore, the "regressive" journey does not complete the study of religion that must also become historical and comparative. Otto's turn to the history of religion as a crucial stage of the critical study of religion serves to distance his work further from rationalist-foundationalism toward a more holistic approach for which theoretical constructs like the "numinous," the "infinite," and "divination" are not uncriticizable introspective discoveries but hypothetical constructs—proposed by critical analysis and introspection—that are in constant need of testing against the concrete empirical data uncovered by the history of religion.[101]

Otto maintains that the scholar of religion, who is equipped with the findings of the philosophy of religion, must embark on a comparative history of religion, realizing that

---

[100]Ibid., 113–14.

[101]Otto is ambivalent in his commitment to a thoroughgoing fallibilism. On the one hand, he claims in *The Philosophy of Religion* (pp. 222–30) that a Christian theology cannot be attempted on the grounds of acquaintance with the history of Christianity alone, but requires as total a comparative study of religion as possible. On the other hand, in *The Kingdom of God and the Son of Man: A Study in the History of Religion* (trans. Floyd V. Filson and Bertram Lee Woolf; Lutterworth Library 9; London: Lutterworth, 1938) Otto criticized the religious experience of rabbinic Judaism in light of the Pauline insights that, not surprisingly, fit his phenomenology of religious experience in *The Idea of the Holy*. In that study, he learned nothing from the Jewish experience. Otto's attempt to gain acquaintance with the religions of India may have been an attempt to test the applicability of his theories to another culture. Otto did not say that his phenomenology may have to be revised in the future, but opted instead to use it as a basis for a claim for the superiority of Christianity.

it is one thing merely to believe in a reality beyond the senses and another to have experience of it also; it is one thing to have ideas of "the holy" and another to become consciously aware of it as an *operative reality*, intervening actively in the phenomenal world. Now it is a fundamental conviction of all religions, of religion as such, we may say, that this latter is possible as well as the former. Religion is convinced not only that the holy and sacred reality is attested by the inward voice of conscience and the religious consciousness, the "still, small voice" of the Spirit in the heart, by feeling, presentiment, and longing, but also that it may be directly encountered in *particular occurrences and events*, self revealed in persons and displayed in actions, in a word, that *beside the inner revelation from the Spirit there is an outward revelation of the divine nature.*[102]

This argument enables us better to comprehend Otto's understanding of the structure and role of the study of religion. Otto holds that a comparative study of religion is the vocation of the modern theologian who is persuaded by the antispeculative implications of Kant's philosophy. The attention of the modern theologian must be focused on the historical evidence regarding the ways humans experience God. The study of religion, qua theology, consists of the cooperation of two complementary movements: the philosophy of religion and the comparative history of religion. The goal of the philosophy of religion, as a branch of the study of religion, is to establish the veracity of religious judgment by exposing the formal ideas of Reason and by validating them as a priori endowments of the mind. Otto argues that the philosopher of religion, however, must remember that, as Kant already taught us, ideas in themselves are formal and empty. Accordingly, religious ideas by themselves do not constitute the religious life. Consequently, the demonstration of the a priority of the religious ideas does not complete the work of the theologian. The philosophy of religion must be supplemented with an examination of the history of religion.

---

[102]Otto, *The Idea of the Holy*, 143. Emphasis mine.

> But at this point the realm of a priori principles has reached its
> limit, and just as in the other sciences, experience now steps in,
> i.e., religious experience, and with it History, as enlarged expe-
> rience; and with them the whole of the science of religion in
> itself, as comprehending religion in its historical manifestation
> and variety, as a comparison and a determination of values, as
> criticism, elucidation, and, if possible, as means of progress, as
> a practical study of how the disposition to religion and religious
> community is formed. And so far as theology has ceased to be
> a supernaturally inspired physics and metaphysics of heavenly
> things, and is a Science of Religion as explained above, aiming
> at the practice and maintenance of religion in actual life, then
> the relation of philosophy is defined as well.[103]

Otto, then, urges the student of religion not to be satisfied just
with isolating and identifying the distinct religious category. Rather,
the scholar of religion must embark on the equally important study of
the history of religion. The scholar of religion must now "give an
explanation of religion as a phenomenon in history, of its multiplicity
and variety in history, of its degrees and stages, the lower and higher
phases of its appearance."[104]

Otto's discussion of the historical manifestation of religion serves
a purpose similar to that of Kant's transcendental deductions. Although
Otto does not draw this analogy explicitly, and even though his discussion is extremely short, it seems to me that in his discussion of the
history of religion Otto aims to prove that the religious category,
which we were able to isolate with the analytical regressive method
and to verify by introspection, is constitutive of a distinct realm of
experience. Otto's discussion is very brief; it does not amount to
detailed "proof" of this position. We may recall in his defense, however, that Kant's own deductions, especially in the *Third Critique*,
were by no means always detailed demonstrations. Like Otto's, they

---

[103]Otto, *The Philosophy of Religion*, 101–2.
[104]Ibid., 145.

consisted mostly of illustration and exposition of Kant's view rather than of its demonstration.[105]

6.D.3.a. Reason and History

In emphasizing the importance of history Otto cautions the student of religion to acknowledge the delicate balance between the religious a priori and history, between Reason and the reality it constructs, and to delegate to each its proper status. Against "empirical" approaches, which do not acknowledge a distinct religious category, Otto emphasizes that history cannot be understood properly until it is regarded as the construct of Reason. Otto objects both to a philosophy of religion that does not acknowledge the importance of history and to a study of history that does not acknowledge the religious a priori:

> Plainly, then, religion is only the offspring of history in so far as history on the one hand develops our disposition for knowing the holy, and on the other is itself repeatedly the manifestation of the holy. "Natural" religion, in contrast to historical, does not exist, and still less does "innate" religion.[106]

Otto's discussion of the history of religion is, I maintain, directly related to a final stage of his proof of the noeticity of religious feeling. Otto began his proof by showing that religious feeling has a direct reference to a religious object. He continued by pointing out the a priori determinability of the feeling by the category of the numinous. The third and last stage strives to show that the religious a priori is constitutive of a distinct realm of meaning. To make his point, Otto draws a comparison between the roles of preexisting potentialities in both a biography of a person and the history of a cul-

---

[105]It could be argued that even in the *Second Critique* Kant really gives only an exposition of his argument regarding freedom. This point was discussed by Beck in *A Commentary on Kant's Critique of Practical Reason*, 110, 171–72. Otto may have relied here on the fact that Kant argued that the judgments about the sublime need only an exposition and do not require further deduction (see Kant, *Critique of Judgment*, 142/280).

[106]Otto, *The Idea of the Holy*, 176–77.

ture. This comparison is interestingly analogous to Kant's dictum regarding the emptiness of ideas and the blindness of impressions. Both biography and history presuppose, according to Otto, the existence of a priori potentials that come into their fullness of being in interaction with external stimuli. Moreover, ipso facto, the reality of a history of religion is evidence of the constitutive force of the religious a priori. No account of the history of religion can be valid that will ignore the capacity of the mind to apply the category of the numinous to spatiotemporal events:

> There is something presupposed by history as such—not only the history of mind or spirit, with which we are here concerned— which alone makes it history, and that is the existence of a *quale*, something with a potentiality of its own, capable of *becoming*, in the special sense of coming to be that to which it was predisposed and predetermined. . . . We only have the history of a people in proportion as it enters upon its course equipped with an endowment of talents and tendencies; it must already *be something* if it is really to *become* anything. And biography is a lamentable and unreal business in the case of a man who has no real unique potentiality of his own, no special idiosyncrasy, and therefore a mere point of intersection for various fortuitous causal series, acted upon, as it were, from without. Biography is only a real narration of a real life where, by the *interplay of stimulus and experience on the one side and predisposition and natural endowment on the other*, something individual and unique comes into being, which is therefore neither the result of a "mere self unfolding" nor yet the sum of mere traces and impressions, written from without from moment to moment upon *tabula rasa*.[107]

Otto states his case succinctly in his subsequent assertion: "In short, to propose a history of mind is to presuppose a mind or spirit determinately qualified; to profess to give a history of religion is to presuppose a spirit specifically qualified for religion."[108] Although Otto does not say so explicitly, his discussion of the history of religion

---

[107]Ibid., 175–76; the next to last emphasis is mine.
[108]Ibid., 176.

provides the final confirmation to the noeticity of religious ideas and feelings. It is true that in metaphysical and introspective analyses we arrive at principles that we trust to be the property of reason itself, nevertheless, as Leonard Nelson had pointed out, this trust is not infallible. Our all too human reason may put its trust in ideas that are not genuine transcendental principles. Our analysis may have failed by beginning with a partial and misleading set of religious judgments for its basic data. Only through continuously widening the scope of religious data in an investigation of the history of religion can we lend further confirmation to the conclusions of the Metaphysical Deduction which were affirmed by our introspective investigation. By interpreting the diverse phenomena of the history of religion in light of these principles, the science of religion confirms that the principles we identified and in which we put our trust are indeed the constitutive ground of religion.[109]

6.D.4. Divining the Infinite in the Finite

Thus far Otto has led us in a sympathetic method of introspection, striving to make us recognize the distinct character of religious experience. He exhibited a distinct religious a priori and argued that the religious capacity stems from the "bottom of our mind," that it is the most profound cognition of which we are capable. He also told us that the distinct religion category is constitutive of a religious history and that the historical manifestations of the idea of the holy should not be ignored by the theologian and the philosopher of religion. In doing so Otto wanted to prove that religion is a distinct realm of meaning which must be understood and evaluated in its own terms. He wanted us to realize that religious judgments should be distinguished from theoretical, moral, and aesthetic judgments. Thus far, however, Otto did not quite explain to us what is in essence the unique religious perspective on reality. We must now inquire what, according to Otto, is the unique outlook that religious judgments convey. We can begin our search for answers to these questions in

---

[109]For a discussion of the open-endedness of the critique of Reason, see Nelson, *The Socratic Method*, 113–14.

Otto's discussion of history. As we recall, in this discussion Otto asserts that religion presupposes that the sacred reality is encountered directly in particular occurrences and events.[110] This fact, he says, is expressed in religious judgments:

> Religious language gives the name of "sign" to such demonstrative actions and manifestations, in which holiness stands palpably self-revealed. From the time of the most primitive religions everything has counted as a sign that was able to arouse in man the sense of the holy, to excite the feeling of apprehended sanctity, and stimulate it into open activity.[111]

Suggesting a name for the faculty of apprehending the holy in history, Otto says, "Let us call the faculty, of whatever sort it may be, of genuinely cognizing and recognizing the holy in its appearances the faculty of divination."[112]

Criticizing reductionists who deny the existence of a distinct religious category and explain the judgments Otto calls divination as delusions of the understanding, Otto argues that such interpretation fails to understand the logic of religious language and the nature of the judgments it expresses:

> Genuine divination. . . has nothing whatever to do with natural law and the relation or lack of relation to it of something experienced. It is not concerned at all with the way in which a phenomenon—be it event, person or thing—came into existence, but with what it *means*, that is, with its significance as a "sign" of the holy.[113]

---

[110]Otto, *The Idea of the Holy*, 143.

[111]Ibid.

[112]Ibid., 144.

[113]Ibid., 145. It may prove interesting to compare Otto's position here with Ludwig Wittgenstein's remarks on religious belief, particularly his remarks on Sir James Frazer's *The Golden Bough* (*Remarks on Frazer's Golden Bough* [trans. A. C. Miles and Rush Rhees; Atlantic Highlands, NJ: Humanities, 1979]).

In *The Idea of the Holy* Otto does not discuss the faculty of divination at length. Instead, Otto explains that his understanding of divination relies on the teachings of Schleiermacher, Kant, and Fries. He claims to have given a more precise assessment of their theories in *The Philosophy of Religion* and refers his readers to that book.[114] In *The Idea of the Holy* Otto provides a brief summary of his earlier discussion. Brief as it is, this summary helps us understand what constitutes for Otto the unique character of the religious outlook and the capacity of divination.

Otto hints very briefly that the faculty of divination enables us to think about reality in terms of purposiveness. He argues, as he previously argued in *The Philosophy of Religion* and in *Naturalism and Religion*, that the religious outlook concerns itself with questions regarding the purposes, aims, and significance of things.[115] The essence of religion, he says, consists of believing in and experiencing God's works and self-revelation in the midst of finite reality.[116] The capacity that enables us to perceive the working and the manifestation of the infinite in the finite is divination, which Otto, building upon Schleiermacher's theory of religious feeling, characterizes as

> the faculty or capacity of deeply absorbed *contemplation*. . . . Wherever a mind is exposed in a spirit of absorbed submission to impressions of "the universe," it becomes capable. . . of experiencing "intuitions" and "feeling" (*Anschauungen* and *Gefühle*) of something that is, as it were, a sheer over plus, in addition to empirical reality. . . though these intuitions are limited and inad-

---

[114]Otto, *The Idea of the Holy*, 145–46.

[115]Rudolf Otto, *Naturalism and Religion* (trans. J. Arthur Thomson and Margaret R. Thomson; ed. W. D. Morrison; New York: Putnam's, 1907) 80–81.

[116]Ibid., 370. In *The Philosophy of Religion*, Otto explains that "for the religious man in the stricter sense of the word, for the really godly man, godliness first becomes a living thing when he becomes aware of the Infinite in the Finite. In life itself comes the immediate testimony that Nature, ourselves, all that exists and all that happens, are in fact appearances of a transcendental Reality. Transcendental Idealism—the conviction that is already latent in the most primitive religious faith—is experienced in Feeling as a Truth" (p. 131).

equate, they are none the less indisputably *true*. . . they must certainly be termed *cognitions*, modes of *knowing*. . . . . Their import is the glimpse of an Eternal, in and beyond the temporal and penetrating it, the apprehension of a ground and meaning of things in and beyond the empirical and transcending it.[117]

As I said before, Otto asserts that his theory of divination relies heavily on Schleiermacher and Fries. Like them he regards the ability to view reality in terms of purposiveness as the essence of religion.

When Schleiermacher, in expounding the nature of the (religious) experience, tries to elucidate its object by giving examples, he is for the most part led to adduce impressions of a higher τέλος, an ultimate, mysterious, cosmic purposiveness, of which we have a prescient intimation. Here he is quite in agreement with the exposition of Fries, who defines the faculty of *Ahndung* as being just a faculty of divining the "objective teleology" of the world.[118]

Unfortunately, these few sentences are the only explicit indication Otto gives to readers of *The Idea of the Holy* of what he takes to be the content of the religious outlook. It is as if Otto refuses to relieve the tense aura of mystery he so persistently tried to impress upon us as we advanced in our reading of *The Idea of the Holy*. Otto never speaks directly of the content of the category of the numinous. Throughout *The Idea of the Holy* he persistently refers to it as to a mysterious X that eludes conception. It is only from his repeated references to Fries and Kant that we can surmise that the object we encounter as a mysterious X is that to which Fries had said the Ideas of Reason give symbolic rational translation. From the beginning of *The Idea of the Holy* Otto follows very closely upon Fries's analysis and characterization of the moment of awareness of the mystery of the infinite, of the manner in which we divine the meaning and purpose of reality. The structural and substantial resemblance between Otto's and Fries's discussions of the subject, as well as the fact that

[117]Otto, *The Idea of the Holy*, 146–47.
[118]Ibid., 147.

Otto continuously refers to Fries and to his own exposition of Fries's philosophy of religion in *The Philosophy of Religion*, provides a strong indication that whenever possible Otto's elliptical pronouncements should be interpreted in light of his Friesian heritage. Such interpretation is called for all the more since it lends systematic coherence to Otto's all too brief and enigmatic writing.

When we examine Otto's characterization of religion in terms of the search for purposiveness, we must ask how he perceives the relations of the religious world view to the scientific, the moral, and the aesthetic. Before we can try to answer this question we must see if and how Otto justifies his theory of the faculty of divination. It is here that we find final proof that in his discussion of the numinous Otto builds upon Kant's *Third Critique*, and that this discussion should therefore be interpreted along the lines of the Kantian conception of our cognition of purposiveness in finite reality. Otto argues that the fact of the faculty of divination cannot be proved by logical demonstration. Instead of giving such a proof he tries to establish his case by drawing an analogy between Kant's discussion of aesthetic taste in the *Third Critique* and the faculty of divination.

> No intellectual, dialectical dissection or justification of such intuition is possible, nor indeed should any be attempted, for the essence most peculiar to it would only be destroyed thereby. Rather it is once again to aesthetic judgments that we must look for the plainest analogy to it. And the faculty of judging (*Urteilsvermögen*), here presupposed by Schleiermacher, certainly belongs to that "Judgement" (*Urteilskraft*), which Kant analyses in his Third Critique, and which he himself sets as "aesthetic judgment" in antithesis to logical judgment. Only, we may not infer from this that the particular several judgments passed in this way need be judgments of "taste" in their *content*. Kant's distinction between the "aesthetic" and logical judgment did not mean to imply that the faculty of "aesthetic" judgment was a judgment upon "aesthetic" objects in the special narrow sense of the term "aesthetic," as being concerned with the beautiful. His primary intention is simply and in general terms to separate the faculty of judgment based upon feeling of whatever sort from that of the understanding, from *discursive, conceptual thought and inference*; and his term "aesthetic" is simply meant to mark

as the peculiarity of the former that, in contrast to *logical judg-ment*, it is not worked out in accordance with a clear intellectual scheme, but in conformity to obscure, dim *principles* which must be felt and cannot be *stated* explicitly as premises. Kant em-ploys sometimes another expression also to denote such obscure, dim *principles of judgment*, based on pure feeling, viz. the phrase "not-unfolded" or "unexplicated concepts" (*unausgewickelte Begriffe*)[119] . . . . [T]hose judgments that spring from pure con-templative feeling also resemble judgments of aesthetic taste in claiming, like them, *objective validity, universality, and neces-sity*.[120]

The analogy Otto draws between Kant's discussion of aesthetic taste and divination brings me once again to wonder why Otto thinks that these are two different faculties and that the former is but a pale shadow of the later. Since Otto's theory of the autonomy of religion depends on his ability to show that the religious feeling—through which alone we perceive the numen—is distinct and unique, I think that Otto should have conducted a more detailed comparison between the feeling of the sublime and the numinous. As I have already indi-cated, I think that readers of Kant's descriptions of the emotions of dread and elevation we feel toward the "holy will," the moral law, and the sublime, need more than Otto's reassuring assertion to be convinced that the numinous feeling is indeed unique.[121] It is a pity that Otto's discussion of the unique character of the numinous feeling, which is one of the stronger aspects of *The Idea of the Holy*, should do no more to alleviate such doubts.

■ 6.E. Conclusion

As the argument of this chapter unfolded, we met Otto as a theo-logian who is interested primarily in establishing the cognitivity of

[119]The term "*unausgewickelte Begriffe*" is the term Kant also uses, and it is better translated as "indeterminable concepts."

[120]Ibid., 147–49. Otto exaggerates here; the validity Kant claims for aes-thetic taste is only subjective.

[121]As I mentioned above, I hope to devote a future study to a detailed comparison of Kant's theory of the sublime and Otto's theory of the numinous.

religious judgments. Throughout, I interpreted Otto's analysis of religion in *The Idea of the Holy* in light of Otto's description of it as "directed towards Christian theology and not towards religious history or the psychology of religion."[122] I argued that in his attempt to secure the veracity of religious convictions, Otto turned back to Kant in whose critiques of Reason and its domains he found methodological anchorage and in whose discussion of reflective purposiveness he found both an inspiration to and a confirmation of his theological insights. I suggested that in turning back to Kant, Otto managed to offer an integrative theory of the relations between the affective and cognitive elements of religious experience, and that in so doing he took Kant's insights into the nature of religion a step further and presented religion as a universal human propensity rather then the exclusive property of an intellectual elite.

My analysis showed that Otto accepted the Kantian dualism of nature and freedom and rejected idealistic claims to intellectual intuition of things-in-themselves. Like Kant, Otto could find no way of bridging the abyss between the finite and the infinite other than by a reflective judgment in which the infinite is felt to be manifest in the finite. Unlike Kant, who found disclosure of ultimate meaning in rare reflective moments, which are accessible only to an aesthetic and scientific elite, Otto thought that such moments of awareness were possible to all people at all times since they are based on the a priori category of the numinous, a category that is an original constituent of Reason. Whereas in Kant's discussion of reflective judgment, the appeal to the divine designer of the universe is always a contemplative reflection upon a prior cognition, Otto strives to show that an insight into ultimate meaning in life is available at all levels of culture.

Building upon Kant's analyses of the beautiful and the sublime, Otto offers a theory of religion as an ability to perceive the infinite in the finite, in a judgment that combines affective and cognitive moments. He identifies a moment of consciousness, the numinous experience, in which the distinct religious feeling has an immediate reference to a "numinous object." His theory challenges prevailing philosophical interpretations that tend to separate the affective and the

---

[122]Otto, *Religious Essays*, 31.

cognitive aspects of religion and to emphasize one at the expense of the other. Otto's category of the numinous promises to reunite religious cognition and affectivity in one moment of awareness, thereby overcoming their problematic bifurcation.

In considering the significance of Otto's claim to have identified a distinct religious a priori, we must inquire how this identification affects his understanding of the relations between religion and other realms of meaning. Otto does not discuss the issue systematically. Since, however, he considered the essence of religion to be the ability to perceive the infinite in the finite, it seems to me that Otto must have considered the possibility that in religion nature and freedom find their unity. After all, this in essence was the theory that Fries, his mentor, expounded in his *Knowledge, Belief, and Aesthetic Sense*, a book which is intended to highlight and develop what were, according to Fries, Kant's religious interests in the *Third Critique*. As I demonstrated, Otto's theory of divination is an application of Fries's theory of *Ahndung*, the capacity to apprehend purposiveness in nature.

> If we compare this life in the world of appearance with our own essential nature as we recognize it in belief (i.e. morality), we see it as our own fault that we can never come to a really complete understanding of ourselves. Our own essential being becomes, as does the entire world of nature, mere appearance. At that point there arises for our aesthetic sense a desire to be freed from the bonds of the finite and to find ourselves once again in the presence of God.[123]

> We know about the finite in nature; we believe in the eternal. But for our reason, this cognition of the finite and the eternal must ultimately be one and the same. There is but one truth, and it must be that the same reality of the eternal is repeated in the finite. We look at the finitude of nature as the appearance of the eternal. . . . Neither the understanding, to which the concept (of nature) belongs, nor reason, to which the idea (of freedom)

---

[123]Fries, *Knowledge, Belief, and Aesthetic Sense*, 149.

belongs, is at work here. Only independent, free, reflective judgment can grasp the eternal in the finite with its pure feelings.[124]

Fries clearly identifies these pure feelings as the feelings of religion:

> In fact all truly religious people would admit, even if this may not be the way they would want to express it, that one could call the feeling that actually constitutes religiosity *the aesthetic sense of the eternal in the finite.* . . . I prefer the term "aesthetic sense" (*Ahndung*) to define that feeling in the life of belief where religion actually begins.[125]

I would like to suggest that Otto did not develop the idea that religious judgment unifies the judgments of science and morality, because his theory deviates significantly from Fries's in one fundamental respect. I read Fries's work as a commentary on Kant's discussion of the Highest Good in the *Third Critique* and as a further elaboration of it. For Fries, as for Kant, we arrive at the highest good as a supreme unifying principle through reflection on the achievements of science and morality. Fries admits that the "aesthetic sense" (*Ahndung*) "is only the possession of one who is more cultivated."[126] Like Kant, Fries and Nelson feared a religious fanaticism that would abrogate the autonomy of science and morality and argued most emphatically that a genuine religious feeling can only come into play in a fully developed moral consciousness. Eventually, for them, the ultimate value of religion consists in its producing "an enthusiasm that confers higher value on our actions. . . religion first acquires a distinctive motivating quality as a motive for fulfilling our duties."[127] It has become clear through our study of Otto that he rejects these ideas and considers religion to be essentially independent of science

---

[124]Ibid., 95.

[125]Ibid., 121.

[126]Ibid., 119.

[127]Ibid., 122. Nelson developed these ideas in his *Socratic Method*, 75; for his discussion of the danger in a religion that does not stem from morality, see p. 47.

and morality and accessible to all levels of cultural development. According to Otto, genuine religious feeling can be totally devoid of morality.[128] It seems that between the interests of the unity of reason and the autonomy of religion, Otto emphasized the latter.

The difference between Otto and his predecessors can be understood as a difference in emphasis on two elements of the *Third Critique*. In our study of the *Critique* we found it necessary to distinguish between reflective judgment, which identifies and characterizes an object, and contemplative thought, which builds upon the reflective judgment and constructs an ideal perspective for the interpretation of the domains of Reason. In my concluding remarks on Kant, I suggested that he saw in the contemplative idea of the Highest Good a starting point for a philosophical theology. It seems that while Fries and Nelson begin to recognize a distinctly religious feeling, they wish to retain its contemplative-interpretive status as the guarantor of the unity of Reason.

In contradistinction, Otto wants to say that we experience holiness in an object or in an event just as we experience harmony in an object of aesthetic pleasure. Both are judgments without determinative concepts. Both are therefore reflective judgments to which only symbolic expression can be given, but they involve a claim that their object, aesthetic or religious, exists. Otto insists that we can divine holiness in particular events and occurrences in the world. His primary example for a holy object so divined is the figure of Christ in whose person holiness was "made manifest."[129] Based on their own indeterminate principle, the category of the numinous, religious cognitions can come into fruitful interaction with other realms of meaning which, in the more advanced religions, provide a rational

---

[128]Otto, *The Idea of the Holy*, 51.

[129]Ibid., 155. Otto explains the phenomenon of Christ as "a person in whose being, life, and mode of living we realize of ourselves by 'intuition' and 'feeling,' the self-revealing power of the Godhead." It may be interesting, at some point, to compare Otto's discussion of Christ in *The Idea of the Holy* to Kant's discussion of the Genius in sections 46–50 of part one of the *Critique of Judgment*.

schematization to its essentially nonrational apprehension.[130] While it is possible through rational schematization for religion to be integrated with the other domains of Reason, and while such integration is considered by Otto the mark of an advanced religion, it is not necessary for religion to be so integrated and even if it is, it is not clear that the autonomy of the other realms will be respected.

Even if Otto never intended it, his idea of an independent numinous category placed highest in the hierarchy of Reason provides theoretical ground for a religious view that sets itself beyond all other realms of culture and interprets them in the service of its own interests, seeing in them mere symbolic ideograms for its own profound insights. Some intimation of such a view may already be found in Otto's suggestion that morality is a schematization of the numinous, and that the idea of a moral transgression is an ideogram for the numinous notion of sin.[131] In contrast to Otto, Paul Tillich, to whose theory of religion we now turn, was acutely aware of the problem of the relation of religion to other realms of meaning and sought to preserve their autonomy in his theory of a theonomous consciousness.

[130]Otto develops a theory of the schematization of the numinous by the "lower" categories of reason in *The Idea of the Holy*. This is a difficult theory to interpret, and it has bewildered commentators like Paton who tried to understand in terms of Kant's theory of the Schematism in the *First Critique*. For reasons of time and space I shall postpone discussion of this theory to a more encompassing study of Otto that I plan for the future. Suffice it to note here that Otto's model is to be found in Kant's discussion of beauty as a symbol of morality in the *Third Critique*. The crux of the Schematism is a theory of association of ideas, which, as we have seen, also informs Otto's introspective investigations.

[131] Otto, *Religious Essays*, 27.

7

TILLICH'S THEORY OF THE
THEONOMOUS CONSCIOUSNESS

■ 7.A. Introduction

7.A.1. Religion and Culture

The philosophical theology of Paul Tillich offers us a chance to see how Kant's notion of the contemplative unity of consciousness can be extended and developed into a philosophy of religion and a theology. In the following pages I shall show that Tillich sought to resolve the problem of the relation of religion to the various realms of culture in the radical claim that religion is a product of the mind yet neither an independent function of the mind nor an aspect of one of its various functions. Tillich defines religion, suggestively, as the depth dimension of all realms of culture. It will be a major task of this chapter to interpret this enigmatic formula.

While Tillich's positive views are typically cryptic, provocative, and puzzling, his acute critical remarks orient our understanding of his views. Tillich's criticism is directed against both secular culture, which finds no place for religion in its domain, and neo-orthodox theology, which sets religion somehow outside of culture and in opposition to it. He claims that cultural secularism and theological conservatism fail to recognize the central place of religion among the creative forces of the human spirit. While secular culture depicts religion as either a transitional developmental phase that must be superseded or as one cultural option among many others, conservative theologians, like Barth, strive to fortify the position of religion in modern life by presenting religion as an independent realm that need not be accountable to secular science and ethics. Due to their failure to appreciate the essential role religion must play in the creative life of the human spirit, Tillich argues, religion deteriorates into irrational fanaticism and secular culture falls into barren formalism in science, ethics, and aesthetics.

Tillich claims, as we shall soon see and attempt to interpret, that religion is a "depth dimension" that unifies all realms of culture since it is expressed in all acts of cultural creation. If we are to understand religion correctly and allow it to assume its important place in modern culture, we must realize that religion involves our emotional, volitional, and intellectual faculties. Faith is understood accordingly neither as a nonrational leap nor as a spiritual force alongside volition, knowledge, and valuation, but as the unifying force of a personality. Tillich says of faith:

> [It] happens in the center of the personal life and includes all its elements. Faith is the most centered act of the human mind. It is not a movement of a special section or a special function of man's total being. They are all united in the act of faith. But faith is not the sum total of their impacts. It transcends every special impact as well as the totality of them and it has itself a decisive impact on each of them.[1]

> Religion does not allow a person to be also religious. In fact, it does not grant that a person is "religious" at all. It tolerates no

[1]Paul Tillich, *Dynamics of Faith* (New York: Harper & Row, 1958) 4.

coordination of the functions, not even the hierarchical form in which religion stands at the top.[2]

Our discussion will attempt to explain the unifying role Tillich thinks religious faith is to play in our lives and why he thinks it is capable of performing it. In order to do so we shall analyze *The System of the Sciences*, focusing especially on Tillich's conception of metaphysics as unifying reflection on science and morality.

7.A.2. Religion and Philosophy of Religion

Our inability to appreciate the place of faith in culture is reflected, according to Tillich, in the failure of philosophy to understand religion. Traditional philosophy of religion has failed because it sought to subsume religion under other realms of culture and to explain it as a function of our cognitive, moral, or aesthetic life. The result was that each of these realms came to recognize its self-sufficiency and either swallowed faith altogether or rejected it. Yet, Tillich claims, "religion, like God, is omnipotent; its presence, like that of God, can be forgotten, neglected, denied. But it is always effective, giving inexhaustible depth to life and inexhaustible meaning to every cultural creation."[3] When we turn later to interpret Tillich's use of the metaphor of depth to describe the function of religion, we shall have to explain why the religious dimension of the various realms of culture is so often overlooked. It is, Tillich thinks, a typical failure of the philosophy of religion, and of secular culture with it, not to realize that in modern times—perhaps more than ever before—religion is an indispensable dimension of culture.

Philosophy of religion errs in trying to understand religion as a kind of knowledge, an aspect of morality, or an aesthetic orientation in life. Subsumed under scientific rationality, religion becomes unsubstantiated belief, which at best precedes science and is superseded by

[2]Tillich, *What is Religion?* 126
[3]Paul Tillich, *The Protestant Era* (abridged ed.; ed. and trans. James Luther Adams; Phoenix Books; Chicago: University of Chicago Press, 1957) xi–xii.

it. Practical reason may underwrite some of the normative dimensions
of religion, but must suppress other dimensions of religion lest they
undermine the autonomy of the moral will. While art may accept
religion as a poetic form of life, this is an identification religion must
resist if it is to retain its claim to truth and goodness. Tillich describes these relations in his sketch of the history of the philosophy
of religion:

> Religion is not a special function of the human spirit! History
> tells us the story how religion goes from one spiritual function
> to the other to find a home, and is either rejected or swallowed
> by them.
>
> Religion comes to the moral function and knocks at its door,
> certain that it will be received. Is not the ethical the nearest
> relative of the religious? How could it be rejected? Indeed, it is
> not rejected; it is taken in. But it is taken in as a "poor relation"
> and asked to earn its place in the moral realm by serving mo-
> rality. It is admitted as long as it helps to create good citizens,
> good husbands and children, good employees, officials, and sol-
> diers. But the moment in which religion makes claims of its
> own, it is either silenced or thrown out as superfluous or dan-
> gerous for morals.
>
> So religion must look around for another of man's spiritual
> life, and it is attracted by the cognitive function. Religion as a
> special way of knowledge, as a mythological imagination or as
> a mystical intuition—this seems to give a home to religion. Again,
> religion is admitted, but as a subordinate to pure knowledge,
> and only for a brief time. Pure knowledge, strengthened by the
> tremendous success of its scientific work, soon recants its half-
> hearted acceptance of religion and declares that religion has
> nothing whatsoever to do with knowledge.
>
> Why not try to find a place within the artistic creativity of
> man? religion asks itself, through the mouths of the philoso-
> phers of religion. And the artistic realm answers, through the
> mouths of many artists, past and present, with an enthusiastic
> affirmative, and invites religion not only to join with it but also
> to acknowledge that art *is* religion. But now religion hesitates.
> Does not art express reality, while religion transforms reality? Is
> there not an element of unreality even in the greatest work of
> art? Religion remembers that it has old relations to the moral

and the cognitive realms, to the good and to the true, and it resists the temptation to dissolve itself into art.[4]

In light of these past failures, Tillich suggests, religion must realize that it cannot be confined to any realm of culture and must come to recognize that "it is at home everywhere, namely, in the depth of all functions of man's spiritual life. Religion is the dimension of depth in all of them."[5]

7.A.2.a. Tillich's Metaphor of Depth

The metaphor of "depth" pervades Tillich's suggestions for a solution to the problem of the philosophy of religion. The metaphor is hardly self-explanatory and proves quite difficult to interpret as a philosophical concept, yet interpret it we must if we are to understand Tillich's theory of religion. The following quotation from Tillich—metaphoric and difficult in its own right—begins to unpack the meaning of "dimension of depth of all spiritual functions." Tillich's formulations here will guide our exegetical efforts.

> Yet there is a function of the spirit which neither stands along-side the other functions nor is their unity, but rather comes to expression in and through them. . . there is, therefore, no special religious function alongside the logical, aesthetic, ethical, and social functions; nor is it confined either in one of them or in the unity of them all. It is rather that which breaks through each and all of them, and it is the reality, the unconditional signifi-cance of each of them.[6]

Tillich's claim that religion is related to all realms of culture as their elusive "depth dimension," not external to them nor swallowed

---

[4]Paul Tillich, *Theology of Culture* (ed. Robert C. Kimball; New York: Oxford University Press, 1964) 6–7.

[5]Ibid., 7.

[6]Tillich, *What is Religion?* 142–43.

up in them, seems to require both that religion not be imposed on the autonomous functions of reason, as an authority from without, and that religion not be identified with the autonomous functions of reason. But is that logically possible? If religion has claims regarding both truth and goodness, can its claims be neither identical to the claims of science and morality nor different from them?

7.A.3. Theonomy: Beyond Autonomy and Heteronomy?

Using terminology suggested by Kant and Troeltsch,[7] the problem can be set as a challenge to show that religion is neither heteronomous nor autonomous. To fit Tillich's usage, autonomy can be defined as the free spontaneous function of the human spirit in obedience only to cognitive and volitional rules it sets itself. Heteronomy will be acceptance of beliefs or norms on other authority than that of the self-legislation of the spirit. The principle of religion, the principle of the rule of God, will be called theonomy. The problem can now be set as follows: Can theonomy be neither autonomy nor heteronomy? Is there a third alternative?

The problem as we presented it is a reformulation of Socrates' inquiry of Euthyphro whether he can claim to have knowledge of the requirements of piety that is distinctly religious.[8] Are acts of piety just, Socrates seems to ask, because the gods love them, or do the gods love them because they are just? Socrates' query reverberates throughout the tumultuous history of the relations between reason and revelation and appears in modern guise in Kant's *Grounding for the Metaphysics of Morals.* Kant raised the question in order to prove that the supreme principle of morality cannot be religious.

---

[7]For a discussion of the concepts of autonomy, heteronomy, and theonomy as they were developed in the eighteenth and nineteenth centuries, see James Luther Adams, "What Kind of Religion Has a Place in Higher Education?" *JBR* 13 (1945) 184–92. See also Paul Tillich, *A History of Christian Thought: From its Judaic and Hellenistic Origins to Existentialism* (ed. Carl E. Braaten; New York: Simon & Schuster, 1968) 320–25.

[8]Plato *Euthyphro* in *Plato: The Collected Dialogues* (Bollingen Series 71; Princeton: Princeton University Press, 1987) 169–85. Note especially *Euthyphro* 11e: "See if you do not think that of necessity all that is holy is just."

Having just offered a formulation of the Categorical Imperative and shown that all types of moral duty can be derived from it, Kant asks whether other conceptions of morality may rival his. Among the contenders he mentions the ontological concept of perfection and the theological concept of morality. Kant finds the concept of perfection empty and indeterminate, yet preferable to the theological:

> Nevertheless, it [the concept of perfection] is better than the theological concept, whereby morality is derived from a divine and most perfect will. It is better not merely because we cannot intuit divine perfection but can only derive it from our own concepts, among which morality is foremost; but because if it is not so derived (and being thus derived would involve a crudely circular explanation), then the only remaining concept of God's will is drawn from such characteristics as desire for glory and dominion combined with such frightful representations as those of might and vengeance. Any system of morals based on such notions would be directly opposed to morality.[9]

Kant's argument here is that a religious morality must either be autonomous or heteronomous, and in both cases it cannot be the supreme principle of morality. If our ideas of a divine will are derived from the concepts of Practical Reason, religion dissolves into autonomous morality. If religion is to be an independent source of value, Kant sees no alternative for its ideas of a divine will but to be based on biblical (or similar) images of the wrath of God and the rewards that are promised to the obedient. In this case, religion is heteronomous and contrary to the moral ideal of a good will.

In his moral writings Kant proceeded to develop a conception of religion within the limits of Practical Reason, wherein the moral law is thought of as a divine command and the voice of our conscience is externalized as omniscient divine judgment.[10] As Tillich puts it, religion is swallowed by moral autonomy. Kant's argument addresses the relation between religion and morality, but it can easily be extended to the relation between religion and knowledge. When the

---

[9]Kant, *Grounding*, 47.
[10]See part one, section 2.D.2. above.

argument is thus extended we may speak, as Tillich does, of the autonomy of both Practical and Theoretical Reason and of the threat of heteronomy to both of them.

In previous chapters I argued that Kant's philosophy of religion, which I designated his "official" view, does not include the most important things he had to say about religion or the most interesting. I tried to show that he returned to think about religion in his later writings in which we find a contemplative conception of religion according to which religious thought establishes a unity of the domains of Reason, a unity of nature and freedom. We must ask ourselves now whether Kant's contemplative conception of religion transcends the dichotomy of autonomy and heteronomy, whether the contemplative perspective of Reason opens a third alternative. This is a question that Kant should probably have asked, since he maintained that the moral law is seen from the contemplative perspective as the preestablished guiding principle of history. This contemplative realization is, furthermore, the only guarantee the moral agent has that the moral law is realizable in the natural world, and only this guarantee saves the agent from moral paralysis. Is this still a picture of the autonomous moral agent who obeys only a law she legislates to herself?

In the following pages I shall explain that in Paul Tillich's theory of religion as a theonomous consciousness we can find an extension of Kant's contemplative conception of religion and that the purpose of this extension is to show that it is possible for a religious consciousness not to be heteronomous and yet not to be exhausted in the autonomous functions of reason. Tillich tries to show that religion necessarily recognizes the theoretical and the practical functions of reason and respects their autonomy. At the same time, he argues, religion is not identical to these functions but adds to them a substantiating dimension that they themselves must recognize as essential.

7.A.3.a. A System of the Functions of Reason

In order to show that the theoretical and the practical domains of reason retain their autonomy even as they require a validation beyond their spontaneity, Tillich had to present a systematic conception of the relations between the various functions of reason. Only by juxtaposing the many applications of reason, in order to study the various ways in which they are dependent on or independent of each other, is it possible to establish the relations of religion to other realms of the creativity of the human spirit. In order to explain the special role religion needs to play in our spiritual life, Tillich wrote his *The System of the Sciences* in which he attempted a sketch of a complete system.

As we shall soon see, Tillich tried to show in this book that due to their spontaneous and constructive nature, the autonomous theoretical and practical human sciences[11] require a confirmation beyond their autonomy and that they find this confirmation in the religious consciousness. This argument is an expression of Tillich's metalogical method according to which philosophy begins with criticism and transcends it in order to secure a metaphysical[12] confirmation of its critical conclusions. If religion is to provide a confirmation that science and morality are to be shown to need, it must further be shown that religion can provide the required confirmation without infringing on the theoretical and the practical autonomy of the spirit.

Tillich's *The System of the Sciences* was written as part of the early twentieth century debate in Germany about the status of the human sciences. Due to its overly technical style and its largely outdated subject matter, the book is dreadfully boring and rather difficult to read. Furthermore, Tillich was influenced by many writers and borrowed freely from their theories and formulations, usually without acknowledgment. Yet, whatever Tillich borrowed from others received

---

[11]Translation of "*Geisteswissenschaften*" to "human sciences" rather than to "spiritual sciences" or to "sciences of the spirit" may be problematic in Hegelian contexts which require that the "Absolute Spirit"/"God" connotation of "*Geist*" be retained. Tillich's usage is usually rendered "human sciences" by his translators. This translation rightly emphasizes Tillich's rejection of the idealism of Schelling and Hegel and his fundamental acceptance of the neo-Kantian critical stance which initiates an open-ended quest of the human spirit to achieve tentative self-knowledge through study of its ever restless activity.

[12]Tillich's special notion of "metaphysics" will be explained below. We shall see (part two, sections 7.A.4.a and 7.C.4.a–b) that his conception of metaphysical thought closely resembles Kant's notion of contemplative thought.

new meaning as it was integrated into the effort, which continued throughout his life, to express his profound and influential insight that a genuine religious consciousness establishes the unity of the human personality and redeems it from an alienated existence. In *The System of the Sciences* we find Tillich's only attempt to explain the unifying function of religion, and this is reason enough to delve into the book and to extract the gems that it conceals.

Through careful reconstruction of a central part of *The System of the Sciences* in which the unifying function of religion is presented and by distancing ourselves from its dense definitional style, we shall come to understand the meaning of Tillich's metaphor of "depth dimension," and how it serves to show that "theonomy" can be a third alternative to autonomy and heteronomy. I shall then explicate Tillich's claim that a theonomous consciousness—the essence of religion according to Tillich—is an attitude of mind that recognizes the validity of the autonomous functions of the human spirit and seeks to become aware of an underlying fundamental unity of the principles and the categories that guide the spirit in its free construction of conceptual models and to relate these models to the reality they are intended to capture.

From these discussions I shall draw a concept of religion that is very similar to the one we found in Kant's *Critique of Judgment*. We shall see that human religiosity, according to Tillich, is an expression both of an uneasiness of reason with the hypothetical nature of constructions of the world that it generates freely of itself and of a need of reason to reflect on the significance of its autonomous constructions in an attempt to relate them, contemplatively, to an unconditioned ground. Tillich's formulations cannot fail to remind us of Kant's ultimate grounding of science and morality in a contemplative thought about a supersensible substrate of reality. It is in the desire to go beyond the creations of reason and to assess their significance that Tillich sees the essence of a theonomous consciousness that eschews heteronomy and transcends autonomy. In the concluding sections of this chapter I shall return to inquire to what extent Tillich's theonomy lives up to its promise.

7.A.4. Tillich's Understanding of Kant

Since we have found in Tillich's writings theories and ideas that promise a further development of Kant's embryonic contemplative theory of religion, it is appropriate to ask whether such development might indeed be Tillich's intention. Without clear textual evidence no conclusion regarding influence and intent can be definite, yet we should hardly be surprised to learn that Tillich's understanding of Kant's *Third Critique* closely resembles the one I have labored to expound. Tillich was well aware of the significance of Kant's contemplative conception of religion and of its influence on the history of religious thought.

Tillich admired the *Critique of Judgment* as an attempt to restore the unity of nature and freedom which were separated in Kant's first two *Critiques*. He went so far as to designate Kant the "philosopher of Protestantism." Kant's Protestantism is manifest, according to Tillich, in his confinement of humans to the prison of finitude and in his subsequent attempt to find ways of escaping this prison.[13] According to Tillich, Kant locked us in the prison of finitude when he limited the scope of the categories of the understanding and of the forms of intuition to the realm of finite objects and by pointing out the gap between what we ought to be and our actual situation. In his *Second Critique* Kant suggested that obedience to the moral law, and acceptance of the postulates of Practical Reason that such obedience implies, should elevate humans beyond the world of nature of the *First Critique*. Kant, however, recognized the gap between what is and what ought to be and realized that this gap results in humans' estrangement from their essential being.[14] According to Tillich, Kant

[13]See Tillich, *A History of Christian Thought*, 362–63, 366, 512–23; and idem, *Systematic Theology* (3 vols.; Chicago: University of Chicago Press, 1951–63) 1. 81–82. For similar reasons, we may recall (part two, section 6.A.3.c), Otto found in Kant a philosophical elaboration of Luther's religious insights.

[14]Tillich translated these insights into "existentialist" formulation in his mature writings which discuss human estrangement.

sought a solution to this problem in his theory of Reflective Judgment. Tillich says that in the *Third Critique* Kant "tried with great caution to escape the prison of finitude."[15] Teaching the *Third Critique* Tillich explained:

> In this *Critique of Judgment* Kant tried to bring together the two divergent critiques of reason, theoretical and practical reason. He showed possible union between the two. These cannot, however, be affirmed assertively, but only in terms of possibility, or better, as a human vision of realities without knowing that the realities really correspond to the vision.[16]

> In his *Third Critique*, the *Critique of Judgment*, Kant found a principle for uniting the theoretical and the practical reason in the aesthetic intuition of reality. In this he found that which transcends the scientific consideration of nature, the Newtonian as it was called at that time, as well as the moral principle. The moral always commands while the theoretical analyses. Is there a union between them? Is there something in nature which, so to speak, fulfills the commands of the moral imperative and transcends the mere scientific analysis of nature? He discovered. . . the organic in nature and the aesthetic in culture.[17]

In Tillich's own theory of religion I see an extension of Kant's search for an "escape from the prison of finitude" and an elaboration on it. Like Kant, Tillich found his escape in the reflective contemplation he called "theonomy": theonomy being, according to Tillich, the directedness of the spirit toward the meaning of its constructs. It is the reflective apprehension of the unity of the ideal and the real. Tillich often substitutes "spirit" for "reason," in order to avoid Kantian "faculty language" and to express and emphasize the spontaneity of the mind and the integrated cooperation of its functions. He defines spirit as the unity of cognitive, conative, and emotive powers.[18] Ac-

---

[15]Tillich, *A History of Christian Thought*, 365.
[16]Ibid.
[17]Ibid., 379. See also Tillich, *Systematic Theology*, 1. 81–82.
[18]See Paul Tillich, *The System of the Sciences: According to Objects and Methods* (trans. Paul Wiebe; East Brunswick, NJ: Associated University Press,

cordingly, Tillich characterizes theonomy as a fundamental attitude by which the spirit achieves its unity. Tillich seems to have followed Kant's suggestion that the directedness of the spirit toward an ultimate reality—the substrate of the lawfulness of nature and the purposiveness of freedom—is the solution to the spirit's quest for unity. In *The System of the Sciences* Tillich contends that it is the task of religion, conceived as the directedness of the spirit toward the unconditioned, to establish the unity of spirit and of culture.

In *The System of the Sciences*, Tillich argues that though the spirit is inevitably driven to impose its concepts and principles on the givenness of experience, it also needs to believe that these concepts reflect a structure of reality that was not shaped by them. This idea echoes Kant's belief in a need of reason to think of its theoretical constructions as discoveries and of its moral ends as realizable in the world of nature. Kant believed that the reflective principle of the supersensible substrate of reality paves the way toward satisfaction of these needs. Tillich, in comparison, identifies the need as the theonomous interest of the spirit and presents religion as its solution.

7.A.4.a. Religion as a Solution: A Preview

In anticipation of our elaborate discussion, we may say that Tillich has a rather simple basic idea. Thought, he seems to say, must be understood as an attempt of the mind to apprehend reality, as an Eros of Reason to comprehend Being. In its desire to grasp reality the mind constructs theories and methods and strives to establish their rational validity. Likewise, the mind attempts to construct and vali-

---

1981) 137–39. For the German edition, see idem, "Das System der Wissenschaften nach Gegenständen und Methoden" (1923; reprinted in idem, *Gesammelte Werke* [Stuttgart: Evangelisches Verlagswerk, 1959] vol. 1). See also idem, *What is Religion?* 160. For Tillich, religion is the directedness of all the functions of the spirit. This view is the foundation of Tillich's rejection of the emotivist interpretation of religion, on the one hand, and the intellectualist interpretation of religion, on the other. This conviction should remind us of Otto's view of the unity of emotive and cognitive elements in the numinous consciousness. Tillich discusses this issue primarily in *Systematic Theology*, 1. 15, 43–44, 91–92, 153–55 (in the discussion of "ontological reason"); and 3. 111, 131–34.

date systems of ethical value. These attempts are the sphere of critical reasoning and autonomous construction. Tillich stresses that rational validity, however, is not enough. It does not satisfy the demand of reason to comprehend reality. Rational validity is internal to theoretical and hypothetical constructions; it does not relate them to the objects of which they are supposed to be true. Rational validity is not truth. While he recognizes that the Eros of Reason to know Being cannot be satisfied in achievements of internal theoretical validity, Tillich is no naive realist who believes that thought can step outside itself, to compare itself with reality. Tillich's ontology, or metaphysics—in which the quest of reason for knowledge is to be satisfied—cannot therefore be understood as a further science through which rational validity becomes truth.

As we proceed, I shall explain that the Eros of Reason is satisfied, according to Tillich, not in a further development of scientific knowledge but in a reflective evaluation of the relation between the constructs of thought and our intuitive experience. We shall see that this is somewhat like an attempt to decide between alternative theories of equal claim to rational validity, according to a further indeterminate principle of intuitive acceptability that leads to a conviction, not knowledge, that a valid theory is indeed true. It follows from this relation between metaphysics and scientific reason that no metaphysical conviction is ever absolute and final. Metaphysics is always a reflection on the achievements of science and ethics, which, due to the restlessness of reason, are ever evolving. Metaphysics, or ontological reason, is therefore an ongoing task; it is the task to relate the constructs of reason to reality. It is in our recognition that this is a task we must undertake that Tillich sees the essence of a religious attitude in life.

Tillich does not reject instrumental and theoretical application of reason in the name of a metaphysical or a religious attitude. He accepts the various functions of reason as autonomous, legitimate, and necessary in their own spheres. What he does object to is the claim that this is all there is to reason. Tillich's conception of reason, like Kant's, is a dynamic-erotic conception. Driven by a Platonic Eros, reason strives out of an internal necessity to achieve its ends. On the one hand, reason strives to assimilate itself to reality by comprehending it. On the other hand, reason strives to bring reality into conformity with its ideals. Like Kant, Tillich insists that reason cannot be satisfied that its ends are realizable unless it becomes reflective and contemplative. From this point of view it is clear that once religion is understood as a contemplative application of reason, religion cannot be an additional function of reason alongside the theoretical and practical. Accordingly, religion cannot be a distinct realm of culture alongside science, ethics, and art. While religion transcends the limited concerns of the various realms of culture, it is essentially dependent upon their creations in its contemplative efforts to attain a world view (*Weltanschauug*[19]) infused with conviction that the spirit is in touch not merely with its own forms and constructs but with reality. In Tillich's language, religion is the directedness of the spirit to the unconditioned forms that it apprehends as manifested in being.

7.A.5. Implications of Tillich's Theory of Religion

From his analysis of the functions of the mind and their interrelatedness, Tillich derives an ideal concept of religion, a concept of a pure religion of the spirit. We shall see that Tillich utilizes this concept to serve as a criterion by which to evaluate historical manifestations of religion. Tillich distinguishes accordingly between two concepts of religion: a narrow concept that refers to the traditional religion of organized communities and a wider concept that denotes the contemplation of the unity of thought and being. Tillich later came to characterize the wider concept as "Ultimate Concern." We are already familiar with its designation as "theonomy." To avoid repetitive use of lengthy definitions, I will henceforth refer to the narrow and to the wide concepts of religion, respectively, as "religion$_2$" and "religion$_1$." While his discussion of religion$_1$ relies on Kant's theory of contemplation, Tillich's discussion of religion$_2$ relies on Otto's theory of the numinous consciousness and draws heavily on Otto's phenomenology of "mysterium tremendum and fascinans."[20] The

---

[19]Tillich sometimes calls metaphysics the doctrine of world views, "*Weltanschauungslehre.*" See Tillich, "Das System der Wissenschaften," 256.

[20]See Tillich, *Dynamics of Faith*, 12-13. I propose that although, unlike Kant, Tillich acknowledges the intrinsic value of myth, dogma, and ritual, his definition of the relations between religion$_1$ and religion$_2$ echoes Kant's dis-

distinction between religion$_1$ and religion$_2$ enables Tillich to warn against the danger of the "demonization of religion"—that is, assigning infinite value to the finite manifestations of religious symbols and metaphors, against the elevation of a particular manifestation of religion to absoluteness.[21]

We shall have a chance to examine some of Tillich's statements on the distinction and its significance toward the end of the chapter. Conclusions regarding the science of religion and theology follow immediately from the distinction, and Tillich does not hesitate to draw them. Like Otto, he claims that a science of religion must integrate a history and a philosophy of religion. The historian of religion must approach the phenomena guided by concepts provided by the philosophy of religion. These philosophical concepts are in turn abstracted from the findings of the historical study and verified by it, insofar as the philosophical concepts succeed in providing explanation and endowing coherence to historical phenomena. Tillich advocates a theology that will dedicate itself to construction of symbols through which we shall be able to achieve an integrated world view.

■ 7.B. The Search for Unity in *The System of the Sciences*

7.B.1. Introduction

In an effort to defend his claim that religion has an important role to play in the creative life of the human spirit, Tillich set out in *The System of the Sciences* to determine the spiritual role of religion and to place the science of religion within the "human sciences." He conceived the "human sciences" as a collection of disciplines which study the ways humans endow reality with meaning and value. Regarding

---

cussion in *Religion within the Limits of Reason Alone*. These are issues of considerable interest, and Tillich's indebtedness to Otto deserves serious discussion. This chapter must however focus primarily on the analysis of religion$_1$. I explore the relations between religion$_1$ and religion$_2$ briefly in my conclusions.

[21]See Tillich, *Systematic Theology*, 1. 3, 13. I suggest that in making the wider concept the criterion of the narrow concept, Tillich may have found a way of overcoming the reductionist implications of Otto's theory.

these sciences as constructive, Tillich suggested that the study of religion could only become an important science once it is acknowledged that the religious propensity is an "attitude of the spirit" which lies at the heart of every spiritual act of construction of meaning. In order to establish the study of religion as a respectable science, Tillich proposed to identify a distinct "religious" attitude of the spirit which underlies all its activities. In *The System of the Sciences* he sought to show that religion is not an additional function of the spirit alongside its theoretical and practical functions, nor an additional realm of meaning alongside the realms constructed by the theoretical and practical functions of the spirit (for example by science, law, and art). He presented religion as an underlying attitude in each of these functions.

> *[R]eligion* is not one sphere of meaning alongside the others; it is an attitude within all spheres: the immediate directedness to the Unconditioned. When the unconditionality of the Holy has been grasped, there can be no question of classifying religion alongside the other areas or even of placing it above the others. Consequently, the normative science of religion cannot be concerned with one object alongside others; it is concerned with an intention that is possible within all the areas of meaning. The normative science of religion is the theonomous human science.[22]

Construction of a system is, for Tillich, primarily an intellectual effort to achieve self-knowledge. It is the way we become aware of our activity as knowing, willing, and evaluating subjects. It is, at the same time, the only means by which we can realize our personal unity. Tillich's comments on the issue are remarkably reminiscent of Kant's discussion of the transcendental unity of apperception. We may recall that in response to Hume's claim that the self is but a "bundle of impressions," Kant argued that the world of our experience exhibits a structure that cannot be attributed to impressions but to the mind that imposes order upon them. Kant argued further that insofar as the world of experience shows unity, it reflects a unity of the ordering mind. The unity of nature is a mirror of the unity of the Understand-

[22]Tillich, *The System of the Sciences*, 156.

ing. Likewise for Tillich, only a systematic unity of the constructions of the spirit can show the unity of the person.

> The significance of the system of the sciences becomes even clearer when the system is considered in light of the presuppositions of Kant's epistemology, i.e., when the categories of objects are interpreted as the basic functions of consciousness. Then the system of the sciences becomes the expression of the system of the functions of spirit, and the structure of spirit becomes discernible from the different directions in which science locates and delineates its objects. *The structure in the subjective realm is apprehended by means of the structure within the objective realm.*[23]

Tillich, however, has a further goal for the system. Like Husserl, he hopes that the systematization of the sciences will provide direction and guidance to the future development of culture.

> A system of the sciences is a necessary act of scientific self-consciousness for every era. It prevents the sciences, each of which seeks to arrange every individual belonging to its sphere within its own comprehensive context, from standing alongside and in competition with each other in a disordered, chaotic way. It is concerned with form, but it is not formalistic; it is, rather, the living and therefore constantly changing expression of the scientific consciousness of an era.[24]

These sentences also disclose a fundamental Kantian conviction that Tillich incorporates into his own thought. Like Kant, Tillich believes that a systematic organization of the sciences is both necessary for our self-knowledge and is a reflection of a fundamental quest of the spirit for unity.[25] Due to the restlessness of reason and the

---

[23]Ibid., 31. Emphasis mine.

[24]Ibid., 32.

[25]Clarity concerning Tillich's conception of the unity that is to be sought between the diverse functions of reason is an important first step in understanding the status of theonomy in his work and the manner in which it

ever-evolving sciences, the systematic task is open-ended; no system is ever final, and every generation must achieve it for itself.

7.B.2. The Idea of a System

In order to present theology as a branch of the science of religion and clarify the role and the method of the study of religion in general, Tillich must establish their status in the comprehensive context of the system of the sciences. Tillich consequently undertakes a normative study of the sciences themselves, a study that will indicate what should be the proper objects and methods of the various sciences and how they should relate to each other. Before he embarks on this enterprise, Tillich confronts an obvious objection: "Is it not most unprofitable to be concerned with a science of the sciences?. . . . Is it not better to pursue science itself than to create a system that the living process of knowledge continually renders obsolete?"[26] Would it not be more profitable to pursue the study of religious phenomena themselves? Will not the continuous progress of the sciences render the results of his systematization obsolete? Tillich's reply to this question is instructive. It gives an important clue to his theory of religion as a unifying factor. "Even granted that the problems we face are formal, their solution would still give the spirit immense satisfaction. For to solve them would fulfill the spirit's highest desire, which is *to apprehend the unity* of all individuals."[27]

Tillich's brief remark concerning unity remains unexplained. He does not say why he thinks the spirit's highest desire is unity or how

---

purports to establish the unity of the human personality and to redeem it from alienation. It is especially important to observe that Tillich's idea of a systematic unity owes more to Kant's critical-reflective conception of reason than to Hegel's mystical system of Absolute Spirit, even though Hegelian terminology abounds in his writings. The terminological situation is hardly surprising since Hegel is heavily indebted to Kant's later work even as he sought to develop it in a noncritical direction. In any case, Tillich makes all borrowed terms his own, and their meaning has to be established from within his writings. Tillich makes it perfectly clear that he thinks philosophy must be critical in order to avoid the idealistic excesses of Schelling and Hegel.

[26]Tillich, *The System of the Sciences*, 30.

[27]Ibid. Emphasis mine except for the word "unity."

the quest for unity is satisfied by the systematization of the sciences. Since Tillich justifies his systematic approach in this way and since the quest for unity is the major theme of his book, we should, however, attempt to fill the gap and offer a probable interpretation.

7.B.2.a. An Ongoing Architectonic Task

Lest he frighten his readers away, Tillich reassures them that the unity of the sciences cannot be achieved through a detailed systematization of all particular scientific cognitions. Tillich realizes that a particularized system is impossible. He claims, however, that the spirit finds satisfaction for its highest desire, the desire for unity, in a formal system. Instead of uniting the contents of cognition, the systematization of the sciences should aspire to unite the forms, or principles, of cognition.

> Yet what is both possible and necessary for every generation is a formal system of knowledge in which one becomes conscious of the realm governed by the spirit, of the objects within this realm, and of the way in which the spirit governs this realm (i.e., the methods).[28] The desire of the spirit to achieve a living unity of knowledge produces this edifice of the system of the sciences. . . . The power and vitality of the spirit are manifest not in its extensive knowledge of details, but in its ability to unify this knowledge. And although the material of knowledge remains a strange, inexhaustible ocean, form is spirit's native element; after periods of attention to this material, spirit must repeatedly become conscious of form, each time in a richer and more penetrating way.[29]

Tillich's depiction of an ongoing spiritual drive toward a formal unification of knowledge is reminiscent of Kant's explanation why knowledge requires systematic unity.[30] Comparison between the two

[28]Notice the resemblance of Tillich's language to Kant's Introduction to the *Third Critique*.

[29]Tillich, *The System of the Sciences*, 31. I shall demonstrate, momentarily, the resemblance of Tillich's argument to Kant's.

[30]This is not the place to write a commentary on Kant's architectonic, and the reader's general knowledge of it will be assumed. It is, however, impor-

is instructive. Toward the end of the *First Critique*, in a discussion of the "architectonic of pure reason," Kant explains:

> By an architectonic I understand the art of constructing systems. As systematic unity is what first raises ordinary knowledge to the rank of science, that is, makes a system out of a mere aggregate of knowledge. . . our diverse modes of knowledge must not be permitted to be a mere rhapsody, but must form a system. Only so can they further the essential ends of reason.[31] By system I understand the unity of the manifold modes of knowledge under one idea. This idea is the concept provided by reason—of the form of a whole—in so far as the concept determines *a priori* not only the scope of its manifold content, but also the positions which the parts occupy relatively to one another. The scientific concept of reason contains, therefore, the end and the form of that whole which is congruent with this requirement.[32]

This passage provides an instructive background to Tillich's claim that a systematic arrangement of the sciences is a necessary condition of knowledge. Kant's architectonic serves to illuminate Tillich's conception of the interests of the spirit and of its ends. It also clarifies some of Tillich's considerations regarding the actual division and arrangement of the system of the sciences.

7.B.2.b. Synthetic Unity of Thought

Tillich considers the final end of our cognitive life to be the comprehension of the applicability of thought to reality. This is a vital key of which we must constantly be aware in order to understand what Tillich tries to do in his proposal of a system of the sciences. According to Tillich, we encounter thought in its attempt to comprehend reality in diverse ways. The variety of these ways is reflected in

---

tant to warn against the mistaken presumption that an architectonic is an attempt to force all possible findings into preconceived notions. A misconception of the architectonic drive as "prefabrication," lends an unjustified pejorative sense to the term "architectonic."

[31]Notice the resemblance between Kant and Tillich's understanding of the system as a precondition of knowledge.

[32]Kant, *Critique of Pure Reason*, 653/A833=B861.

the specific sciences, in and through which we gain an understanding of the world, and the conclusions of which we try to synthesize into our most general conceptions of reality, our world view (*Weltanschauung*).[33] I shall argue shortly that Tillich's notion of a world view as the highest goal of thought in which the findings of all the descriptive and the normative sciences are brought together in a unified conception closely reflects the Kantian notion of the reflective unity of Reason in the *Critique of Judgment*.

Just as Kant before him could raise the question regarding the reflective unity of Reason only after having established separately the unity of the Understanding and of the will, so must Tillich's systematic organization of the sciences establish the unity of the respective sciences so as to be able to raise the question of the unity of thought and being. While Tillich's ambitions parallel those of Kant, Tillich faces much greater difficulties due to the astonishing development of the sciences and their ever-growing diversification into specific fields of inquiry. In his attempt to secure the unity of thought Tillich must face a problem that Kant could have not imagined, the rise of non-Euclidian geometries and the prospect of alternative general theories of the physical world. Doubts concerning the possibility of even raising the metaphysical question arise, naturally, from the apparent diversity of the sciences and the impossibility of securing a unified scientific method. If thought about being is divided internally, neither a unified conception of being nor a unified conception of thought can be achieved, and the comprehensive world view, which we must all to some degree assume in our daily life, must be a haphazard and unstable mixture of thoughts and insights.

Unlike the positivists who attempted to secure the unity of thought by proposing a unified science which should encompass the physical, the biological, and the human sciences by means of a unified scientific method, Tillich does not believe that scientific unity can or should be achieved at this level. Tillich claims therefore that unity must be sought at a higher level in which a lower level diversity can be overcome. This overarching goal informs Tillich's attempt to outline a systematic organization of the sciences. To achieve its goals, a sys-

[33]See Tillich, *The System of the Sciences*, 186.

tematic organization must show why the particular sciences and their respective methods are as diverse as they are, and it must also show how this diversity reflects a higher unity which can then be apprehended. Tillich's system is accordingly structured to reflect a formal theoretical unity in each of the sciences, an encounter with the resistance to thought of the diversity of being, and a higher level synthetic apprehension of the applicability of a form of thought to a particular segment of being. It is through a structural analysis of this sort that Tillich suggests we apprehend the internal synthetic unity first of the descriptive sciences (which are grounded formally in logic and mathematics) and then in the normative sciences. It is only after this is achieved that Tillich can propose the further task of reflection, namely, to secure the unity of thought beyond the diversity of its application as theoretical and practical. Due to the transparently Kantian inspiration of the program we should not be surprised to find Tillich suggesting that the reflective unity, in which a world view is achieved, can only be secured through a synthetic comprehension of the unity of the theoretical and the practical in the unconditioned ground of being and that this comprehension is achieved primarily through the metaphysics of history.[34]

7.B.3. Toward a Synthetic Unity of Thought and Being

We have learned that according to Tillich a systematic conception of an individual discipline (e.g., physics or theology) must identify the place of the discipline in the system of knowledge. Tillich suggests that the identification should consider both subject matter and method. As we shall see shortly, Tillich believes that this is especially true for the normative cultural sciences, "in which subject matter and method belong more closely together, and in which they are to a much higher degree disputable, than in the purely formal and empirical sciences."[35] To arrange the sciences systematically within a system of the sciences, Tillich thinks, a principle must be found by which to organize the system:

[34]See ibid., 186, 202.
[35]Ibid., 30.

> Every systematic classification of the sciences must proceed from
> one *principle* that can only be the essence of science itself. . . .
> A principle is always both a point of departure and a continu-
> ation, a foundation and a regulative idea. Such a principle for a
> system of the sciences can be found only in the idea of knowl-
> edge itself.[36]

Tillich's organizing principle is the idea of knowledge. Accordingly, his system of the sciences reflects his understanding of the
constituents of the basic cognitive act, the act of knowledge. The
principle expresses Tillich's view that cognition is the result of the
interaction between the empty forms with which thought constructs
realms of meaning and the given material upon which thought in-
scribes these forms. Above all, it conveys Tillich's conviction that
there must be also a synthetic unity between the two. Accordingly,
Tillich distinguishes three constituents of cognition: "thought," "being," and "spirit."

Having identified "thought" and "being" as elements of cognitive
acts, Tillich claims that we can define thought only as an act that is
directed toward being and that we can define being only as that which
is intended by thought, as that toward which the act of thought is
directed. Tillich warns that it is utterly impossible to transcend this
reciprocal definition of the fundamental concepts of being and
thought.[37] A third element of cognition that Tillich identifies is the
establishment and the apprehension of a synthetic unity of thought
and being.[38] Tillich calls this synthetic unity "spirit," and defines it,
not very helpfully, as "existent thought."[39]

His analysis of the three constituents of the cognitive act enables
Tillich to suggest a tripartite division of the sciences into the sciences
of thought, of being, and of spirit. The goal of the science of thought

---

[36]Ibid., 33–34. Notice the resemblance to Kant's argument in *The Critique
of Pure Reason*, 537–38/A651=B679.

[37]Tillich, *The System of the Sciences*, 34–35.

[38]I list establishment and apprehension together because Tillich considers
the apprehension of synthetic unity a spontaneous creative act of the spirit.

[39]Ibid., 34–35.

is the knowledge of the pure forms of thought, "the universal forms to which every content must be adapted,"[40] considered in abstraction from their relation to being. The goal of the science of being is knowledge of empirical existents. It examines the material or "content" which "compel thought to adapt itself" to it. The human sciences should focus on the way the reflective spirit posits itself through the legislation of norms. Its goal is to interpret realms of culture as the constructs of the creativity of the spirit.[41] My analysis will focus on Tillich's system of the human sciences, since it is there that he develops his concept of religion and his idea of the theonomous consciousness. It is also in the system of the human sciences that Tillich suggests a program for a metaphysical unity of theory and praxis and of thought and being.

Tillich argues, reiterating the conviction of proponents of the distinctness of the human sciences, that the peculiar characteristic of thought is that it can be directed not only toward given objects but also toward itself. Thought can observe itself and thereby become a part of existence. In examining itself, thought makes itself into an object alongside other objects. In this process of self-examination,

> thought subjects itself to all the conditions and determinations that apply to being and into which thought has dissolved being. . . . If we ask where this existing thought is found, we can only answer: in the "interior" of the conscious being, and for humans, above all, in the spiritual life of humanity.[42]

Defining "spirit" as "the mode of existing thought" and as the "self-determination of thought within being,"[43] Tillich argues that spirit is characterized by free creativity which is informed by the infinite

---

[40]Tillich, *The System of the Sciences*, 37.

[41]Ibid., 37–38.

[42]Ibid., 36.

[43]Ibid., 137. In *Systematic Theology* (3. 111) Tillich defines spirit as "the actualization of power and meaning in unity." I think that the definition of spirit in *The System of the Sciences* is altogether more intelligible and straightforward.

opposition between thought and being. Explaining what he means by "creativity," Tillich says that "creation and spirit are nothing but the unity of *intention toward the universal and realization within the particular*."[44] He also says that "the nature of spiritual creations, their existence as spirit, is the self-determination of thought within being. Every spiritual act is the positing of a norm."[45] Tillich adds that history is the locus of this creativity.[46] We shall turn now to examine these claims through an analysis of Tillich's system of the human sciences.

■ 7.C. The Quest for Meaning in the Human Sciences

7.C.1. Introduction

In presenting his suggestion for the organization of the human sciences Tillich offers a complex system that embodies several principles of division. In what follows I shall examine only those elements of Tillich's system of the human sciences that have a direct bearing on his theory of theonomy and are crucial for understanding Tillich's conception of the study of religion.

Although his mapping of the sciences is merely a concise outline, more assertive than explanatory—always maintaining that a justification of the outline and its usefulness will only be achieved in detailed discussions of the various specific sciences—it is possible to extract from it a rather clear idea of the essence of Tillich's understanding of religious thought. Central ideas such as unconditioned form (*unbedingte Form*), unconditional meaning (*unbedingten Sinn*), theonomous attitude (*theonome Geisteshaltung*), and import of meaning (*Sinngehalt*) are explained in brief in Tillich's analytical outline of what he suggests as the necessary unchanging structure of the human sciences. It is therefore through examination of these ideal structures that Tillich suggests we are to be introduced to his basic convictions regarding religion and its appropriate science.

[44]Tillich, *The System of the Sciences*, 142.
[45]Ibid., 149.
[46]Tillich says (ibid., 167) that "the principles of meaning are concretely realized in history. History is the arena of creative fulfillment of meaning."

Since Tillich's language is so obtuse I shall try to explain in my own words what I think it is supposed to mean, distancing myself, as much as I can, from Tillich's own language. I shall first attempt to present Tillich's fundamental insights concerning the notion of meaning, as I have come to understand them. Once I have explained what I think are Tillich's basic organizational insights, I shall proceed to show how their implications are spelled out, step-by-step, in Tillich's work.

7.C.2. The Logical Structure of Meaning

Tillich explains his notion of the human sciences through an analysis of the logical structure of explanation that is appropriate to these sciences. Maintaining that the goal of the human sciences is to ascertain the meaning (*Sinnbegriff*) of their subject matter, Tillich proceeds to analyze the logical structure of an explanation in terms of meaning.[47] In order to do so, he first explains the notion of meaning. Through his analysis of what he calls "the structure of meaning" (*Sinngebilden*) we learn that meaning is found when we become aware that a particular phenomenon exhibits the fulfillment of an ideal of spirit. The meaning of a given phenomenon is the ideal of the spirit, the realization of which it exhibits. The human sciences are in essence attempts to ascertain the meaning of their objects of study, which are the creations of the spirit, as they are to be found in history and in the ongoing creative action of the spirit.

Since, according to Tillich's analysis, explanation in terms of meaning is the comprehension of the realization of the ideal in the real, the structure of explanation in terms of meaning involves three interrelated elements. It involves, first, the encounter with the historical evidence of the products of the spirit as they are unfolded before it by historical research. The second element, which analysis will show had already implicitly informed the first, but which becomes crystallized only through critical analysis of the findings of history, is the ideal or ideals which inform the spirit as it creates its own products. We have, with these two elements, an essential tension in which the spirit comes to know itself as creative: first, through the givenness of

[47]See ibid., 149–51.

history that shows how things happened to be, and second, through the spirit's recognition of the ideals that informed its acts of creativity. I suggest that Tillich had in mind here two focuses of tension. It is first a tension between the way spirit comes to know itself as creative through what happened to be the case in history, a perspective in which the spirit sees itself as ever changing and creating through a wide variety of impulses and influences. This is perhaps the primary source for a relativistic self-understanding of the spirit: it finds itself and its creativity mirrored in history in a multitude of diverse forms. Seeing itself mirrored in this way, the spirit cannot know if it creates freely or through some process that it undergoes. As the spirit comes to know itself through critical analysis of its products, however, as creating according to ideals, it knows itself as free and self-determining. The other element of tension is to be found in the perennially problematic relation between the ideal and the real, wherein the real falls short of the ideals to the extent that it is possible to doubt whether it is indeed the ideal which is effective in bringing it about.

Meaning is achieved only in a third "element of meaning," a synthetic element that combines the awareness of the ideal and the real in a reflective judgment that the ideal is realized in the real. In Tillich's words this is the comprehension of the fulfillment of a meaning giving act.[48] It should be clear from this analysis that meaningfulness, the cognitive goal of the human sciences, must reflect this triadic logical structure in which alone meaning is to be found. This structure determines, therefore, Tillich's conception of the organization of the system of the human sciences. The human sciences should always reflect this triadic logical structure in a division to three interrelated sciences, whatever the specific objects of these sciences may be. Since meaning involves three interrelated elements: the givenness of fact, the abstracted form or ideal, and their synthetic unification, these three elements should become the objects of study of the human sciences.[49]

[48]See ibid., 150.
[49]See ibid., 151.

Tillich thinks that each of these elements requires a distinct methodology. He suggests, therefore, a corresponding threefold methodological division of the human sciences. Each addresses one of the three elements of meaning with a methodology appropriate to it. In essence, these three types of science are historical, philosophical, and systematics.[50] Tillich's notion of systematics will be explained shortly. It is important to note that at this level of abstraction we are concerned not with specific sciences (e.g., philosophy of law or history of art) but with an outline of a general methodological approach. A division of the specific human sciences that will ensue will have to reflect the interrelatedness of the three most general movements that are necessary for a science whose goal is to ascertain the meaning of its phenomena.

It is already clear from these considerations that neither a historical study of a phenomenon alone, nor a philosophical study of it alone, is capable of ascertaining its meaning. While to some extent it is possible to conduct historical and philosophical studies on their own, the ultimate goal of explanation in terms of meaning in these sciences can only be achieved by "systematics" in which the other two are brought to synthetic unity. We shall now turn to Tillich's text to follow his presentation of these ideas step by step.[51]

Tillich outlines his organization of the human sciences according to the three modes in which he thinks the creative human spirit is aware of the cultural creations that arise out of its own spontaneous creativity. The conviction that underlies Tillich's discussion is that the human sciences differ from the natural sciences because their subject is not something alien to human activity but is rather its product. In

[50]See ibid., 151, 156.

[51]Anticipating an upcoming discussion, I would turn the reader's attention to the fact that Tillich identifies systematics as theonomous theology (see ibid., 212). This means that the work of the theologian cannot ignore either philosophy or cultural history. The implication of this idea for the study of religion is that the science of religion should include three interrelated disciplines: philosophy of religion, cultural history of religion, and theology. We may recall at this point that Otto had reached very similar conclusions regarding the relations between history and philosophy (see Otto, *The Philosophy of Religion*, chap. 16, pp. 222–30).

studying the products of human thought and action, the spirit, in a manner of speaking, studies a reflection of itself and comes to know itself as the creator of its subject of study.[52] Contemplating the idea of a human science from a most abstract point of departure, before any knowledge of a specific science is introduced, Tillich suggests that in studying its own creations the spirit has a threefold approach to its creations. First, it knows them as given facts of human history. Second, it has the capacity to analyze the general rules that it abstracts critically from the findings of history. There is, however, a tension inherent between these two modes of knowing the products of the spirit. In the first, the historical, the creations of the spirit are known as they happened to be realized in an infinite multiplicity of ways throughout history. They have the factuality of the given. On the other hand, the general rules according to which the spirit fashions its creation are understood as ideals, abstracted from the realizations but understood as independent of them, as their guiding principles. The ideals that the spirit abstracts critically are perceived as the norms to which historical realization ought to conform. The tension between the antithetical focus, on the actual and on the ideal, is resolved in the awareness of the spirit of its own activity in creating the empirically given according to norms.[53] This is a higher and third moment of self-awareness of the spirit in which it reflects on its creations, which are now empirically given to it, and on the rules which guide its activity in creating them (the ideal laws which it abstracts from the given) and secures an awareness that the norm is realized in the given. These three modes in which the spirit is aware of its creations, and therefore of itself as creating, inform the whole of Tillich's system of the human sciences.[54]

---

[52]See Tillich, *The System of the Sciences*, 149–50. We have already noted the Kantian origins of this metaphor in the image of nature as the mirror of the mind; the special application of this idea to the human sciences is a noteworthy contribution of Wilhelm Dilthey (*Introduction to the Human Sciences* [trans. Ramon J. Belenzos; Detroit: Wayne State University Press, 1988]).

[53]See Tillich, *The System of the Sciences*, 151–53.

[54]See ibid., 149–50.

It is important to note in connection with these considerations Tillich's use of the terms "context of meaning" (*Sinnzusammenhang*) and "system." Unless these are clearly understood his suggestions will not be intelligible.[55] A context of meaning, namely, the context in which the cognitive goal of the human sciences is fulfilled, is no other than the ideal norm, which the spirit comes to know as its guiding creative principle and as the ideal that it finds realized in empirical historical moments. A system, for Tillich, is essentially an act of creative comprehension of meaning. It is an act in which we comprehend the meaning of the empirically given. It is an act in which we are simultaneously aware of the empirically given, of the normative ideal, and of the way in which the two are synthetically interrelated as the latter is realized in the former through a creative act of the spirit. In other words, the system is both an awareness of the synthetic unity of the ideal and the real, and the creative synthesizing act itself.[56] It is for this reason that for Tillich the human sciences are essentially productive and methodologically constructive. An explanation of these two notions will be forthcoming.

Thus, a system of the human sciences refers not only to the abstract organization of the different functions of human activities but first and foremost to the self-reflective moment in which the fulfillment of the ideal norms of the spirit is perceived as realized in its historical creations. This is the synthetic activity of the system. Tillich defines this concept of a system as a unique and creative comprehension of meaning. He says about it two things that are of importance to us: First, he claims that it is not a "thought form," which means that it is not an abstract rule that can be expressed in propositions. Second, he says that it is not an "existential form," which means that it is not an empirical fact that can be described as such in theoretical and scientific knowledge.[57] These explanations will surely remind us of the essential characterizations of a Kantian Reflective Judgment. The system, according to Tillich, exists (primarily) only as an act. It is an act of comprehension of both the meaning of the empirical

[55]See ibid., 150–51.
[56]See ibid., 150.
[57]Ibid.

elements of the history of culture and of the fulfillment in history of the ideals of the spirit.[58] In light of our previous discussion of Kant and of Tillich's understanding of the *Critique of Judgment*, I find it irresistible to suggest that Tillich has in mind here something very similar to a Kantian moment of the contemplative apprehension of the unity of nature and freedom or of theory and praxis.[59]

Throughout this discussion Tillich is concerned with general considerations about what the human sciences must be like, not yet with any science in particular. He is, however, willing to say at this point that in light of this understanding of a system and of a context of meaning, particular human sciences will involve propositions that express the context of meaning, i.e., the ideal norm.[60] Since particular sciences are concerned with distinct areas of spiritual activity and seek to discover the meaning of these activities, their quest will necessarily be to discover the way in which the creative systematic act of the spirit finds expression in that specific realm. Namely, each science asks what norms are realized within its jurisdiction.[61]

In light of these considerations, Tillich can claim boldly that meaning is system,[62] a definition which I suggest we understand as claiming that meaning is the reflective comprehension of a fulfillment of an ideal standard of the spirit as it is found in the empirical givenness of experience. Meaning is therefore an apprehension of the fulfillment

---

[58]See ibid., 150–51.

[59]See ibid., 150.

[60]See ibid., 149.

[61]Since system is a reflective act it cannot be founded on propositional reasoning or, in Kantian terminology, on determinate concepts. It is clear, however, that the specific human sciences are not of this nonpropositional nature; the history of culture is descriptive and philosophy is analytic. They are descriptive and analytic rather than reflective. Since the specific sciences are clearly propositional Tillich must explain that their propositions are not about the system (which, as stipulated, is nonpropositional); rather, the propositions are within the system. I suggest that what Tillich means is that the propositions of the specific human sciences (e.g., varieties of history and philosophy) do not have the system as their subject matter but rather the empirical and the analytical elements of the context of meaning. Systematics will have to find its own mode of expression.

[62]See ibid., 151.

of the ideal that is grounded in the unconditional. Tillich says that the human sciences are systematic, in his special sense, because they are normative.[63] This means, I would suggest, that the human sciences involve a reflective comprehension of an ideal. I find striking similarity here to Kant's portrayal, at the end of his discussion of judgments of taste, of aesthetic judgment as a comprehension of ideals of reason in particular objects. In my chapter on Otto, I discussed the use that Fries made of this Kantian discussion in his theory of religion, a theory which Otto elaborates in his *The Idea of the Holy*.[64]

7.C.2.a. Elements of the Human Science

Having analyzed, at the most abstract level, the ways in which we become aware of the spirit as creating the realms of human experience, or of culture, Tillich begins to draw conclusions regarding the organizational structure of the human sciences. This is in essence a translation of the previous considerations into what Tillich calls the "elements" of the human sciences. Beside the elements, as we shall soon see, the human sciences include spiritual attitudes and the objects of the sciences. To anticipate, the elements are philosophy, history of culture and systematics; the spiritual attitudes are autonomy and theonomy;[65] and the objects are the different realms of human activity that are studied by the particular sciences, such as law, art, etc.

As we noted above, the discovery of "meaning," for Tillich, is a reflective comprehension of the fulfillment of the ideal in reality. We also noted that the structure of meaning involves an inevitable tension between ideal determinations of what ought to be and empirical discoveries of what happens to be the case. We are painfully aware that reality usually falls so short of our ideals that it is often possible to doubt whether they have anything to do with it. Tillich, however, believes that this tension exists between two elements that are merely analytical constructs. The spirit encounters meaning reflectively as

[63]See ibid.
[64]See part two, section 6.D. above.
[65]Heteronomy is not mentioned because it is considered a spiritual failure. See my discussion of metaphysics in part two, section 7.C.4.a–b below.

fulfilled; it does not impose ideals on the given, nor does it discover them empirically in the given. Both idealism and empiricism are mistaken, according to Tillich, in this regard. The spirit encounters meaning as fulfilled and analyzes its discovery through the two abstract elements of historical givenness, on the one hand, and philosophical form, on the other. These two elements serve the spirit in its analysis of the manner in which fulfillment of the ideal in the real appears to it immediately as a third synthetic element. These three are the elements of what Tillich calls the structure of meaning.[66]

In other words, as I understand Tillich's intention, every act of a human science that attempts to establish the meaning of any human phenomenon will necessarily encounter this logical structure: an ideal that is posited by the spirit, an empirical creation of the spirit that the spirit now finds as historically given, and a synthetic moment of the unity of the ideal and the given. Without any one of these three there cannot be such a thing as meaning.[67] Each of these essential elements of the structure of meaning can become an object of study in itself.[68] The element in which the spirit knows itself as positing ideals results in what Tillich calls "the doctrine of the principles of meaning" and finds expression in the work of philosophy which studies the functions of the spirit and its categories.[69] The empirical givenness of the creation of the spirit results in what Tillich calls the doctrine of the material of meaning which finds expression in the various disciplines which study the history of the spirit: the empirical human sciences.[70] The synthetic element of the apprehension of the fulfillment of meaning results in what Tillich calls the "doctrine of the system of meaning";[71] it gives rise to the science of "systematics" which is concerned

[66]See Tillich, *The System of the Sciences*, 161; and idem, *What is Religion?* 42, 52.

[67]The same rule applies, of course, to the study of religion.

[68]See ibid., 151–52.

[69]See ibid., 159–64.

[70]See ibid., 167–70.

[71]Later on Tillich calls it "the doctrine of the Norms of Meaning" (see ibid., 170–73).

with the clarification of the relations between all three elements and their corresponding sciences.[72]

While each of the first two—philosophy and cultural history—can to some degree be independent sciences, systematic is essentially inseparable from the other two. There is no science of systematic independent of philosophy and cultural history, because the subject matter of systematic is nothing but the complex relations between the ideals, which philosophy studies, the real, which is presented by history, and the way in which the fulfillment of the ideal in the real is comprehended and expressed. Since Tillich will argue that religious awareness is essentially an awareness of fulfillment of meaning,[73] we find in this discussion the basis for his subsequent claim that there can be no independent theology and no independent study of religion$_1$.

7.C.2.a.(1) Understanding (**Verstehen**): It is also in light of these considerations that Tillich brings forth his conception of the specific mode of understanding in the human sciences (*Verstehen*).[74] Since the cognitive goal of the human sciences is the apprehension of meaning, and since the apprehension of meaning is achieved in reflective comprehension of the ideal in the real as an act of the spirit, *Verstehen* is nothing but the self-realization of the spirit as creating meaning, as creating its objects. Understanding in the human sciences is the spirit's awareness of itself as creating the object of the sciences.[75] In Tillich's special mode of expression, understanding is "conscious participation in the creative act."[76] Although Tillich does not say so, the logic of his position seems to me to imply necessarily that the specific mode of understanding in the human sciences is essentially reflective.

---

[72]See ibid., 151. We shall soon see that this is the task of theonomous theology.

[73]Theology is essentially a third branch alongside philosophy and history (see ibid., 156). Religion is not an object of study but a part of the structure of meaning. It is the awareness of the fact that the spirit encounters meaning as fulfilled.

[74]See ibid., 152–54.

[75]See ibid., 152. As we shall see shortly, this too is the task of theonomous theology (see pp. 207–8).

[76]Ibid, 152. See also Tillich, *What is Religion?* 36–37, 155–56.

I would suggest that if this is so, then we have good reasons to think that the methodology of the human sciences must indeed be different from that of the natural and the logical sciences. It is not merely that the subject matter of the human sciences is not alien to us, as is nature, but that it gives rise to a demand for a special method for the human sciences. It is rather the reflective character of *Verstehen* that sets it apart from scientific explanation. Tillich seems to be committed to this view, which I find most interesting, because, as I interpret his position, he claims that understanding (*Verstehen*) is conscious participation in the creative act of meaning and implies that the creative act of meaning is a reflective comprehension.[77]

7.C.2.b. *Spontaneity and Construction*

Having explained that system is an act in which understanding takes place—the two terms being used in the special technical meaning Tillich has given them—Tillich proceeds to explain that understanding in the human sciences is not passively receptive but productive and constructive.[78] His explanation proceeds according to the triadic structure that the human sciences must have as they follow the logical structure of meaning. Tillich explains therefore how the understanding is productive in all three elements of meaning: in philosophy, in history, and in systematics.[79] We shall see that the spontaneity of the spirit finds greater expression as we proceed from the least spontaneous activity of historical studies and reaches its maximum in the pure spontaneity of systematic.

With regard to cultural history, Tillich says that it is both receptive and productive. It is receptive to the empirical givenness of concrete

[77]My interpretation of the synthetic apprehension of meaning as reflective is based on Tillich's characterization of it as involving neither "a thought form" nor an "existential form" (*The System of the Sciences*, 150; also see my discussion above). I suggest that this insight underlies Tillich's discussion of "Knowledge and Revelation" in *Systematic Theology*, 1. 129–31.

[78]Although Tillich's discussion is rather complicated, it is worth attending to because it serves to explain not only the structure of the system of the sciences in general, but also, in particular, the structure of the science of religion and the structure of theological activity.

[79]See Tillich, *The System of the Sciences*, 152–54.

realizations of acts of the spirit. It is productive insofar as its receptivity to the phenomena is guided by the norms of the spirit. History of culture, according to Tillich, is not merely an unguided, purely empirical collection of impressions, but an examination of phenomena with the informed interest of finding in them the footprints of the creative activity of the spirit. As in all Kantian (and Hegelian) conceptions of an empirical science, the spirit contributes to the empirical study both the interest and the norms that govern that study and direct it. We are not purely receptive to the given; we are looking for something in it. Tillich calls the distinct mode of cognitive achievement in historical sciences a "receptive understanding."[80]

Philosophy is to some degree receptive also, although it deals with the abstract forms that inform the activity of the spirit. It is receptive insofar as philosophy extracts the principles from the findings of history. Philosophy, for Tillich, is essentially a critical activity, the task of which is to map the principles and the categories through which the spirit functions. Philosophy comes to know these principles and categories in its analysis of the findings of history. The distinct mode of cognitive achievement in philosophy is therefore given the name "critical understanding."[81]

Unlike the first two, in which the understanding is mediated through the receptivity of the historical studies, systematics directs itself to the consciousness of an act of positing norms. It is therefore a self-reflective awareness in which the spirit knows itself as setting out of itself the norms that it finds fulfilled in history. The distinct mode of cognitive achievement in systematics, which is pure spontaneity, is called by Tillich "productive understanding."[82]

---

[80]Ibid., 153

[81]Ibid.

[82]Ibid., 152. While the resemblance to Hegel's theory of the history through which the spirit becomes aware of itself is obvious, it should be kept in mind that for Tillich the spiritual process is open-ended, and its moments of self-awareness *do not proceed in degrees of clarity.* For Tillich, the spirit can become aware of itself only through reflection on the critical findings of philosophy as the latter analyzes the findings of the ever-evolving sciences.

To the three modes of productivity in understanding Tillich posits corresponding scientific procedures or methods. The methods, which Tillich deems appropriate to the three elements of meaning according to their levels of spontaneity, are three corresponding levels of constructive activity. By "construction" (*Konstruktion*) Tillich refers to the activities of the distinct sciences in their "presentations of contexts of meanings from the perspective of normative principle."[83] In all three elements of the sciences, philosophy, history, and systematics, we find an attempt, with various degrees of effectiveness, to discern or present the meaning of a specific phenomenon in light of a normative principle of the spirit.

In cultural history this is an attempt to place the phenomenon in an appropriate context, as part of a certain type of activity, from which the norm could then be abstracted and analyzed. The function of cultural history, then, is an "arranging construction."[84] Cultural history attempts to construct out of the material that it finds organized historical unities (identifiable types of human activity), which later can be subjected to further analysis. It is important for Tillich to emphasize here once more that historical study is not merely passive receptivity to the facts; rather it is the construction of the facts of history. It is, however, a low-level construction, limited to an arrangements of its findings, the findings themselves remaining absolute givens.[85]

Philosophy, according to Tillich, is an activity of "analytical construction."[86] Philosophy attempts to understand the meaningfulness of phenomena in light of the various ideals, norms, and categories that define various realms of meaning. As it tries to understand the meaning of the given phenomena, in light of the ideals relevant to it, philosophy exhibits an awareness that ultimately the phenomena reflect a creative act of the spirit. The subject matter of philosophy, however, is not the creative act itself but the principles that inform it.

[83]Ibid., 153.
[84]Ibid.
[85]Similarly, the history of religion₂ is typological. Tillich conducted such a typological study in *Dynamics of Faith*.
[86]Tillich, *The System of the Sciences*, 153.

Philosophy is analytical, according to Tillich, because by the term "analysis" he means an activity of constructing the principles out of the context in which they are founded by history. From this perspective philosophy is seen as limited in its spontaneous construction by its necessary critical relation to the empirical findings of history. It is spontaneous, however, insofar as it does not find the principles and categories given to it by history but must suggest them out of itself. It seems to me that what Tillich wants to emphasize here is that philosophy does not simply discover the principle within historical findings. The principles can only be established by a constructive contribution of philosophy that hypothetically suggests principles to see if they are capable of accounting for the phenomena as found. Philosophy thus stands midway between the pure spontaneous creativity of the spirit and the empirical givenness of the history of culture. It is only in systematics, which generates the normative principle out of itself, that the spontaneity of the spirit is purely effective. Tillich calls the spirit's mode of functioning in systematics a "synthetic construction."[87]

7.C.2.c. Modes of Certainty

Since the objects of the history of culture, philosophy, and systematics are never simply given to the spirit, especially not in the more fully constructive elements of philosophy and systematics, the mode of certainty that can be achieved in each cannot be determined by the relation of the science to its object. The mode of certainty must reflect the validity of the constructive act in which the object is represented. Thus, for example, systematics, which creates meaning out of itself in full spontaneity, can find certainty only in its awareness that the meaning it finds fulfilled in an empirical given is a meaning that it creates out of itself. I would suggest that we have here something very similar to the appeal to the self-confidence of reason that we found in Nelson. For Tillich, however, this self-confidence, or certainty, is found in different modes in the various elements. In philosophy, which deals with abstract norms and principles in themselves, the self-confidence of spirit tends to appear as self-evidence. In his-

[87]Ibid.

tory, the certainty that an historical phenomenon was appropriately constructed manifests itself in terms of probability. The probability of which Tillich speaks in the context of historical sciences seems to me to refer to an awareness that, given our general acquaintance with the creative activity of the spirit, it is most likely that certain findings represent a certain type of activity. This estimation of probability is directed toward the validity of the scientific act of the construction of the historical fact out of the material of history.

Thus the highest level of certainty, a level in which error is impossible, is the level of systematics, which is the self-awareness of the spirit as creating the meaning that it represents to itself. Philosophy, in trying to ascertain the principles and norms that inform the creative activity of the spirit, is not immune to error. Its certainty that it succeeded in finding the right principles manifests itself in an appeal to self-evidence, an appeal that can be misleading. Tillich calls these three modes of certainty, which are appropriate to the human sciences, various modes of conviction. The name seems to reflect an awareness that we cannot ascertain that we got things right by checking our findings against something external to them; we are simply convinced, in different degrees, that we have things right. In Tillich's words, "conviction is based on the standpoint not on the relation between knowledge and the object."[88]

7.C.3. A Will to the Unconditioned

Up to this point Tillich has tried to draw the conclusions that follow from his initial analysis of the logical structure of explanation in terms of meaning in the human sciences. The analysis led first to the identification of the three elements of the structure of meaning: the historical, the philosophical and the systematic, along with the methods appropriate to them. The elements of meaning form the matrix within which the human sciences can achieve their cognitive goals. The cognitive goals of the human sciences are, however, not simple; they express the complexity of the interests of the spirit in its attempt to understand its mode of functioning. The interests of the spirit as a

[88]Ibid., 154.

knowing subject[89] are always directed, according to Tillich, by an essential drive, a drive which he calls the Eros of the spirit.[90] It expresses itself as a will to the unconditioned. The idea of a will to the unconditioned requires some explanation. Much of what Tillich says about it is far from perspicuous and requires sympathetic interpretation that I shall try to provide.

Spirit, it seems, is essentially motivated to comprehend the meaning of the phenomena it discovers. Being so oriented it finds itself between the two poles of thought and being. For Tillich, thought is essentially an attempt to comprehend the givenness of experience through concepts. Being, on the other hand, is what can provide content for an otherwise empty form. Tillich seems to be playing with the Kantian duality of concepts, which are generated by thought in order to comprehend the givenness of experience without which the concepts are empty, and intuitions, which are meaningless without concepts that give them form and structure. It is only in the convergence of the two that a meaningfulness of being can be comprehended. Thought in itself is ideal, abstract, and empty. It is not a form of anything. Being in itself, uninformed by the forms of thought, is merely an absolute given, totally meaningless. Spirit finds itself attempting to ascertain meaning between the two poles of the pure ideality of thought and the absolute givenness of being.

If spirit is to succeed in discerning meaning in being (what Tillich calls "*der Gehalt*," and is translated as the "import" of meaning), it must discover the form of thought that truly informs being, that is, the principle, the fulfillment of which being represents. In its attempt to comprehend being, thought endlessly brings forth a multiplicity of concepts in order to shape and fit the manifold of the given. These are all conditional attempts, with varying degrees of success, of hypothetical explanations.[91] The Eros of the spirit, its will to the Unconditioned, can be understood in light of the hypothetical status of

---

[89]Up to this point, it seems that Tillich was concerned with describing the different aspects of the spirit as a creating subject; he turns now to examine the interests of the spirit as knowing, as knowing itself and its creations.

[90]See ibid., 148, 145.

[91]See ibid., 154–55.

conceptualization of being as an attempt to discern the one form that truly informs being: the one unconditioned form. We thus have two poles of unconditionality which converge. We have the unconditionality of the given and the unconditional form of thought that informs the given. It is to these that the spirit directs its efforts as it tries to understand the meaning of being. We can already surmise how this may become possible in light of what Tillich had already said about the nature of the special mode of understanding in which the spirit apprehends reflectively the fulfillment of meaning in reality.

7.C.3.a. Autonomy and Theonomy

As opaque as our last paragraph may be, I hope that one thing becomes clear by means of it: that in its attempt to comprehend being the spirit can be driven by two different attitudes and can operate in two distinct manners. The spirit can be driven by what Tillich calls theonomous and autonomous attitudes. In its autonomous attitude the spirit is driven to grasp being through abstract concepts. In its theonomous attitude the spirit is driven to grasp being through reflective recognition of the realization of ideals. The first attitude of the spirit leads it primarily to focus on a critical philosophical understanding of reality. The theonomous attitude leads the spirit to focus on the systemic act whereby the synthetic unity of the ideal and the real or thought and being is realized.

On the one hand, spirit can suggest hypothetically a multiplicity of concepts by means of which it tries to grasp the givenness of the phenomena and its meaning. As it does so, it generates out of itself general forms to see if it is possible to suggest that it is these forms that inform the phenomena. If more than one possible form can be found, the basic question that arises is which form best satisfies the claim to validity. Which form best accounts for the phenomenon as we encounter it? Since the forms are generated by the spirit spontaneously, out of itself, and are merely found to fit the phenomenon, this mode of comprehension of being is called by Tillich "autonomy."[92] We could perhaps say, in another manner of speaking, that in an

---

[92]Ibid., 155.

autonomous comprehension of meaning the spirit imposes its own forms on the givenness of the material.

On the other hand, the spirit finds within itself an essential drive to move beyond the merely hypothetical construction of meaning to the conviction that the meaning that it constructs is indeed a meaning that is already given in being.[93] The spirit can comprehend meaning through its reflective ability to discern, in the givenness of being, the realizations of the ideals that being manifests. Rather than trying to impose meaning on a phenomenon, spirit now tries to comprehend the meaning of the phenomenon reflectively and searches for the concept or the principle that best expresses its antecedent reflective discovery. Tillich calls this directedness of the spirit to the unconditioned "theonomy."[94] Theonomy differs from autonomy in that it does not attempt to suggest, out of itself, hypothetical forms that may fit the phenomena and thus endow it with meaning. Rather, the theonomous attitude attempts to discern the meaning that it discovers reflectively. Having discerned the given meaning of the phenomena, the spirit then tries to find a principle that would capture or express its discovery. It should be noted that theonomy is concerned with an attempt to grasp the inherent meaning of a particular object or event. Having grasped it, it asks what principle of the spirit could have brought it about. Whereas autonomy sets out from its own forms and tries to endow meaning to the phenomenon, theonomy starts from the discernment of the meaning of the phenomenon and tries to discern the principle or norm that informs it.[95]

The parallelism between philosophy and autonomy and between systematics and theonomy is evident. Tillich seems to suggest that the

---

[93]I see here an allusion to Kant's conviction, which he expressed both in the *First Critique* and in the *Third Critique*, that the scientist needs to believe that the particular laws of nature and their unity reflect the real structure of things in themselves; and that the moral agent needs to be able to believe that the moral end is realizable in the natural world and that, eventually, perhaps with divine assistance, the Highest Good will be realized as the kingdom of God on earth.

[94]Tillich, *The System of the Sciences*, 155.

[95]Ibid., 154–56, 203–6. Note the parallelism to Kant's characterization of reflective judgment.

autonomous attitude of the spirit directs it to philosophize. The theonomous attitude directs the spirit to systematics. Systematics is the act of synthesis in which the spirit apprehends the meaning that is realized in reality. Theonomy is the interest of the spirit to understand theonomically, through systematics. Systematics is the only way in which the theonomous attitude is realized.[96] Systematics, however, is not an isolated discipline: it depends on the disciplines of history and philosophy. Theonomy, too, cannot be understood as independent of autonomy. Since Systematics is the synthetic unity of the ideals of philosophy and the empirical findings of history, theonomy is the directedness of the spirit to the realization that the autonomous ideals are indeed those that are realized in being.[97]

7.C.3.a.(1) Theonomy as an Eros for Unity: Tillich's argument in the system of the sciences thus far is that while it is generally recognized by scholars and intellectuals that the spirit has an insatiable drive to impose its concepts on the givenness of experience and thereby to achieve knowledge, it must also be recognized that the spirit has a further drive to achieve a certainty that the concepts through which it tries to understand the world and to shape it are indeed the concepts through which the world is shaped. It is the further drive to know that the constructs of reason are not merely hypothetical attempts at construction of meaning, but genuine discoveries of true meaning. There is a striking resemblance between Tillich's notion of the theonomous interest of the spirit and Kant's depiction, in the Dialectics of the *First Critique* and in the *Third Critique*, of the interest of Reason to think of its constructions as discoveries.

Tillich's argument that the widely recognized autonomous Eros of the spirit must be supplemented with a recognition of its theonomous Eros is based on his initial analysis of the triadic structure of meaning. Having argued that the cognitive goal of the human sciences is

[96]See ibid., 206–10.

[97]In this context it is important to keep in mind that Tillich identifies systematics with theology. Though Tillich does not say so explicitly, it seems to me that the logic of this argument leads him to the view that theology— understood in the broad sense of creation of myth—is a decisive manifestation of religion.

to ascertain meaning and that meaning is secured only in the synthetic unity of the ideal, which autonomous philosophy describes, and the real, which is described by history, Tillich is in a position to claim that without a theonomous attitude, which calls for the systematic comprehension of the unity of the real and the ideal, the goal of the human sciences cannot be achieved. Theonomy is thus presented as essential to the realization of the goals of the human sciences.

Reflecting on the significance of these formal delineations of the structure of the human sciences as Tillich projects it, I have come to see that his conception of the spiritual interest—which he calls a theonomous attitude—is closely related to, if not actually identifiable with, his discussion earlier in the book of the spirit's desire for unity. Noticing that theonomy is an Eros of the spirit, a motivational force directed toward the unconditioned form (to the ideal norm that in fact shapes reality and forms it), we realize that this Eros is directed to, and satisfied by, the element of the human sciences that Tillich calls systematics. It is in systematics that the synthesis of form and being is achieved. It is through systematics that the unconditioned form, which informs being independently of the spirit's attempt to interpret being, is recognized.

Since systematics is the synthetic unity of the elements of meaning, and since systematics is the reflective comprehension of the unity of the ideal abstract forms of philosophy and the concrete empirical findings of history, systematics achieves unity. Insofar, therefore, as theonomy is an Eros of the spirit to the unconditioned form, an Eros that finds its satisfaction in the achievements of systematics, and insofar as the achievement of systematic is synthetic unity, theonomy must be understood as an Eros for unity.[98]

7.C.3.a.(2). Two Concepts of Religion: As we come to recognize the theonomous attitude, which informs the spirit's understanding of all realms of meaning—an attitude that I have interpreted throughout as religion$_1$, and have consistently tried to interpret in light of the Kantian critique—we are in a position to suggest that Tillich's notion

[98]See Tillich, *What is Religion?* 80; and idem, *The System of the Sciences*, 148–49, 154–55.

of the spirit's desire for unity reflects and builds upon Kant's analysis of reason's quest for reflective unity. Remembering that Kant's discussion of reflective unity and its contemplative conclusions ended with the suggestion that these conclusions are the point of departure for a philosophical theology, we are in a position to suggest further that Tillich's philosophy of religion can be seen as an attempt to fulfill the promise of Kant's conclusion. *The System of the Sciences* allows us to see in general outlines what reflective role religion is to play for Tillich in a holistic conception of meaning in the human sciences. Religion is to be the interest of the spirit in every realm of meaning[99] to secure the unity of its understanding of the ideal and the real. This religious interest—in which the spirit no longer sees itself as merely autonomous and imposing its forms on the material of experience, but as discovering that these forms are already embodied in being—finds expression not only in its contribution to the specific sciences but also in cultural objectifications that symbolize and express this inherent desire of the spirit to surpass its autonomous tendencies and to strive for the realization of the quest for unity by adopting a theonomous attitude. These symbolic expressions of the theonomous interest are to be found throughout history, and they constitute what Tillich considers the cultural historical manifestation of religion— what I called religion$_2$.

This theory has two interesting implications regarding religion$_1$ and religion$_2$. Being the relatedness of the spirit toward the unconditioned, religion$_1$ is essentially theonomy. As such, religion$_1$ is an indispensable part of the structure of meaning in the human sciences. Insofar as religion$_2$ is the historical manifestation of the spirit's relatedness to the unconditioned, the historical and the philosophical study of religion$_2$ are essential for the understanding of the theonomous conscious-

---

[99]Tillich uses this term in a narrow and a wide sense. In the narrow sense, there are two realms of meaning: the theoretical and the practical. In the wider sense, realms of meaning are also specific manifestations of the theoretical and practical activities of the spirit. These latter manifestations constitute the objects of the specific human sciences.

ness and should constitute a distinct and important specific science within the humanities.[100]

7.C.3.b. Tillich's Ontological Thought

Our discussion thus far has shown Tillich's conception of the spirit to be constructive and reflective. I note, however, that Tillich's thought has often been described as metaphysical or as existentialist. In light of what has already been said, it is possible to explain what elements in Tillich's thought may seem to be existentialist. In the "systematics" element of the sciences, in which alone meaning is secured, Tillich strives to distance himself from abstract ideals, concepts, and norms and emphatically stresses that meaning is to be found in the particular itself. This focus on the particular in its unconditioned meaningfulness is an interest in existence, in being, rather than in the merely abstract forms of thought. It is an emphasis that, when isolated from the context of the three elements of meaning, is liable to be misunderstood as an immediate prerational apprehension of the meaning of the particular which receives conceptualization only at a second stage. Understood in this way, Tillich's focus on the givenness of the meaningfulness of the particular seems to fit the existentialist slogan "existence precedes essence." It is clear, from what we have read, that the apprehension of meaning in the particular, the directedness of the spirit toward existence, is not prerational but a synthetic reflective unity of the forms of thought and the givenness of being. We recall that Tillich states that there can be no independent science of systematics that alone discerns the meaning of the particular. Systematics depends on cultural history and philosophy and brings their findings into synthetic unity.

It is Tillich's focus on the centrality of systematics and on the importance of theonomy in antithetic contradistinction to autonomy and formal philosophy that lends Tillich's thought its metaphysical character. Here too isolation of theonomy and systematics from their

---

[100]This issue is explored further in the conclusion to this chapter (section 7.D.3).

place in the structure of meaning leads to a misrepresentation of Tillich's thought. Rather than trying to overcome the formal conclusions of critical philosophical analysis, in which the spirit posits its own forms and categories, and attempting to reach out to Being itself as unconditioned by human concepts, Tillich tries to secure the validity of the constructs of autonomous reason by grounding them, reflectively, in a synthetic apprehension of the meaning of Being.

When Tillich claims that Critical philosophy is a starting point that must be surpassed and its conclusions anchored in being, he follows, as I have argued throughout, Kant's insistence that his analytical studies must be supplemented with a dialectic. In order to see that this is so, we must now proceed in our examination of Tillich's delineation of the structure of the system of the sciences, to examine his characterization of the role of metaphysics and ethics.

7.C.4. Theoretical and Practical Sciences

Having outlined both the elements (history, philosophy and systematics) of the system of the human sciences and the two spiritual attitudes (autonomy and theonomy) that provide the driving force of the spirit, Tillich proceeds to depict the structure of the "objects" of the system of the sciences. The objects of the system are the particular realms of meaning that are to be found in history and alone give content and application to the formal structure of the system (its elements and attitudes). Tillich does not attempt at this stage a thorough discussion of all the particular sciences, nor does he think such an a priori discussion is possible because the activity of the spirit is open-ended and capable of generating an ever-growing variety of specific activities. What Tillich attempts instead is a depiction of the general structure according to which the specific sciences should be organized, whatever they may turn out to be.[101]

The basic structure of the objects of the sciences follows, according to Tillich, from a distinction between two highest-level realms of meaning: the theoretical and the practical. The division of the sciences into these two realms is derived, directly, from Tillich's under-

---

[101]See Tillich, *The System of the Sciences*, 156–58.

standing of spiritual activity as involving essentially a dual act through which it relates to reality. On the one hand, it "absorbs reality into itself," while on the other hand, it attempts to "penetrate reality." The first aspect of this dual act in which the spirit attempts to assimilate itself to reality, to conform to what it finds, is Tillich's notion of a "theoretical activity." The spirit's effort to insert itself into reality, to make reality conform to its forms and demands, is what Tillich understands in "practical activity."[102]

These two types of activity constitute the highest-level organizing principle of all the sciences into theoretical and practical. Since the objects of the sciences, which have now been divided into theoretical and practical, provide the content to the elements of the sciences and to the spiritual attitudes (autonomy and theonomy), we should expect to find the internal division of the elements and the attitudes reflected within the practical and theoretical sciences.

Whereas in our discussion of the elements we spoke in general of "history," "philosophy," and the synthesis of their findings in "systematics"—when philosophy referred to the totality of the possible forms and ideals of the spirit, and history represented the totality of cultural facts that may ever be discovered—when we turn to the specific sciences, our discussion is limited to a specific fact, to a specific form, and to their synthetic unity. Thus we shall find within each specific science, theoretical or practical, an internal division of its structure of meaningfulness that reflects the essential structure of meaning previously discussed.

In Tillich's terminology, the first two elements are the historical "individual being" and the philosophical "individual form," whereas the third systematic unity of these two can be described as the unconditioned that supports all individuals and is the foundation of individual meaning-fulfillment. In other words, the synthetic third element identifies the form according to which the particular is the particular that it is; the particular is identified as realizing a specific form. This realization, achieved in synthetic reflection, provides support for the first two scientific constructs: the historical fact and the philosophical

[102]See Tillich, *What is Religion?* 62–63; idem, *The System of the Sciences*, 157; and idem, *Systematic Theology*, 1. 76.

norm. Both are merely hypothetical constructions in attempted explanations of phenomena until their conditionality is overcome in the
judgment that the ideal, or the "unconditioned form," is indeed manifest in the particular. It is in light of these considerations that Tillich
calls the first two elements of the particular sciences "supported" and
the third systematic element "supporting."

The two supported elements of the particular sciences are involved
in attempts to find adequate concepts to capture and to describe the
given material. As such, they are interested in finding or constructing
concepts and forms. Being so directed, they necessarily exhibit the
autonomous attitude of the spirit, its interest in the forms, which, out
of itself, it imposes on the material. Of the two supported sciences,
one is interested more in the abstract form itself and its logical relations to other forms, while the other is interested more in the empirical fact and the way its factuality is constituted by the abstract form.
The supporting functions, in which alone the findings of the supported functions are unified synthetically and grounded, requires a
shift in spiritual attitude as well as in intellectual function. It can no
longer be autonomous, descriptive, and analytic. It must instead become theonomous in attitude and reflective-synthetic in function.

7.C.4.a. Theonomous Science: Metaphysics and Ethos

Following the guidelines of this general analysis of the structure of
meaning and of the attitudes of the spirit, Tillich concludes his analysis of the structure of the human sciences with a further delineation
of the elements of both theoretical and practical sciences.[103] In the
theoretical sphere he sees the two supported elements as the functions
of science and art. Science is less interested in the particular phenomenon and concerns itself primarily with general concepts and structures of explanation. In Tillich's words, science is "determined by
form." Art, on the other hand, is interested in the particular manifestation of a form. It tries to embody a form; it tries to express a form,
an idea or an ideal, in a particular artistic creation. It is interested
more in the particular, as exhibiting the form, than in the form itself.

---

[103]See Tillich, *The System of the Sciences*, 158; and idem, *Systematic
Theology*, 1. 77–80.

In Tillich's language, art is "determined by the import."[104] In the theoretical sphere, the supporting function is no other than metaphysics.[105]

Metaphysics, in this role and in this place in the structure of meaning, cannot be thought of as "speculative construction" or "poetic idealism." Tillich assigns to metaphysics the specific role of securing the reflective unity of science and art and of finding the most adequate modes for expression of its findings. The mode of expression most fitting for representing the reflective findings of metaphysics, according to Tillich, is the language of myth.[106]

In the practical sphere, Tillich sees the two supported elements as the functions of law and community. Law, according to Tillich, is determined by form. It is interested in the principles according to which social life should be conducted. Law as such is not primarily interested in particular manifestation of lawful behavior. Community, according to Tillich, is determined by import. It is the attempt to create a political community.[107] The supporting element in the practical sphere, the element that provides the ultimate grounding and justification of communal activity and of legislation, is the function of ethos. It is the role of ethos to bring into synthetic unity the abstract legislation of the spirit and the empirical reality of political-communal life and to ground them in a realization that the norms according to which they function are indeed the unconditioned norms that inform the process of history.[108] It is only through ethos, so conceived, that the law is seen not only as abstractly just, but as applicable, and communal life is understood as embodying not merely freely constructed legal principles, but principles that are now seen as reflecting absolute norms which ought to inform and direct history. It is worth commenting at this point that Tillich's special notion of ethos

[104]See Tillich, *What is Religion?* 64; and idem, *The System of the Sciences*, 158, 175–81.

[105]See Tillich, *The System of the Sciences*, 158, 181–87.

[106]See Tillich, *What is Religion?* 35–36; idem, *The System of the Sciences*, 181–82; and idem, *Systematic Theology*, 1. 80–81.

[107]See Tillich, *The System of the Sciences*, 158, 187–201; and idem, *What is Religion?* 65.

[108]See Tillich, *Systematic Theology*, 1. 149.

closely resembles Kant's notion of reflective interpretation of historical human events as embodying norms and thus as commendable or
damnable. In daily life this reflective judgment is the noble duty of
the judge.

According to Tillich's analysis both metaphysics and ethos must be
theonomous. As we have seen, however, metaphysics and ethos require a shift in attitude both in spiritual orientation and in intellectual
function; the spirit must become theonomous and reflective. Tillich
believes that modern culture reflects a general failure to appreciate
the necessity of the shift and to deny it in the name of a misguided
secularism which seeks to celebrate the autonomy of the spirit and to
rest on its laurels. Tillich must therefore acknowledge that it is spiri-
tually possible to fail to shift from autonomy to theonomy in metaphysics and in ethos. It is possible to attempt to absolutize the
autonomous constructions of reason in metaphysical and ethical systems as purely philosophical projects. Such projects abdicate their
reflective unifying responsibility and will inevitably fail to fulfill the
requirement of the human sciences to secure meaning. Tillich, therefore, presents the attainment of meaning in the human sciences as a
religious challenge to secular society.

7.C.4.a.(1). Metaphysics and Ethos: An Explanation: Tillich's all
too brief discussion of metaphysics and ethos as theonomous functions is of special importance for our study since it is through these,
he claims, that the "ideal unity of the elements of meaning" is
achieved.[109] It is a unity that envelopes both the theoretical and the
practical attitudes toward the unconditioned and is recognized, therefore, as "the fundamental act of spirit as such."[110] We note the parallelism between Tillich's suggestion and Kant's attempt to discover
the highest principle that unites nature and freedom in the contemplative thought about the supernatural substrate of reality.

In order to understand Tillich's notion of metaphysics and his notion
of ethos we must be careful to distinguish the two from traditional
meanings of the terms that he rejects. Metaphysics and ethos must be

[109]Tillich, *The System of the Sciences*, 186.
[110]Ibid. See also Tillich, *What is Religion?* 56–57.

theonomous and direct their attention to the unconditionality of the norm that they apprehend reflectively as realized in particular empirical or practical events. Should metaphysics and ethos fail to be theonomous and adopt instead an autonomous attitude, they will give up their attentiveness to the unconditionality of their respective norms and will attempt instead to endow the status of unconditionality to the autonomous constructs of the spirit. Examples of such failures can be found in an attempt to construct a metaphysics from the conclusions of science. A stamp of unconditionality is put on science with no attempt to reflect on the constructive nature of science and to ground it in our contemplative understanding of the ground of being. An example from the practical sphere would be an autonomous attempt to absolutize the formal requirements of a moral law constructed purely out of the spirit itself, thus making its demand unconditional with no ability to respect the significance that a moral law must have as an expression of the ideal end of human activities. Tillich is, accordingly, highly critical of Enlightenment attempts to create a scientific metaphysics and a system of morality. Both fall short of the ideal of securing meaning; they are illegitimate attempts to extend the validity of autonomous legislation, in theory and in praxis, beyond their appropriate roles. We should be careful, therefore, not to mistake Tillich's metaphysical claims for scientific knowledge, or his ethical claims for moral rules.

The specific role of metaphysics, in Tillich's projected system of the sciences, is to answer three questions. With regard to being, metaphysics attempts to comprehend the relation of the unconditioned forms to existence.[111] With regard to history, metaphysics attempts to comprehend the relation of the unconditioned to the creative spiritual

---

[111]It is interesting to think of this quest in close comparison to Kant's demand that we come to think of the particular laws that govern the events of nature not simply as hypothetical constructs of reason but as reflections of the divine thought which determines the process of nature. In light of this comparison we can think of Tillich's quest for the unconditioned form as the demand to understand a formal law of science not merely as hypothetical but also as unconditioned. For discussion see, for example, Tillich, *Systematic Theology*, 1. 149.

process.[112] Metaphysics' further task is to comprehend the unity between the natural and the spiritual processes. Tillich's metaphysical
project clearly corresponds here to Kant's critical attempt to establish
the transcendental unity between nature and freedom.[113]

7.C.4.b. Metaphysics of History

In *The System of the Sciences* Tillich does not attempt to supply a
full-blown metaphysics that would answer his three questions. He
tries to say what sorts of answers these should be, and some of his
comments are of importance to us.

As a metaphysics of Being, ontology should attempt to find an
adequate mode of discourse to express its reflective comprehension of
the unity of all that is as an expression of pure meaning. As I propose
to understand it, this is a demand for an idea of the cosmos as a
totality: not as a totality that is alien to reason and opaque to thought,
but as the manifestation of an ideal, an ideal of which we must think
as a divine thought or as an immanent idea within the cosmos, as an
organizing principle that is inherent to the cosmos.[114] It is clear that
no such account could ever strive to be scientific, but according to
Tillich, this does not give it free poetic license. Since metaphysics
should be the comprehension of the synthetic unity of thought and
being, the language of metaphysics must be conceptual, borrowed
from science and philosophy, but used symbolically.[115] Being reflectively dependent on science, from which it borrows its formal means
of expression, metaphysics must follow the developments of science;

[112]Comparison to Kant is informative here too. We should consider here
Kant's demand that we not merely attempt to understand history in light of the
diversity of possible motivations which may be suggested as guiding particular human actions, but should evaluate history in light of the moral law as this
law reflects its ultimate end, the Highest Good. In light of this comparison,
we can think of Tillich's demand to relate our understanding of the creative
spiritual process not merely to formal laws but to the unconditional ends of
spiritual activity.

[113]See Tillich, *The System of the Sciences*, 185.

[114]We note here the resemblance to the Kantian idea of the universe as an
expression of the thought of an archetypal reason.

[115]Ibid., 181–85.

it cannot dictate to science or ignore unpalatable scientific theories, nor can it pretend to be a supreme science. The foremost symbols of unconditioned meaning in ontology are, according to Tillich, the symbols of "Being" and "Unity."[116]

A metaphysics of history plays a crucial role in Tillich's thought. Primarily it attempts to express an idea of a universal history. Tillich understands this task as an attempt to comprehend and to find adequate means of expression for the reflective comprehension of unconditioned meaning in historical process.[117] I can only understand this metaphysical project as an attempt to represent the totality of history—a totality that we can never experience and can never describe, but within which we must understand ourselves—as a free, norm-directed activity seeking to realize a supreme end. We are hardly surprised to find Tillich asserting that as the metaphysics of history addresses itself to the foundations of human activity, it bridges the gap between the theoretical interest of the spirit in understanding the universe and its practical interest in shaping it.

> But both the metaphysics of being and the metaphysics of history[118] unite in the investigation of the universal process, in which the contrast between the intention of meaning and meaning-fulfillment is also conquered. Only the union of the two creates the ultimate, highest symbol of the Unconditioned, the ideal unity of the elements of meaning, a unity that is both the goal and the ground of all being and becoming. . . . Metaphysics can be called the doctrine of world views. But if we use this term, we must divest it of everything suggesting subjective opinion or scientific hypothesis. If "world view" is to be the concept

---

[116]Ibid., 184. We have here a clue to the foundations of Tillich's later development of a theory of symbolism that plays a central role in his mature writings.

[117]See ibid., 186–87, 202.

[118]Although here Tillich discusses both metaphysics, his ensuing discussion indicates that it is primarily the metaphysics of history in which he is interested. Whoever had traversed the course of the Kantian critique had already learned to expect that any attempt at a philosophy of history would have to overcome the duality of nature and freedom, of theory and praxis. Here, too, Tillich is true to his Kantian self.

that combines metaphysics and ethics, or the theoretical and the practical attitude toward the Unconditioned, then it is the fundamental act of spirit as such. It is the foundation of all theoretical and practical functions, and it contains the unconditioned seriousness and the unconditioned responsibility that are appropriate to directedness toward the Unconditioned.[119]

The procedure of knowledge in metaphysics is the intuition of the unconditioned import within the conditioned forms; this method was called the "contemplation of the *coincidentia oppositorum*" in Renaissance philosophy, and it is essential to the metaphysical procedure. Concepts such as "intellectual contemplation," "pure intuition," comprehension of "the absolute identity" and of "the paradox" express the *method of coincidence*. But we must emphasize that these concepts describe the metaphysical method, not a scientific method; they are fatally misunderstood when the independence of the metaphysical function and its forms of expression is not recognized.[120]

The metaphysics of history is therefore that point within the human sciences in which the theoretical and the practical are indissolubly connected.[121]

History, according to Tillich, provides the arena in which the spirit's creative activity is realized. As the theoretical activity of the spirit (the attempt of the spirit to assimilate itself to being) addresses itself to history, it addresses itself to products of the spirit's practical activity. It seeks to apprehend the unconditioned end of the practical activity of the spirit within a unified conception of the cosmos. We should not be surprised to learn that Tillich assigns the task of formulating this unified conception of the cosmos for all the culture, not to the scientist or the philosopher whose orientation is primarily autonomous, but to the theologian. I shall have more to say on the role of theology in the conclusion of this chapter.

---

[119]Ibid., 186.
[120]Ibid., 187.
[121]Ibid., 202.

Having followed Tillich's development of the proposed structure of
the sciences and seen how closely it corresponds to Kant's intentions
in the *Third Critique* but develops them further, we are adequately
prepared for Tillich's bold declaration that in the metaphysics of history the foundations are laid for a unified world view in which the
unity of metaphysics and ethics can be represented. It is just such a
world view that Tillich projects as the highest possible achievement
of metaphysics. He gives it the pretentious name "metaphysics of the
absolute idea."[122]

In his brief outline Tillich did not explain how the unity of theory
and praxis can be achieved. In light of our previous discussion of
Kant's corresponding attempts, we can only suggest what Tillich might
have had in mind. I can find his suggestion intelligible only if he
suggests we think of the unconditioned ideal which motivates and
directs ethical activity, as an immanent idea which pervades the cosmos.[123] If this is what he means, then he is clearly echoing the Kantian
notion of the supernatural substrate of reality, thought about which
unites the lawfulness of nature and the purposiveness of freedom. As
we may recall, the contemplative thought about this supersensible
substrate and about the Highest Good as its inherent principle constitutes Kant's solution to the problem of unity. There is some confirmation for this interpretation of Tillich's text in his brief comments on
ethos, which he considers the practical analogue to metaphysics. Here
he seems to maintain that at the point where metaphysics and ethos
meet, in the metaphysics of history, metaphysics represents their shared
content, the unconditioned, through the symbol of "is," while ethos
represents it through the symbol of "ought."[124] Ethics tries to represent the shared content through the symbol of "ought" as an unconditioned end of human action. Like metaphysics, ethics is limited to
symbolic representation of its apprehension; it cannot translate it into
a set of practical rules or a program for an utopia. The significance

[122]See ibid., 186.
[123]Were it not for Kant's *Third Critique*, this idea would have been identified as Hegelian. We are now aware of the special Kantian meaning it can
have.
[124]Tillich, *The System of the Sciences*, 202.

of the ethical awareness for the practical life is found in its ability to inform our formal structures of practical obligation and infuse into them a realization of the end toward which they are directed. Tillich's notion of ethical awareness with its peculiar mode of expression, piety, serves a similar practical function to the Kantian conception of the Highest Good in its relation to the moral law.

7.C.4.c. Religious Awareness

Having examined Tillich's delineation of the system of the sciences, noting the place of the theonomous attitude within its structure and the realization of its requirements in metaphysics, we are in a position to understand his claim that religion is not a distinct realm of meaning beside others, but an attitude within all of them. Tillich calls this attitude theonomy, and its goal a systematics. We learned that the role of metaphysics, and of the theonomous attitude that motivates it, is to secure a conviction that the meaning that the spirit finds exhibited in the particularity of things and events is unconditionally valid. It is then this attitude, together with the desire of the spirit to fulfill its requirement, that constitutes the essence of religion, according to Tillich.

A religious awareness is, accordingly, an awareness of the unconditioned ground of our cultural constructions, and it appears as a demand within the autonomous functions of science and philosophy and of law and communal life as a demand to relate their constructive activity to their unconditioned import. Religion appears within culture as a demand that culture become aware of its own significance, that it become aware that its constructions are discoveries, and that its ideals conform to the end of history. In essence, the demand of religion is an exhortation against the hubris of the spirit, which closes its eyes to its relation to the unconditioned ground of meaning and imagines itself as imposing its forms and ideals on a reality that is otherwise absurd and meaningless.[125]

In its practical aspect, religion represents its comprehension of the unconditioned meaning as an absolute "ought," as a captivating ideal to realize a life of "blessedness" or to bring about "a kingdom of God

[125]See Tillich, *What is Religion?* 74–76.

on earth."[126] These symbols serve to express the significance that ethos finds in our communal relations and in our moral legislations. It is the task of the theologian to produce these symbols and to interpret them for the community, so that through them the community will see its communal and moral obligations as directed toward a best possible world. Theology, as ethos, supports this understanding with an alluring image of what such a world must be like and what it is for a moral agent to strive to bring it about. It is an image of an absolute achievement, and as such it is a critical pole against which every actual achievement must be evaluated and of which it must inevitably fall short. Thus, religion may never be a sanctification of any existing social organization but always a critical voice that points the way toward further improvement.[127] Like metaphysics, ethos depends for its concepts on autonomous rational constructs. Ethos cannot interfere with the autonomous legislation of law and community, on the significance of which it reflects and from which it derives its concepts. Just as metaphysics cannot become a science, ethos cannot pretend to replace morality and law.[128]

The System of the Sciences enables us, furthermore, to account for Tillich's persistent antifanaticism. Tillich insists throughout his writings that religion is not an independent function of the spirit but intrinsically dependent on the autonomous functions and supportive of them. This claim, the implications of which are elaborated in Tillich's various works, finds its systematic justification in his discussion of the structure of meaning that we examined above.[129]

We recall that in his discussion of the logical structure of meaningfulness, Tillich identified "meaning" as the function of the inter-

[126]See Tillich, *The System of the Sciences*, 202.

[127]This, in essence, is Tillich's response to Barthianism, and this is the background that explains Tillich's discussion of religion as the awareness of the abyss of reality.

[128]See ibid., 202–3. This delineation of the logical status of ethos according to the structure of meaning of the human sciences provides the foundation for Tillich's claim in his later writings that theonomy does not violate the autonomy of the moral law. I shall address this issue in the conclusions of this chapter.

[129]See ibid., 210–15.

relatedness of three elements: history, philosophy, and systematics. Of the first two elements, Tillich said that although they are dependent on systematic insights to direct them intuitively or consciously in their constructive autonomous efforts, they can function as independent projects. Of systematics, however, he said that it cannot possibly be an independent insight into the essence of being, for the spirit is incapable of intellectual intuition or of mystical penetration into the mysteries of "the beyond."

Systematics achieves its goal in the discovery of the meaning of the autonomous constructs of the spirit, through its ability to see that the creations of the spirit fit what Tillich calls "the import of meaning." I understand this as a recognition that the theoretical constructs of the spirit reflect a structure of reality that is independent of them.[130] For this reason, I believe, Tillich considers the spiritual attitude that manifests itself in systematics religious. The theonomous attitude realizes that the spirit encounters a given reality that it did not create. Since the function of metaphysics, as a religious attitude of the spirit, is to reflect on the autonomous functions and to discern the unconditioned meaning they express, metaphysics is intrinsically dependent on the autonomous functions of the spirit and cannot replace them. Understood in this way, religion can never dictate to science, philosophy, or morality.[131] What religion can do is to ascertain the meaning of our philosophical, scientific, and moral activities in the total context of our world view. This reflective understanding may then function as regulative ideas which guide the sciences in determining their interests. It is in this way only that religion penetrates the autono-

---

[130]Tillich clearly does not think that we have a capacity for intellectual intuition of a mind-independent reality. Like Kant, he believes that our knowledge is dependent on the conceptual constructs of reason. I think we have to understand him as saying that we can judge reflectively that there is an affinity between the autonomous constructs of the spirit and the import of meaning, but we cannot go beyond this reflective judgment to know directly the meaning of things-in-themselves. In this view of the role of systematics I find a resemblance to Kant's theory of reflective judgment regarding the supersensible substrate of reality.

[131]This view is elaborated in *The System of the Sciences*. See also Tillich, *Systematic Theology*, 1. 12, 26, 28, 130–31, 147–50; and 3. 187–88.

mous realms of culture. Any attempt of religion to replace science in informing us of what the world is like or to replace morality in directing our actions would be a heteronomous abdication of its theonomous responsibility. It would lead, Tillich says, to a pseudo-scientific metaphysics, and to an arid moral formalism.

Being reflective and synthetic, metaphysics must reflect on the best scientific theory that we have at any given time and on the best moral system that we are capable of developing. It is impossible, therefore, for metaphysics to absolutize and sanctify a theory or an ethical norm that has been invalidated by rational criticism.[132] It is the inevitable task of metaphysics to follow closely upon the footsteps of the process of culture and to provide its reflective services at every junction. Metaphysics, like science, is an ongoing process. Should metaphysics or ethos attempt to overstep their bounds and to dictate scientific theories or moral laws they would cease to be reflective, become dogmatic, and destroy themselves as they destroy science and morality.[133]

In my presentation of Tillich's views on these issues I have distanced myself as much as possible from Tillich's difficult language. I tried to present his views (as I understand them) according to my understanding of their internal logic. This being done, it is important to see how these ideas are expressed in Tillich's text. Tillich's ideas regarding the nature of religion and its relation to various realms of meaning are given their best formulation in the following quotations:

> Theonomy is a turning toward the Unconditioned for the sake of the Unconditioned. The autonomous spiritual attitude is directed toward the conditioned, and toward the Unconditioned only in order to support the conditioned; theonomy employs conditioned forms in order to grasp the Unconditioned in them. *Theonomy*

---

[132]This insight is the foundation of Tillich's rejection of what he calls heteronomous religion; a religion which gives the historical and the relative absolute value.

[133]This is the foundation of Tillich's assertion that separate "religious science" and "religious ethics" are signs of the decline of culture. See Tillich, *Theology of Culture*, 42; and also idem, *Systematic Theology*, 1. 79–80, 218; 3. 97, 403; and idem, *The System of the Sciences*, 212–15.

and autonomy are thus not different functions of meaning, but different directions of the same function. They do not stand in a simple opposition, but in a dialectical one: they are based upon the dialectic between the elements of meaning, thought and being.[134]

> Theonomy, the orientation of all forms toward the Unconditioned, can be realized only within forms that are subject to the law of form and thus tend toward autonomy; autonomy cannot be directed to forms without grasping the import they express and thus without the theonomous element.
>
> There is a conflict between the two elements when theonomy sanctifies and preserves forms that contradict the consciousness of validity and when autonomy rationalizes symbols that express import, either establishing or opposing them, When this happens, theonomy becomes heteronomous: it creates one particular function alongside the others, religion, which, by virtue of its inherent unconditionality, violates and suppresses the others. And autonomy becomes secular: it creates culture, or the totality of meaning-fulfillment outside religion. Thus we have the great, irresolvable *conflicts between religion and culture*, between ecclesiastical and secular metaphysics and ethics, and so on. But this situation is inherently unsound, for it creates two independent functions of meaning from the necessary tension between the elements of meaning, leading to the destruction of both functions. Religion gives unconditioned validity to the conditioned forms of expression within the autonomous process,[135] and culture rationalizes the symbols of the Unconditioned, depriving them of their meaning and essence.[136]

When Tillich says that religion is the depth dimension in every realm of culture what he means is that religion is an awareness, within morality, that the autonomous laws of the spirit are not merely arbi-

---

[134]Tillich, *The System of the Sciences*, 203.

[135]Here I correct Wiebe's translation, which reads, "Religion gives unconditioned validity to the unconditioned forms. . . " The German text ("Das System der Wissenschaften," 272–73), as well as the context, demands the correction.

[136]Tillich, *The System of the Sciences*, 204. Tillich argues that this causes a bifurcation that disrupts the unity of spiritual life (p. 207).

trary constructs but the rules that should lead to the realization of the "kingdom of God on earth," and within science, that the theoretical constructs of explanation are not merely arbitrary hypothetical impositions, but attempts to discover the structure of reality. Morality and science can only understand their activity as such with the reflective help of the theonomous consciousness.

7.C.4.d. Constructivism and Knowledge

I would suggest that Tillich's notion of the will to the unconditioned, which informs his idea of religion, is best understood as an expression of a problem that is inherent to many constructivist accounts of reason—a problem of which Kant was acutely aware. Whoever holds that we have no intellectual intuition by which to apprehend mind-independent objects is led to explain experience through ingenious creation of theories. No theory captures the fullness of experience, nor is any theory necessarily unique. Facing a variety of theoretical alternatives, or even one theoretical construct that cannot be shown to be unique, we are forced to evaluate the adequacy of the theories not by their claims to validity (since theories may have conflicting claims to validity), but by appeal to our deepest intuitions about their subject matter or their worth for our lives. The necessity of such an appeal informs the recognition in the philosophy of science of the role aesthetic considerations play in the acceptability of scientific theories. It is through such reflective appeals to intuition that many find Kantian deontology more true to the essence of morality than its utilitarian rivals. Nothing in all of this suggests that appeals to intuition could ever generate a Kantian conception of the moral law; what it does suggest is that the final ground of acceptability of a Kantian construction is our intuitive acceptance or denial of its adequacy. Tillich's notion of metaphysics reflects his demand that we find an adequate mode of discourse to account for our reflective intuition and to express it. In Kantian terms, we may say that Tillich's notion of the will to the unconditioned is an expression of the unwillingness of Reason to rest upon "as if" constructions of the structure of experience and its recognition of the need to go beyond such a construction to a contemplative grounding of it in the unconditioned. I see Tillich's portrayal of religion as embodying the realization both of this demand and of the attempt to satisfy it, that is, a further development of Kant's suggestion that the critique of Judgment culminates at the point where philosophical theology and religion begin.

■ 7.D. Concluding Reflections

7.D.1. Religion and Reason

From a very special point of view, according to Tillich, the human spirit presents itself to us as religious. It appears as interested not merely in exercising its powers to fashion a world to its needs, but in relating itself to the ultimate meaning of reality.[137] From this special perspective we realize that the religiosity of the spirit is not a special function of our spiritual life, but the dimension of depth in all of its functions.[138]

We are capable of attaining this perspective only when we recognize that reason is not merely a mirror of reality, but a source of meaning, structure, norms, and principles. The religiosity of the spirit must elude us if we limit ourselves to a technical-pragmatic conception of reason as an instrument for controlling our environment.[139] To such a conception of reason, religion must appear alien. Tillich thinks that we find rivalry between faith and reason only when we adopt the technical conception of reason: when we limit reason to scientific method and to technical calculation. When this happens religion becomes an external power, seeking to control and direct the activities of a subservient reason. If religion understands itself and its relations to reason in this way, it becomes heteronomous. When we come to see reason as free and creative and identify it with our humanity, we

---

[137]Tillich frequently prefers not to use the term "God" to describe the spirit's religious attitude. He would later explain that the word "God" is but one historical symbolization of the spirit's recognition of an ultimate reality, a symbol that has been dangerously literalized and personified. He would come to speak of a "ground of being" and of "an object of ultimate concern."

[138]See Tillich, *Theology of Culture*, 5–6.

[139]For discussion of the two conceptions of reason, see Tillich, *Systematic Theology*, 1. 71–75. In this discussion Tillich develops his notion of "ontological reason" and argues (1. 82) that Kant developed a similar notion of "ontological reason" in the *Third Critique*.

must oppose a heteronomous religion. We realize that if faith were the opposite of reason, religion would tend to dehumanize us and eventually destroy itself.[140]

When we adopt a normative and creative conception of reason and identify the religious attitude of the spirit, we find, Tillich claims, that religion does not stand alongside the theoretical and practical functions, cannot be confined to any one particular function, but finds expression in and through them. Tillich identifies religion with the search for unconditional significance and validity.[141] He sees as religious the demand to believe that the laws of theoretical reason and the ends of practical reason reflect the structure of a reality they did not create; and defines "religion" as the directedness of reason which searches for this unconditioned meaning. From the perspective of such an understanding of religion, he believes, we inevitably recognize the intrinsic interdependence of religion and culture. We realize that religion does not provide alternative principles and does not require that we hold standards of "double truths." There is no room for separate "religious ethics," "religious science," or "religious aesthetics." Rather, religion is actualized in all spheres of spiritual or cultural life.

To explore the religious dimension of our life we must, therefore, direct our attention to the various realms of culture. We should attempt to detect a "special circle, a special sphere of influence of 'the religious.'"[142] We should focus on that directedness of reason which searches for the unconditional, for the ultimate ground of the meaning of the constructs of reason. The directedness of reason, Tillich suggests, is manifest and actualized in a special religious-cultural sphere of meaning. It is expressed in religious perception—myth or dogma; in a sphere of religious aesthetics—the cultus; in a sphere of religious molding of the person—sanctification; and in a religious form of society—such as the church with its special canon law and communal

---

[140]See Tillich, *Dynamics of Faith*, 74–76.

[141]See Tillich, *What is Religion?* 142–43, 160–61.

[142]Ibid., 161. For discussion of moral theonomy, see idem, *Systematic Theology*, 3. 157–60, 204–12, 267–75, 402. For discussion of cognitive theonomy, see 3. 201–4, and 253–55. For discussion of theonomous aesthetics, see 3. 196–201, 256–57.

ethics.[143] Tillich claims that this view of the religious dimension of culture enables him to preserve both the autonomy of science, morality, and art and the distinctness of religion.[144] I shall now say a word in evaluation of his claim.

7.D.1.a. Is Theonomy Heteronomy in Disguise?

In the introduction to this chapter, I expressed the hope that an understanding of Tillich's theory of theonomy as a "depth dimension" of the spirit would help us to determine whether indeed theonomy can be a third alternative to autonomy and heteronomy. It is time now to see if what we have learned from *The System of the Sciences* brings us closer to an answer.

When we reflect on Tillich's picture of religion as the depth dimension of culture we must ask ourselves whether, from the point of view of culture, Tillich's theonomy should be suspected of being a Trojan horse. We should inquire, especially from a Kantian point of view, whether theonomy is not actually heteronomy in disguise. To what exactly, we should ask, does Tillich's "special circle of religious influence" amount? What, for instance, is its status in the moral realm?

Looking, for example, at the alleged religious-ethical sphere of meaning, we should ask whether it might not be just another manifestation of heteronomous religion that aims to subject the moral imperative to the alien authority of God's revelation. Tillich would like to say:

> I maintain my basic assertion that the unconditional character of the moral imperative is its religious quality. No religious heteronomy, subjection to external command, is implied if we maintain the immanence of religion in the moral command.[145]

---

[143]See Tillich, *What is Religion?* 161.

[144]See ibid., 162–63.

[145]Paul Tillich, *Morality and Beyond: Religious Perspectives* (New York: Harper & Row, 1963) 25. See also the discussion of theonomy in idem, *Systematic Theology*, 1. 85, 147–50; 3. 249–52, 266–75.

But do we find his assertion convincing? Does theonomy not crush the proud moral agent whose dignity arises from the determination that she will obey no law that she has not set herself?

A challenge to Tillich's claim to have distinguished theonomy from heteronomy can be found in Victor L. Nuovo's criticism of Tillich's religious morality.[146] His critique, I believe, ultimately fails, but it provides an excellent example of the pitfalls awaiting all who attempt to understand Tillich on merely the basis of Kant's analytical works. I suggest that having been profoundly impressed by the heroic self-sufficiency of duty determined by reason alone, one cannot but suspect that Tillich's demand that the Categorical Imperative be supplemented by the theonomous consciousness is at best a misunderstanding of Kant's view of morality (in the *Grounding* and in the "Analytic" of the *Second Critique*), and at worst a perversion of it in the interest of religious apologetics. Nuovo's argument is typical of such an approach. Rather than interpret Tillich as building upon Kant's ethical philosophy, as we have come to know it in the previous chapters, Nuovo sees Tillich as attacking Kantian morality as formal and empty.[147] Consequently, Nuovo concludes:

> Tillich chose to subordinate morality to religion, claiming that the rational form of morality had to be filled with religious substance. But Tillich's argument is based upon a misunderstanding of Kant's ethical formalism. If, as I have argued, autonomous reason does not empty itself of content and substance by following its own laws, then to impose a theonomous norm upon it is heteronomous.[148]

---

[146]Victor L. Nuovo, "On Revising Tillich: An Essay on the Principles of Theology," in John J. Carey, ed., *Kairos and Logos: Studies in the Roots and Implications of Tillich's Theology* (Macon, GA: Mercer University Press, 1984) 37–61.

[147]Nuovo may have understood Tillich's critique of moral formalism as a reiteration of Hegel's claim that Kant's Categorical Imperative is formal and empty.

[148]Ibid., 60.

Our analysis of Kant in the previous chapters allows us to observe that the misunderstanding of Kant's ethics is totally Nuovo's. An understanding of Kant's ethics, based on the ideas of his impressive short work the *Grounding*, is quite common but inexcusable. The *Grounding*, like the analytic of the *Second Critique*, seeks the supreme principle of morality, which it finds in the Categorical Imperative. When the *Grounding* is not supplemented by the two parts of the *Second Critique*, it may create the erroneous impression that the supreme principle of determining whether maxims are right or wrong is the whole of morality and that morality is purely a matter of reason. It is with this in mind, I believe, that Nuovo seeks to defend Kant against the charge of "empty formalism," by interpreting the applicability of the laws of duty through use of the alien model of the Schematism of the *First Critique*.

> What the categorical imperative states is that moral duty cannot be based upon the particular interest of a rational being or of a community of rational beings, and that duty's incentive is always itself. By means of this rule we can determine in whatever situation what is or what is not rightfully our duty. *Rather than driving out content, the rules of moral duty acting through the imagination are likely to bring to mind a manifold of possible uses.* This is just the power of a formal principle when it is properly understood.[149]

The picture of duty that underlies these remarks portrays the Categorical Imperative as a supreme category from which specific general duties are derived, duties which the imaginative moral agent must find ways of implementing in his or her life. It is a picture of moral duty being imposed on our life purely from above, from the legislation of reason alone. It is, however, a misleading picture. Its image of Kantian morality is of a detached speculative exercise of deriving duties a priori from a first principle. This is hardly what Kant envisaged or described.

[149]Ibid., 51. Emphasis mine.

If the Categorical Imperative is not empty, it is not because laws of duty can be derived from it speculatively, but because it can be used to evaluate the rational acceptability of maxims of conduct suggested to the will by a previously determined evaluative structure, be it the structure of natural desires, political custom, or social goods. Rather than determine values, the Categorical Imperative presupposes a premoral valuation to the validation or invalidation of which it applies itself. Furthermore, while the recognition of duty may suffice to determine the will, it is not the sole ground of moral motivation.[150] This insight is expressed in Kant's discussion of the Highest Good as the object and end of morality. On the basis of his narrow picture of Kant's ethics, however, Nuovo argues that

> there is a parallel between Tillich's conception of the criterion of theology and the categorical imperative. The categorical imperative expresses the formality of the moral law, its universality and unconditionality.[151] Tillich rejects the categorical imperative as the sole principle of morality. He argues that because it is formal and lacks specific content, it has no concrete use. It must be supplemented by ethos, the immediate felt-values of a community, and it must be filled with love. But this is a mistaken view of the categorical imperative.[152]

If what I have been arguing so far is true, Tillich made no mistake here. According to the more complete picture of Kant's ethics—the picture generated by the Dialectic of the *Second Critique*, the *Third Critique*, and *Religion within the Limits of Reason Alone* (when

---

[150]A similar interpretation of Kant has come to play an important role in John Rawls's influential *A Theory of Justice* (Cambridge, MA: Harvard University Press, 1971), as well as in his later works. Systematic support for my reading, as opposed to Nuovo's, is to be found in the important work of Onora O'neill (see, for example, *Constructions of Reason* [Cambridge: Cambridge University Press, 1989] chap. 8]).

[151]I regard this assertion as an imprecise presentation of Kant's theory. The Categorical Imperative does not express the formality and universality of the moral law; it is formal and universal.

[152]Nuovo, "On Revising Tillich," 51.

it is interpreted in light of the previous two), and which a careful reading will observe also in the *Grounding*—the Categorical Imperative serves the moral agent to steer a right course in the pursuit of a conception of the good, the good being the ultimate end of the agent's actions. When Tillich supplements the pure formality of the categorical imperative with a value system, he does no more than echo Kant's own understanding of the moral life. I suggest that this is the understanding that underlies Tillich's following question:

> Can the commanding law, which presupposes the contrast between our essential and our actual being, motivate us to transform ourselves in the direction of reuniting the actual with the essential?[153]

Tillich's answer to this rhetorical question is that:

> It is not the moral imperative in its commanding majesty and strangeness that is morally motivating, but the driving or attracting power of that which is the goal of the moral command—the good.[154]

Nuovo's "Kantian" critique of Tillich's idea of theonomy as heteronomy in disguise fails because it misrepresents some elements of Kant's theory and ignores others. The Kantian defense, which we were able to provide for Tillich's theonomy, however, does not suffice to answer our initial question whether theonomy does not crush the self-legislating dignity of the autonomous moral agent by proclaiming that the moral law expresses the "import of meaning." Nuovo's critique may be misguided in part, but it may be correct in what seems to be its underlying insight: Will the heroic dignity of the Kantian good not be negated by the theonomous consciousness? If this is the case then should our question not be addressed not only to Tillich but also to Kant? It is, after all, Kant's Reflective Judgment

---

[153]Tillich, *Morality and Beyond*, 50–51.
[154]Ibid., 60; see also 25, 47, 50; and Tillich, *Theology of Culture*, 136–37.

that taught us that the law the moral agent thought she had set herself is indeed a law that determines the course of history, a law set by the archetypal thought of the moral designer of the universe.

In trying to answer the question, we need to assess the precise relations between theonomy and autonomy. We recall that according to Tillich theonomy is of necessity dependent on autonomy. What this dependence means is that theonomy has no cognitions that are not dependent on science and morality. As theonomy reflects on the autonomous constructions and provides them final validity, it does not become an additional source of theoretical or practical cognitions. Under theonomy there is no duty that is not a moral duty, and there is no knowledge that is not scientific. As far as content is concerned, theonomy does not seem to infringe on autonomy.

Even if there is in fact no theonomous knowledge that is not also autonomous, theonomy may be tempted to claim, condescendingly, that reason is capable of discovering on its own what religion or revelation had known all along to be true. This is a presumption of theonomy that Tillich does not allow. His theonomous consciousness aspires to maintain a delicate balance. It confirms the validity of conclusions of our autonomous faculties without presuming to be able to take their place. If theonomy were to make the latter claim it would become heteronomous and put itself in an independent position that would allow it to attempt to dictate to science, morality, and art. When theonomy limits itself to reflection on the autonomous functions of the spirit it recognizes autonomy as the exclusive source of valid cognitions, even as it provides them final confirmation.

The balance Tillich expects of theonomy appears fragile; it seems to involve a (quasi-) paradoxical recognition of dependent superiority. Theonomy is dependent on autonomy for content even as it passes final judgment on autonomous constructs. Tillich seems to think that the balance is stabilized and sheds its paradoxical aura when we recognize that we are dealing with two distinct senses of validity: internal and external. Autonomous morality seeks internal coherence through valid applications of its rules of practical deliberation. Theonomy is only indirectly concerned with specific practical decisions; it addresses itself primarily to the autonomous project of morality itself. Theonomy bestows external confirmation on morality when, according to Tillich, it relates the formal application of the Categorical Imperative to the ideal of the good. Tillich clearly follows here upon the footsteps of Kant as he related the supreme principle of morality to the quest for the Highest Good which is itself an a priori ideal of Reason.

Where does Tillich's presumed distinction leave us? Recalling our earlier discussion of the logical status of contemplative hope in Kant's thought and its conception of the Highest Good as a means by which to overcome moral paralysis, we may suggest that, according to Tillich, whenever a situation arises which calls for practical deliberation, the religious-moral agent reaches a decision solely on the basis of the autonomous moral law. This agent, however, follows the law out of theonomous understanding of the meaning of morality and of its value in pursuit of the ultimate good. Tillich's religious-moral agent may thus escape the criticism that is often directed toward Kantian morality, namely, that mere conformity to the form of a law is a rationalistic subversion of moral goodness.

Tillich presents then a picture of religious morality in which the theonomous agent is never released from the duty to reach an autonomous moral decision because a religious tradition has already determined what ought to be done. Yet, even so, we might ask, does not theonomy, or contemplative hope, inform the agent that in legislating the moral law the agent is in fact obeying the primordial law that governs history, and does this recognition not nullify the autonomy of moral agency? Does contemplative hope not offer the agent an incentive to obey the law for other reasons than respect for its autonomous majesty? No conclusive answer to this question will be possible without a thorough analysis of the nature of moral agency that is far beyond the scope of this study. Suffice it then to suggest briefly that an answer may be found in an internal tension in the conception of the good will in Kant's moral philosophy.

In trying to determine what it is for the will to have moral worth and to be autonomous, we find that a minimalist answer can be given as well as a maximalist. The difference between them may prove relevant to our inquiry. Minimally, we may suggest, a will is autonomous when it recognizes the Categorical Imperative as a fact of Pure Reason and finds it authoritative for itself. It should make no difference then if the Categorical Imperative happens to inform the will of an omnipotent ruler of cosmic history. Alternately, the autonomy may reside in the dignity of a will that decides to obey only a law it has set itself. The dignity of such a will may be shattered when it learns that the moral law it has legislated is merely a reflection of the hidden structure of history. This last conception of autonomy, which can certainly be found in Kant's moral writings and has contributed to their wide appeal, cannot be accommodated by Tillich's theonomy. Yet it is far from clear that this inability does Tillich's theory much harm. It is, after all, a view of autonomy that conflicts with Kant's own contemplative thought, a view which Tillich would most likely ascribe merely to the hubris of the spirit. Upon reflection we too may come to see it as belonging more to a Nietzschean pride than to a requirement of moral worth.

Tillich is not yet in the clear, however, for even the minimal conception of autonomy may still be problematic. For Tillich as for Kant, theonomy or contemplative hope are intended to lend support to the will by making duty meaningful, without tampering with the ground of duty. Kant, we may recall, was fearful lest belief in the Highest Good would reintroduce incentives into the determination of the will and thereby nullify its moral worth. Does not faith that the moral law is indeed the hidden law of history, or the "import of meaning," have the same effect? Does not belief that the moral law is the means by which the cunning of history secures the Highest Good provide strong incentive to act morally? Even a contemplative thought (less than a theonomous conviction?) to that effect, which does not amount to knowledge, is supposed to help us overcome moral despair.

We need perhaps to distinguish here between a moral determination of the will, which must remain autonomously pure, and a psychological ability to act on our moral decisions regardless of consequences. If such a distinction can be upheld, then theonomy or contemplative hope can address themselves to the agent after he or she has reached a moral decision about what ought to be done.[155]

---

[155]For discussion of Kant's own distinction between intelligible and empirical action see part one, section 4.A.1 n. 5.

They could then comfort the agent by promising that moral action is not absurdly heroic because it is in line with the true course of history. There are reasons to accept the distinction as well as to reject it, and both can be found in Kant. In the *Grounding* Kant seems to have thought that no attitude of the will can be considered a genuine decision if it does not involve doing all we can to carry it out.[156] Inability to act on a determination of the will by the moral law due to moral despair would seem then to render the determination a mere wish. If contemplative hope is psychologically required to make a genuine decision possible, then contemplative hope becomes part of the decision and cannot claim not to effect the moral determination of the will. In his later work, especially in *Religion within the Limits of Reason Alone*, Kant seems to have held a less rigorous view. In his discussion of evil and of moral education he was willing to distinguish between deciding what ought to be done and being motivated enough to overcome natural inclinations to the contrary. It is only according to this later view that contemplative hope can lend moral assistance without infringing on the autonomy of the good will.

If we are willing to distinguish in moral action between recognizing something as a duty and being motivated to act according to this recognition, we may have a way of understanding theonomy as supplementing autonomy without infringing upon it. If the notion of the Highest Good provides a vision of the end of the moral law that can motivate the agent to act on duty, it does so as a reflective contemplation which follows our autonomous determination of duty and does

---

[156]Kant distinguishes between a mere wish which involves an awareness of what ought to be done and a genuine moral decision which requires serious effort to carry it out. In the first part of the *Grounding* (pp. 7–8/394) he writes: "Even if, by some especially unfortunate fate or by the niggardly provision of stepmotherly nature, this will should wholly lacking in the power to accomplish its purpose, if with the greatest effort it should yet achieve nothing, and only the good-will should remain (not, to be sure, as a mere wish, but as the summoning of all the means in our power), yet would it, like a jewel, still shine by its own light as something which has its full value in itself."

not enter our practical deliberations.[157] The same should hold for Tillich's theonomy. Even if we accept the distinction between decision and sufficient motivation for action and allow for additional motivation from contemplative sources, we may wonder whether Kant's Highest Good and Tillich's "import of meaning" are the only options we have for overcoming moral paralysis and for rescuing the moral law from shallow formalism. I shall return to this question in the next chapter.

7.D.2. Two Concepts of Religion

The *System of the Sciences* puts forth a concept of religion, similar to that of Kant, according to which human religiosity is an expression both of the unwillingness of reason to rest upon hypothetical constructions of the world that it generates freely of itself and of its recognition of a need to go beyond such autonomous constructions to ground them contemplatively in an unconditioned. This is an ideal concept of religion, a concept of a pure religion of the spirit. Like Kant, Tillich finds in this concept a criterion for the interpretation and the evaluation of historical manifestations of religion. He argues, again like Kant, that historical religion serves to train and to prepare the spirit to achieve the theonomous attitude.

In his mature writings, Tillich characterizes the theonomous attitude as faith. He defines faith as a state of "ultimate concern" and asserts that "faith as being ultimately concerned is a centered act of the whole personality."[158] Drawing a conclusion from his analysis of theonomy, Tillich contends that since faith is the centered act of the whole personality, if one of the functions that constitute the totality of the personality is partly or completely identified with faith, "the

---

[157]Compare my discussion of the role of Kant's *Religion within the Limits of Reason Alone* in part one, section 5.E.2.

[158]Tillich, *Dynamics of Faith*, 30. Tillich's discussion of ultimate concern and the unity of the personality suggests that religion may be able to offer a solution to the problems I analyzed in my introduction to Kant's quest for systematic unity.

meaning of faith is distorted."[159] In other words, ideally faith is the depth dimension that pervades the theoretical and the practical functions of the spirit and is their point of unity.[160] Tillich accordingly defines religion as "the aspect of depth in the totality of the human spirit,"[161] and explains this definition:

> What does the metaphor depth mean? It means that the religious aspect points to that which is ultimate, infinite, unconditional in man's spiritual life. Religion, in the largest and most basic sense of the word, is ultimate concern. And ultimate concern is manifest in all creative functions of the human spirit. It is manifest in the moral sphere as the unconditional seriousness of the moral demand. . . . Ultimate concern is manifest in the realm of knowledge as the passionate longing for ultimate reality. . . . Ultimate concern is manifest in the aesthetic function of the human spirit as the infinite desire to express ultimate meaning. . . . Religion is the substance, the ground, and the depth of man's spiritual life. This is the religious aspect of the human spirit.
>
> If religion is a state of being grasped by an ultimate concern, this state cannot be restricted to a special realm. The unconditional character of this concern implies that it refers to every moment of our life, to every space and every realm.[162]

> One could rightly say that the existence of religion as a special realm is the most conspicuous proof of man's fallen state. This does not mean that under the conditions of estrangement which determine our destiny the religious should be swallowed by the secular, as secularism desires, nor that the secular should be swallowed by the religious, as ecclesiastic imperialism desires. But it does mean that the inseparable division is a witness to our human predicament.[163]

[159]Ibid. See also the discussion of "ultimate concern" in Tillich, *Systematic Theology*, 1. 11–12, 211; 3. 130–34

[160]This view corresponds to Kant's theory of reflection in the *Third Critique*. As we remember, the reflective principle is not determinative of a distinct realm of experience.

[161]Tillich, *Theology of Culture*, 7.

[162]Ibid., 41.

[163]Ibid., 42. See also Tillich, *Systematic Theology*, 1. 79–80, 218; and 3. 97, 403.

In these quotations Tillich recapitulates the views he had previously expressed in more abstract terms in *The System of the Sciences*. He reiterates his conviction that the religious dimension of the human spirit must penetrate every dimension of culture. Religion cannot be confined to a particular realm of culture and cannot exist alongside other realms as an additional manifestation of human spirituality. Tillich recognizes, however, that as long as culture is not theonomous—as long as humans do not see in "the structures and laws of reality as they are present in the human mind expressions and manifestations of reality which is not structured by them," as long as the ultimate meaning of existence does not "shine through all finite forms of thought and action" which become "the vessels of spiritual content"—there is still a need for what we have called religion$_2$.[164]

Although Tillich regards religion$_2$ as a manifestation of the fallen situation of humanity, he believes that as long as culture is not totally theonomous, religion$_2$ plays a significant role in culture. It serves as a sign post and as a reminder, urging autonomous culture to acknowledge its theonomous substance.

> Religion [religion$_2$] opens up the depth of man's spiritual life which is usually covered by the dust of our daily life and noise of our secular work. It gives us the experience of the holy, of something which is untouchable, awe-inspiring, an ultimate meaning, the source of ultimate courage.[165]

Tillich distinguishes, accordingly, between a "large" and a "small" concept of religion.

> If religion [religion$_1$] is defined as a state of "being grasped by an ultimate concern". . . then we must distinguish this as a universal or large concept from our usual smaller concept of religion [religion$_2$] which supposes an organized group with its clergy, scriptures, and dogma, by which a set of symbols for the

---

[164]See Tillich, *The Protestant Era*, 44, xii.
[165]See Tillich, *Theology of Culture*, 7–9; and idem, *Systematic Theology*, 1. 80; and 3. 246.

ultimate concern is accepted and cultivated in life and thought.
This is religion [religion$_2$] in the narrower sense of the word,
while religion [religion$_1$] defined as "ultimate concern" is religion in the larger sense of the word.[166] . . . The ordinary concepts which we connect with the word religion are: entering a
temple, going to a church, belonging to a church sect or religious movement, and having particular symbols or ideas about
God, particular sacramental and ritual activities. All this is the
concern of religious groups. And when we speak of the world
religion, we usually think of these groups and what characterizes
them: their ideas and their practical and imaginary symbols. But
if we look deeper, we must say that religion is larger than this.
Religion—namely, an ultimate concern about the meaning of one's
life and the meaning of "being" as such—also appears in other
forms. It may appear in a painting which has no religious content in the traditional sense—the painting of a stone, or a por-
trait, or a scene, or clouds. Or it may appear in philosophy as
an ultimate concern through which the philosopher tries to understand reality. Or it may appear in a political idea.[167]

Tillich suggests that this twofold definition of religion can help as
a tool in the fight against heteronomy. He thinks that if we see in
religion$_2$ a historical manifestation of religion$_1$, a manifestation of the
theonomous attitude of the spirit, we can combat the tendency to
regard the particular and historically conditioned religion$_2$ as absolute.

This distinction of the larger concept provides us with a criterion by which to judge the concrete religions included under the
smaller, traditional concept. Specific religions are inherently
susceptible to criticism which keeps them alive or condemns
them to come to an end, if they cannot qualify under the power
of this ultimate principle.[168]

[166]Paul Tillich with D. Mackenzie Brown, *Ultimate Concern: Tillich in
Dialogue* (New York: Harper & Row, 1965).
[167]Ibid., 5–6. See also Paul Tillich, *My Search for Absolutes* (ed. Ruth
Nanda Anshen; Credo Perspectives; New York: Simon & Schuster, 1967)
125–28, 131–32.
[168]Tillich, *Ultimate Concern*, 4.

Relying on his distinction between religion$_1$ and religion$_2$ Tillich wishes to overcome the danger of heteronomy, of assigning absolute value to the relative manifestations of the spirit's quest for the ultimate ground of its creations. In his struggle against heteronomous tendencies which ignore the relativity of the cultural manifestations of religion$_1$ and accordingly ignore the intrinsic dependence of religion on culture, Tillich argues that the act of faith, like every act in our spiritual life, is dependent on language and therefore on culture. The religious language, the language of symbol and myth, the language which endows the act of faith with its concrete content, is culturally formed. For language is the basic cultural creation.[169]

> Against ecclesiastical heteronomy it is always possible to show that all the rites, doctrines, institutions, and symbols of a religious system constitute a religious culture which is derived from the surrounding general culture—from its social and economic structure, its character traits, its opinions and philosophy, its linguistic and artistic expressions, its complexes, its traumas, and its longings.[170]

If Tillich convinced us in his depiction of religion$_1$ and religion$_2$, then his theory poses an interesting challenge to the study of the humanities in general and to the science of religion in particular. This is a challenge to which I shall now turn.

7.D.3. Implications for the Science of Religion

Conclusions regarding the science of religion follow immediately from Tillich's theory of the human sciences, and he does not hesitate to draw them. He rejects both purely empirical and purely speculative approaches to religion. Tillich characterizes the empirical method as attempting to proceed from the religious function of the spirit and to deduce the essence of religion from the religious act, and the specu-

---

[169]See Tillich, *Dynamics of Faith*, 24; idem, *Theology of Culture*, 42; idem, *Systematic Theology*, 1. introduction, and 123; 3. 127–28, 187–88, 193, 196, 248–49.

[170]Tillich, *The Protestant Era*, 57.

lative approach as trying to determine the essence of religion from the object toward which the act itself is directed.[171] He considers the empirical science of religion a procedure that aims to abstract the essence of religion from individual phenomena through a consideration of the origin and formation of religion in an aspect of society, psychology, or the whole of history.[172] He supports his rejection of this approach by arguing that the empirical sciences must have at least an implicit notion of the essence of their object of inquiry, in order to prevent their abstraction of an essence from the range of phenomena they examine from being arbitrary.

The speculative approach assumes, according to Tillich, that the object of religion can be grasped independently of the religious attitude. Tillich accuses speculative metaphysics of attempting to establish the concept of religion by grasping the object of religion independently of the religious act and of using this concept to examine religious phenomena. Echoing Otto's notion of the interdependence of the cognitive and the emotive elements of the numinous consciousness, Tillich argues that the religious object can be grasped only by the religious act. He expresses this view in his famous theory that the object of ultimate concern is reachable only by the subject of ultimate concern in its act of ultimate concern.[173] Against detached speculative philosophy, Tillich contends that the Unconditional—that toward which metaphysics is directed—cannot be grasped other than in religious acts. We have seen that Tillich's ultimate rejection of independent speculation relies on his definition of metaphysics as "the religious act in which the Unconditional is grasped in theoretical and rational symbols."[174]

Tillich's considerations in *The System of the Sciences* pose a challenge to the academic study of religion and to the modern university. They imply that the humanities should address themselves to the his-

171Tillich, *What is Religion?* 40. The last comment is explicitly directed against Hegel.
172Ibid., 38.
173See Tillich, *Systematic Theology*, 1. 11–12, 211; 3. 130–34.
174Tillich, *What is Religion?* 40.

torical manifestations of the spirit's quest for synthetic unity in all realms of human activity (i.e., in all reams of meaning).[175] The university must also include a department of religion which should address itself to the particular traditional and historical manifestations of the theonomous consciousness. In other words, it should study religion$_2$ and must do so according to the methodology of the human sciences that follow the delineation of the structure of meaning. The study of religion should therefore include and relate to each other a comparative history of religion, a philosophy of religion, and a theology. These disciplines should observe the following guidelines:

> Any presentation of the cultural sciences contains three elements: a philosophy, a cultural history, and a systematics. In philosophy the particular sphere of meaning and its categories are articulated. In cultural history the material that the empirical sciences present is systematically understood and arranged. In systematics the concrete normative system is presented on the basis of the philosophical conception of the essence of the particular matter in hand and on the basis of the historical material understood in light of cultural-historical construction. Every genuine cultural science, consciously or unconsciously, proceeds in this threefold way. It proceeds from a universal function of the spirit and the forms through which objects are constituted therein. It then shows in a critical way the actualization of this essential function in the various directions of historical development. Finally, it gives its own systematic solution on the basis of the problems that are brought to the fore by the conceptualization of the essence of the being and by the cultural history. This threefold relationship. . . is evident in philosophy of religion,

---

[175]See Tillich, *The Protestant Era*, 58. Tillich conducted such a study in *The Religious Situation* (trans. H. Richard Niebuhr; New York: Holt, 1932) and in various articles. In these writings he examined the religious dimension in the various realms of culture. I find his approach to the religious analysis of art to be interesting. His argument, in a nutshell, is that an analysis of artistic creations as manifestation of theonomous consciousness must supplement the study of art through such disciplines as aesthetic assessment and historical analysis.

the cultural history of religion, and the systematic theory of
religion or theology.[176]

It should be the role of the comparative history of religion to
present the empirical manifestations of the spirit's drive for reflective
unity throughout history and in diverse cultures. It should be the role
of a philosophy of religion to identify the categories and the principles through which alone the spirit's quest for unity can be manifest
symbolically in historical activity. It should then be the role of theology to synthesize the autonomous formal and critical constructions
of philosophy with the empirical findings of the comparative history
of religion, to reach an understanding of the creative act of the spirit
in securing meaning and in representing it symbolically. If there is
any truth in Tillich's understanding of religion then there can be no
independent comparative history of religion. Likewise, an independent
philosophy of religion would be an exercise in futility. Above all,
Tillich's theory implies that a university that has no department of
religion, so conceived, will necessarily fall short of its task to achieve
the cognitive goal of the human sciences.

I would suggest that Tillich could rely on the tripartite division of
the science of religion in suggesting an interesting solution to the
traditional tension between philosophy of religion and theology, a
tension the solution of which is one of Tillich's primary goals. Once
Tillich presents philosophy and theology as two functions of the human
sciences, he can argue that the traditional rivalry between them should
be eliminated. Theology and philosophy should be regarded as two
interrelated disciplines of the human sciences which both rely on and
complete each other. Tillich makes such a point when he says that

> the task of philosophy of religion. . . is the theory of the reli-
> gious function and its categories. Theology is the normative and
> systematic presentation of the concrete realization of the concept
> of "religion." The cultural history of religion acts as a bridge
> between philosophy of religion and theology. It grasps critically
> the individual realizations of the concept of religion in history

[176]Tillich, *What is Religion?* 32–33.

and thereby leads on to a special systematic solution of its own (which can be the solution of a group, a "school," or a church.). . . . Thus philosophy of religion and theology are two elements of a single normative cultural science of religion. They belong inseparably together and are in continual interaction with each other and with the third element, the cultural history of religion.[177]

The inclusion of both theology and philosophy in the human sciences and the analysis of their interdependence provides Tillich with the solution that has been sought to the traditional rivalry between these two disciplines. This solution implies that ultimately every philosopher is also a theologian and that, conversely, every theologian must acknowledge the intrinsic dependence of the theological work on the philosophical enterprise. Theology has to confront philosophical criticism and cannot hide behind the shield of a theory of "double truth," and philosophy cannot dismiss as meaningless the theological search for ultimate meaning.

[177]Ibid., 33; see also 41–42, 157–58.

8 ⊠

RELIGION AND CONTEMPLATIVE
REFLECTION

M ajor efforts have been devoted throughout this study to an exposition of Kant's conception of religion as contemplative hope.
These efforts resulted in an interpretation of the *Third Critique* that
differs significantly from those commonly found in the literature on
Kant. We saw that the *Critique of Judgment* is a systematic confrontation of the problem of the unity of Reason and that Kant concludes
this endeavor by asserting that contemplation of the unity of nature
and freedom necessarily involves thought about God. We thus saw
that Kant's ideas about religion developed beyond his refutation of
proofs of the existence of God and beyond his moral argument which
limits the validity of rational faith to the practical sphere. In light of
this new understanding, I sought to reinterpret the work of Rudolf
Otto and Paul Tillich in which I found important elaborations of major
elements of Kant's challenging ideas. As a result of these efforts, my
study has portrayed a Kantian tradition in a philosophy of religion
that seeks to secure for religion an essential role in the economy of
reason.

The Kantian school argues that religion is a fundamental human propensity of unequaled cognitive and emotive value. It urges us to find a room for religion within reason and promises that religion can play a decisive role in the structure of consciousness. This claim is directed both against tendencies to seek the essence of true religiosity in a faith that is understood not as a human potential but as a divine gift and against explanations of religion as a by-product of social and psychological processes, a by-product that has, at best, instrumental value, or is, at worst, a superstitious survival. The Kantian school argues that the essence of religion is a distinct perspective on reality that cannot be attained by any other application of the intellect. It is a reflective assessment of the totality of our personality and of our life, a judgment that unifies our knowledge of what is and of what ought to be. Religion becomes, according to this school of thought, a point of view from which alone we are capable of reflecting on the totality of our personality, in its unity, beyond its excellences or failures in the various tasks to which we apply ourselves. It is important, I believe, for contemporary philosophy of religion and for theology to be aware of this tradition and to listen to what it has to say, since in many ways it responded to challenges very similar to those we face today.

In identifying the religious consciousness with a reflective awareness, this Kantian school takes an important step toward reuniting cognition and affectivity as inseparable elements of religious experience. This reflective unity of cognition and affectivity differs significantly from influential Wittgensteinian and empiricist approaches in contemporary philosophy of religion, each of which focuses exclusively on either religious affectivity or religious knowledge. The two contenders successfully pointed out each other's limitations but neither was capable of providing a comprehensive account of religious phenomena. The Kantian approach, I believe, points to the direction in which a future philosophy of religion may proceed in order to overcome the severe limitations of these influential approaches.

The thinkers we studied sought to redefine the relations between religion and reason. Their view can be seen as a radical alternative both to doctrines that proclaim the superiority of religion and to those that uphold the superiority of reason. They go beyond classical permissions for reason to speak on matters of religion as an interpreter of revelation. They even go beyond the more radical claim that religion and reason reach the same view of the world, though by different means. The Kantian philosophy of religion, which emerged from our study, goes beyond all these to characterize an identity between religion and reason, so that religious experience is essentially the highest possible insight of reason.[1] In identifying religious insights with reason, this Kantian school should not be understood as saying that religious insight is "merely" rational, but that profound rational insight is religious. They put forth not only a special conception of religion, but, perhaps more importantly, a special conception of reason.

The attempt to identify religion with reason sheds critical light on efforts to make religion immune to cultural criticism. Accounts of religions as an extrarational phenomenon can be found in the recent philosophical defense of faith as a distinct language game, if not a distinct form of life, and in claims to a special religious perception. These defensive measures resemble the attempts of theologians like Søren Kierkegaard and Karl Barth to secure a place for faith beyond the critical reach of theoretical and practical reasoning. Such defensive measures succeed at considerable spiritual, cultural, and social cost. While it professes support to communities of faith, this type of defense threatens, perhaps unwittingly, to free the dark forces of religious fanaticism and sectarian bigotry from the burden of justifying themselves before a common court of reason and before the claims of morality and science. Such dangers led thinkers of the Enlightenment to bring religion into the folds of reason, and our contemporary political and spiritual scene gives us reason again to listen to these voices from the Enlightenment to see if we can learn from their experience.

In the previous chapters I tried to show that the influential theories of religion of Rudolf Otto and Paul Tillich are attempts to listen to such voices and to bring their message to the twentieth century. Both of them tried to develop the fundamental Kantian theme that religion

---

[1]While this view is not unprecedented and some versions of it can probably be found in radical medieval philosophers, it is not very common.

finds its proper place within the limits of reason and degenerates into superstition and fanaticism when it eschews its task to bring into completion a rational world view. Throughout their discussions we have learned that the call for religious isolationism in contemporary culture may be a premature admission of defeat that leads persons of faith to relinquish the claim of religion to reign supreme within culture. If Kant and his followers have convinced us that there may be an alternative to contemporary Wittgensteinian and empiricist accounts of religion, then it will be an important task of a future philosophy of religion to evaluate this claim and to suggest such an alternative. Theology, likewise, will have to reevaluate seclusive tendencies, which threaten to parochialize communities of faith, and should strive instead to find means to embrace the totality of culture.

What seems to me most attractive in the Kantian approach is its promise to find a place for religion within the limits of reason, without explaining religion away or subsuming it under morality. If a Kantian conception of religion will prove successful, it will be able to account for the claims of religion to provide an understanding of the world we live in, without clashing with science, and to account for its claim to inculcate and encourage pursuit of values without suspending the claims of morality. If it is successful, a Kantian conception of religion will also explain why manifestations of religiosity in human life can become objects of study of diverse natural and social studies, yet not be completely explained by any one of them or by all of them. If the Kantians are right and human religiosity is a depth dimension of the spirit that manifests itself in all areas of our life, we would expect it to have social, psychological, aesthetic, moral, and theoretical implications that could be studied in their own right. Yet it will be clear that the implications of human religiosity do not define its essential core that is to be found in the power of religion to unify our world view and to relate it to a reality that is independent of us, to which we respond and which we try to understand.

In reflecting on our discussions throughout this study, I would suggest we distinguish two questions. Even if we agree that proponents of the Kantian school offer an intriguing defense of the rationality of religion, we may still want to ask if they succeed in arguing for the stronger case that all rational human beings must be religious. The two claims tend to merge in their work. They defend religion by showing its rational necessity. Yet it may be possible to deny their stronger claim that in order to be fully rational we must all be religious and still to accept their defense of the rationality of religion. I tend to think that a strong case can be made for their philosophy of religion, but I have serious misgivings about their success in proving the rational necessity of religion. I see the problems already in Kant's argument. Let us then review the structure of the argument as we presented it.

Our discussion began with a critique of Kant's commonly known theory that religion is an extension of morality, a theory that confines religion to the limits of Practical Reason. We retraced Kant's argument for this conception of religion to his theory of the postulates of Practical Reason and to his claim for the psychological necessity of belief in the future realization of the Highest Good. Critical analysis has shown, however, that Kant's practical conception of religion does not succeed either in accounting for religion or in proving that religion is morally necessary. We came to see, then, that Kant reevaluated his ideas about religion and reformulated them in his account of Reflective Judgment, where contemplative religious ideas were presented as a proposed solution to the problem of the unity of Reason and its domains. In his attempt to secure a point of view from which the unity of Reason could be thought, Kant produced a conception of the unity of nature and freedom based on the idea of an omnipotent and omniscient moral designer of the universe. We have also seen how this thought results in a conception of history as leading to the realization of our highest moral end, the realization of the Highest Good. This is a conception of religion that I have called a conception of contemplative hope.

A crucial step in Kant's justification of contemplative thought about a supersensible substrate of reality—and therefore of the possibility of a unity of nature and freedom in the supersensible—relies on his belief that Reason cannot acquiesce in a purely constructive conception of science or in a morality of pure duty. The argument in the first case is quasi-epistemological; in the latter case it is psychologi-

cal. Kant claimed that we are committed in our theoretical and practical activities to believe that knowledge is discovery and that duty
has an end that is realizable in the world of nature. These are crucial
steps in the argument and Kant gives them the most minimal support.
We must ask ourselves then whether there are reasons to accept them.
Kant seems to have thought that it will be impossible for us to accept
a theory of nature that is not committed to being a description of the
way things are independently of it. He seems also to have thought
that we would find the duty to realize the Highest Good as absurd
unless we could believe that the structure of nature is conducive to its
realization. Philosophers from Friedrich Nietzsche to Albert Camus,
and perhaps even Nelson Goodman,[2] devoted much thought to these
issues and have rejected the Kantian assumption. It may be difficult
for us to accept total responsibility for our beliefs and values and to
relinquish the desire to ground them in the authority of the structure
of the universe, but what is difficult need not be impossible. Nietzsche's
proclamation of the coming of the "Overman" (*Übermensch*) suggests
that a future humanity will be up to the challenge.

Even if the existentialists are right and a "metaphysical" grounding
of our beliefs is not necessary, their work and its impact on twentieth-century culture have shown that accepting the "absurd" is extremely difficult for many, though perhaps not impossible for some.
Kant based his theory of contemplative hope on the assumption of its
psychological necessity. On this basis, he claimed that it is rational
for us to think of our theoretical and normative constructions as
grounded in the supersensible. For a person who is torn between the
Kantian and the existentialist estimation of what is psychologically

---

[2]Nelson Goodman's basic philosophical attitude is in many ways akin to
the existentialist position. In a brief exposition of Goodman's thought, Hilary
Putman wrote, "He starts. . . by rejecting certainty and by rejecting the idea
of an ontological ground-floor independent of our theorizing. . . . If there isn't
a ready-made world, then let's construct worlds, says Goodman. If there aren't
objective standards, then let's construct standards! Nothing is ready-made,
but everything is to be made." (Hilary Putnam, "Forward to the Fourth Edition" of Nelson Goodman, *Fact, Fiction, and Forecast* [4th ed.; Cambridge,
MA: Harvard University Press, 1983] xiv–xv.)

possible for us, the Kantian religious belief will not seem rationally necessary; yet such a person could still recognize the rationality of religious belief for those who side with Kant. I recognize the profundity of Kant's analysis of the role of hope in our spiritual life. Yet I am not sure that it necessarily follows that such a hope must be founded on an idea of a moral designer of the universe who had preestablished a harmony between nature and freedom. The Kantian contribution here is the opening up of the question of the role of rational hope for us. This is a question that will require much further discussion both in moral philosophy and in the philosophy of religion.

A central aspect of our discussion has been the Kantian quest for the unity of reason. This quest, however, is not merely a fact of the history of philosophy. Our philosophical situation today resembles in many ways the situation in which Kant found himself when he set himself the goal to establish the fundamental unity of consciousness. One of the questions that my discussion raises is whether contemporary philosophy, which finds fault in metaphysical realism and seeks to reestablish, in new terms, the fundamental insight of Kant's Copernican revolution, namely, to show that the facts of our experience are never mind-independent and that the intellect is an active force that constantly generates scientific theories and conceptions of value, needs to address itself not only to its distinct constructs but also to the intellect itself as a constructive force. We recall that Kant, after he had traced the constructive activity of the mind in the various realms of culture, raised the question whether Reason might be guided in its constructive activity by a set of interests or by one supreme interest whereby its diverse constructions can be integrated and Reason can come to know itself and to understand its activities. Kantian terminology and faculty language are no longer in vogue and talk of interests of Reason sounds archaic and anachronistic. Yet Kant's modern heirs may also need to lift their eyes from the analysis of specific cultural creations to consider the nature of the intellect itself whose constructing activities they diligently trace. Is it, we may ask, a final fact about us, as intelligent beings, that we inevitably (out of biological necessity?) continuously construct theories and create ideals? Or might there be some interest that guides this intellectual activity, an interest which may be manifested in the manifold of its creations? If such an interest can be found, might it not be of some value in directing our constructive activity? At the very least, an identification of interests that direct our intellectual activity will definitely enhance our understanding of ourselves as intelligent beings. The return to Kant in contemporary philosophy seems to me to require that the Kantian question concerning the ultimate interests of Reason be raised again.

A few words are due here regarding the Kantian solution for the problem of unity. When I presented my interpretation of the problem as it is first encountered in Kant's writings, I suggested that the identification of distinct applications of Reason accounts for various types of clashes with which we are quite familiar (see part one, sections 3.B.1–2). We may now ask whether Kant's doctrine of the reflective unity of Reason addresses these clashes. At first glance, at least, it seems that by seeking unity from a contemplative perspective, Kant evades discussion of specific clashes, in order to show that conflicts between its applications do not threaten the unity of Reason. Contemplative unity, then, does not allow us to adjudicate conflicts. It transcends these clashes and understands them as expressions of Reason's two principles of interpretation: the principle of nature and the principle of freedom. Tillich, as we have seen, came to a similar conclusion. He maintained that only a high-level systematic unity of the sciences can be achieved, while specific sciences may continue to uphold incompatible positions. It seems appropriate to ask here whether the reflective self-understanding that contemplative unity achieves may serve to regulate the specific applications of Reason in a way that will minimize conflicts.[3] This question will be left for future discussion.

Our discussion has shown that the *Critique of Judgment* gave rise to two distinct strategies for a defense of the rationality of religion.

---

[3] By way of tentative suggestion I would say that for a natural science which understands itself as discovering the mechanical structure of teleological historical processes, an incompatibility of a cosmological theory and a moral outlook will awaken the restlessness of reason and motivate further inquiry. I refer the reader to my previous assessment of Kant's solution to the conflict between the interests of reason (see part one, section 5.D).

The two differ regarding the relations between religion and other realms of culture. At heart, I believe, they differ on whether a defense of the rationality of religion and of its uniqueness requires that religion have a foundation in Reason that is independent of science and morality, or whether it suffices to show that religion is a depth dimension in all realms of culture. The relations between the two approaches are complex, and I suspect that they may reflect a tension that is internal to the phenomenon of religion itself. A resolution of the differences between them requires a further study that I can only outline in this concluding chapter.

Eager to secure the rationality of religion, Otto turned to Kant's analysis of aesthetic judgment and developed further some of Kant's ideas regarding the a priori determination of feeling into a theory of religious experience. His discussion of the status of religion and the role it plays in our life is deeply ambivalent. On the one hand, since he tried to convince us that religion must be understood in its own terms, Otto strove to identify a distinct religious a priori as the constitutive element of religious experience. The isolation of a distinct religious a priori could support an argument to the effect that religion is an independent realm of meaning, alongside science and morality. Otto himself argues that the religious potential arises in consciousness independently of the ethical. It seems to me that had Otto wanted to proceed in this direction, to present the religious a priori as a constitutive rather than as a reflective principle, he should have examined more seriously the relations between religion and aesthetics. In my discussion of his theory I pointed out the shortcomings of his analysis of these relations (see part two, section 6.D.1.a.2).

On the other hand, we can find in Otto a different tendency. He argued that religion issues from the depth of reason and that the criterion of a fully developed religion is its a priori relation with ethics. We also find Otto arguing that religion is a reflection on the meaning of science and morality, and therefore does not purport to offer an alternative scientific theory of reality or an alternative set of moral rules. It seems to me that Otto was vacillating between his desire to protect the independence of religion—his wish to demonstrate that religion is not a deficient science and a handmaiden to morality—and his will to present religion as a judgment over the totality of the personality. I fear that the former aspects of Otto's theory could be developed further in directions he himself would not have favored. If the religious a priori is presented as constitutive of an independent religious realm of meaning, it could perhaps be argued that religion is not accountable to morality and science. Otto never argued in this manner, but some of his assertions might open the door for such a seclusionist theory. Otto's defense of religious language from scientific criticism and his declaration of the superiority of Christianity could be interpreted as supporting such development of his theory of the religious a priori.

Beyond this criticism, however, I find in Otto's theory two elements of great importance that I would like to emphasize for future study. Through his phenomenological analysis of the religious consciousness, Otto identified the intimate relation between cognitive and emotive elements of the religious experience. I have already pointed out the significance of this discovery, and I hope it will receive the attention of which it is worthy. The other element I would like to emphasize (although I had no chance to discuss it extensively in this study) is Otto's analysis of "creature consciousness" and of the religious category of "sin" as an evaluation of the totality of one's personality. Otto's concept of "sin" sheds an interesting light on the claim of the Kantian school that religious consciousness is a form of awareness that apprehends the totality of the self, that it is an awareness that accompanies and informs the more partial forms of our self-awareness which are achieved through reflection of the self on itself as the subject of the activities of thinking/knowing and of willing/doing. This conception of religious self-valuation may prove fruitful for a future theology that seeks to find a role for religious valuation beyond the specific claims of morality.

Sharing Otto's basic interests, Tillich also elaborates on Kant's *Third Critique* in order to establish religion as a realm that must be understood in its own terms. Aiming to present the singular role religion plays in the structure of consciousness, Tillich develops further the Kantian insight that religion expresses a fundamental requirement of reason to achieve certainty that the concepts through which it strives to understand the world and shape it are not merely valid constructs but are indeed the concepts through which the world is designed. Tillich placed greater emphasis than Otto on the need to establish harmony between religion and culture, and elaborated on Kant's theory of contemplative hope that assigned to the thought about the divine designer of the universe a contemplative rather than a constitutive status. Tillich thus strove to present religion as both distinct from science and morality and yet not entirely separated from them. He formulated this insight by saying that religion is the depth dimension of the spirit and should be expressed in the midst of and through all realms of cultural activity.

Tillich's conception of religion, which seeks to secure the rationality of religion and its place in modern life, sounds intriguing and provocative. Yet it requires further study. One of the main issues that a comparative analysis of religion should attend to in evaluating its fruitfulness is whether this conception can guide the interpretation of historical phenomena. More specifically, we should ask whether Tillich's conception can help us understand the phenomenon of a pervasive religious tendency to portray religion as a radical alternative to secular culture. A definitive statement of this tendency, as well as an influential defense, was given in Tillich's time by Karl Barth who argued that true faith begins and ends with revelation and as such should protect us from tendencies to attribute absolute value to cultural achievements. Tillich would have liked to reject Barth's theology as dangerous fanaticism. We, however, must ask ourselves whether the history of religion does not provide sufficient evidence for an essential tendency of religion, and perhaps even a serious interest to present a critical alternative to secular culture and to remind us constantly of the dangers of human presumption? Tillich would have answered, I believe, that his distinction between religion$_1$ and religion$_2$ serves this critical purpose without appealing to extrarational standards. That same distinction, he would say, also proves that his concept of religion can be of use in comparative and historical analyses of religious phenomena. In fact, his theory urges us to realize that a scientific study of religion must secure the cooperation of the philosophy of religion, history of religion, and theology. I find this integrative suggestion interesting, and I believe that it deserves serious consideration. I would suggest that Tillich's conception of a science of religion that consists of an interrelated philosophy, theology, and history of religion, a conception which he shares with Otto, may be able to direct the study of religion away from piecemeal reliance on various social sciences and toward a methodology more appropriate to its subject.

From the works of Kant, Otto, and Tillich, we derive a conception of religion as a distinct realm of meaning which requires interpretation in its own terms. This is a conception according to which the historical manifestations of religion, in symbolic language and action, are expressions of a special mode of feeling and cognition, sui generis. They cannot be explained, reductively, by sociological, anthropological, or psychological theories, because they are not merely means for social objectives or stages in the development of the human personality. Our study suggest that this special mode of feeling and cognition—the essential core of religion—is best understood as a reflective and contemplative mode of consciousness which strives to apprehend, in unity, the meaning of our personal and collective existence. This is a suggestion that I offer as an hypothesis for future discussion and evaluation by philosophers of religion and by theologians.

Like Kant, and perhaps also because of him, we are wary of philosophical speculation, especially of speculative metaphysics. Like Kant, we greatly admire rigorous detailed analyses of scientific and moral reasoning. Yet, our study suggests, this is not the whole of philosophy, even if it is its most important and most difficult part. The rejection of a speculative metaphysics in which science and morality are shown to mirror the structure of reality does not mean, according to Kant, that no reflection on the ultimate meaning of these pursuits is possible. Kant sought to distinguish reflective thought on the ultimate structure of reality from metaphysical speculation. The first he thought necessary, the second chimerical. He rejected the attempts of speculative metaphysics to deduce the structure of being from principles of thought, but defended a reflective thought which studies what our modes of thought inexorably lead us to think the universe is like. Kant suggested that reflective contemplation leads to religion, and, as I have shown, this suggestion was embraced wholeheartedly by Otto and Tillich who elaborated on it in their own writings.

Obviously, we cannot prove the Kantian approach apodictically. We cannot prove that all other approaches to the study of religion must fail. Otto and Tillich's efforts, as well as our attempt to show that they follow from Kant, indicate, however, how various ideas are logically related and how the acceptance of some of them requires the acceptance of others. It is therefore required of whoever wishes to deny their conclusions either to show that the conclusions do not follow from the general Kantian conception of Reason as constructive and reflective or to reject this very conception of reason.

There is clearly an alternative conception of reason that is general enough and capable of supporting a rival conception of a study of religion. Such a conception is a naturalistic account of reason, as the manifestation of the natural forces studied by psychology, sociology, various forms of anthropology, and perhaps even biology. A naturalized conception of reason would allow for a reductionist scientific account of religious phenomena in terms of biologically conditioned rituals, forces of organizations of social power, and anthropological accounts of the adaptive significance of various forms of religious behavior. It is not my interest here to debate the relative virtues of these competing conceptions of reason. I willingly admit that I find incomprehensible a naturalistic conception of reason wherein thought should ultimately be understood as an activity of molecules that is about molecules. I should also say that a pragmatic conception of reason, which can be seen as a mediating conception between the two extremes, does not escape the division between them. Pragmatic accounts, as I interpret them, understand rational activity either as the satisfaction of the interests of reason and are thus closely aligned with the critical constructive conception of reason or as satisfying the interests of the organism, in which case they are aligned with the scientistic conception of reason.

A rejection of the conclusions of the Kantian school with less radical implications is also possible. It may be possible, though with some difficulty (e.g., the problem of unity as analyzed in part one chapter three), to accept the constructivist Kantian account of Reason and to reject Kant's reflective and contemplative application of Reason, and with it Tillich's and Otto's concepts of religion. There is, however, a special price to pay for such a rejection in the case of religion. For it will be wrong to claim that a conception of religion as an awareness of the unity of thought and being, of ideals and reality, is alien to religion and imposed on it by an external theoretical interest. There are in religious discourse pervasive elements, both in myth and in dogma, that proclaim that reality is infused with values; that the world responds to transgression, and that there is meaning to being, or that being is not absurd. It is just these pervasive elements that make it difficult to accept modern attempts to distinguish religion from metaphysics and to account for it as a realm of pure value. It is especially such elements, which express conviction in the realization of value in being, that make the reflective-contemplative account of the religious consciousness so appealing. Obviously, none of this proves that the Kantian position is true and that alternative conceptions are false; I hope it does show, however, what price the alternatives must pay.

It is in light of such considerations that I tend to see profound insight and much promise in the general philosophical approach that I find exhibited in the Kantian school in the philosophy of religion. While much that they say is dated, the central message of this school is clear and challenging: it advocates a constructive and reflective conception of reason as the basis for understanding the religious phenomena in human culture.

SELECT BIBLIOGRAPHY

▦ Works by Kant

Citations from translations of Kant's work appear in the volumes indicated. In most cases, references to the German Academy Edition of Kant's works have been supplied. References to the *Critique of Pure Reason* are to the standard A and B pagination of the first and second editions.

Kant, Immanuel. *Kritik der reinen Vernunft* (1st ed. [A] 1781; 2d ed. [B] 1787). In *Kants gesammelte Schriften*, vols. 3–4. Deutschen Akademie der Wissenschaften. Berlin: de Gruyter, 1902.

————————. *Critique of Pure Reason.* Trans. N. K. Smith. New York: St. Martin's Press, 1965.

————————. *Grundlegung zur Metaphysic der Sitten* (1785). In *Kants Gesammelte Schriften*, vol. 4. Deutschen Akademie der Wissenschaften. Berlin: de Gruyter, 1902.

————————. *Grounding for the Metaphysics of Morals.* Trans. James W. Ellington. Indianapolis: Hackett, 1983.

—————————. *Kritik der praktischen Vernunft* (1788). In *Kants gesammelte Schriften*, vol. 5. Deutschen Akademie der Wissenschaften. Berlin: de Gruyter, 1902.

—————————. *Critique of Practical Reason*. Trans. Lewis White Beck. Indianapolis: Bobbs-Merrill, 1983.

—————————. *Kritik der Urteilskraft* (1790). In *Kants gesammelte Schriften*, vol. 5. Deutschen Akademie der Wissen-schaften. Berlin: de Gruyter, 1902.

—————————. *Critique of Judgment*. Trans. Werner S. Pluhar. Indianapolis: Hackett, 1987.

—————————. *Die Religion innerhalb der blossen Vernunft* (1793). In *Kants gesammelte Schriften*, vol. 6. Deutschen Akademie der Wissenschaften. Berlin: de Gruyter, 1902.

—————————. *Religion within the Limits of Reason Alone*. Trans. Theodore M. Greene and Hoyt H. Hudson. New York: Harper & Row, 1960.

—————————. *Die Metaphysic der Sitten* (1797). In *Kants gesammelte Schriften*, vol. 6. Deutschen Akademie der Wissenschaften. Berlin: de Gruyter, 1902.

—————————. *The Metaphysics of Morals*. Part One. Trans. John Ladd. Indianapolis: Bobbs-Merrill, 1965.

—————————. *The Metaphysics of Morals*. Part Two. Trans. James W. Ellington. Indianapolis: Hackett, 1983.

—————————. *On History*. Ed. and trans. Lewis White Beck. Indianapolis: Bobbs-Merrill, 1963.

▓ Works on Kant

Arendt, Hannah. *Lectures on Kant's Political Philosophy*. Ed. Robert Beiner. Chicago: University of Chicago Press, 1982.

Beck, Lewis White. *A Commentary on Kant's Critique of Practical Reason*. Chicago: University of Chicago Press, 1960. Reprinted Chicago: Midway Reprint, 1984.

—————————. "Editor's Introduction." In *Kant: On History*, edited by Lewis White Beck, vii–xxvii. Indianapolis: Bobbs-Merrill, 1963.

—————————. "Editor's Introductions." In *Kant: Selections*, edited by Lewis White Beck. The Great Philosophers Series. New York: Macmillan, 1988.

Broad, C. D. *Kant: An Introduction.* Ed. C. Lewy. Cambridge and New York: Cambridge University Press, 1978.

Caird, Edward. *The Critical Philosophy of Immanuel Kant.* 2 vols. New York: Kraus Reprint, 1986.

Cassirer, Ernst. *Kant's Life and Thought.* Trans. James Haden. New Haven: Yale University Press, 1981.

Cassirer, H. W. *A Commentary on Kant's Critique of Judgment.* New York: Barnes & Noble, 1970.

Cohen, Ted and Paul Guyer, eds. *Essays in Kant's Aesthetics.* Chicago: University of Chicago Press, 1985.

Coleman, Francis X. J. *The Harmony of Reason: A Study in Kant's Aesthetics.* Pittsburgh: University of Pittsburgh Press, 1974.

Despland, Michael. *Kant on History and Religion.* Montreal: McGill—Queen's University Press, 1973.

Gauthier, David. "The Unity of Reason: A Subversive Interpretation of Kant." *Ethics* 96 (1985): 74–88.

Gilead, Amihud. "Restless and Impelling Reason: On the Architectonic of Human Reason According to Kant." *Idealistic Studies* 15 (1985): 137–50.

Green, Ronald Michael. *Religious Reason.* New York: Oxford University Press, 1978.

Greene, Theodore Meyer. *Moral, Aesthetic, and Religious Insight.* New Brunswick, NJ: Rutgers University Press, 1957.

——————————. "The Historical Context and Religious Significance of Kant's *Religion*." First introductory essay to Immanuel Kant, *Religion with the Limits of Reason Alone*, translated by Theodore M. Greene and Hoyt H. Hudson, ix–lxxviii. New York: Harper & Row, 1960.

Guyer, Paul. *Kant and the Claims of Taste.* Cambridge, MA: Harvard University Press, 1979.

Heine, Heinrich. *Religion and Philosophy in Germany.* Trans. John Snodgrass. Albany, NY: SUNY Press, 1986.

Körner, Stephan. *Kant.* Harmondsworth, Middlesex: Penguin, 1955.

Kroner, Richard. *Kant's Weltanschauung.* Trans. J. E. Smith. Chicago: University of Chicago Press, 1956.

Kuehn, Manfred. "Kant's Transcendental Deduction of God's Existence as a Postulate of Pure Reason." *Kant Studien* 76 (1985): 152–69.

McFarland, John D. *Kant's Concept of Teleology.* Edinburgh: University of Edinburgh Press, 1970.

Paton, Herbert James. *The Categorical Imperative.* Philadelphia: University of Pennsylvania Press, 1971.

Pluhar, Werner S. "Translator's Introduction." In Immanuel Kant, *Critique of Judgment,* xxiii–cix. Indianapolis: Hackett, 1987.

Reiss, Hans. "Introduction." In *Kant's Political Writings,* edited by Hans Reiss; translated by H. B. Nisbet. Cambridge: Cambridge University Press, 1977.

Rotenstreich, Nathan. *Experience and its Systematization.* 2d ed. The Hague: Nijhoff, 1972.

————————. "Is There a Primacy of Practical Reason?" In *Experience, Existence and the Good: Essays in Honor of Paul Weiss,* edited by Irwin C. Lieb, 247–59. Carbondale, IL: Southern Illinois University Press, 1961.

————————. "Happiness and the Primacy of Practical Reason." In *Akten 4 des Internationalen Kant Kongress—Meinz 6–10 April.* Berlin: de Gruyter, 1974.

Russell, Bertrand. *Religion and Science.* London and New York: Oxford University Press, 1961.

Savile, Anthony. *The Test of Time: An Essay in Philosophical Aesthetic.* New York and Oxford: Oxford University Press, 1982.

Sessions, W. L. "Kant and Religious Belief." *Kant Studien* 71 (1980): 455–68.

Silber, John R. "The Copernican Revolution in Ethics: The Good Reexamined." *Kant Studien* 51 (1959): 85–101.

————————. "The Ethical Significance of Kant's *Religion.*" In Immanuel Kant, *Religion within the Limits of Reason Alone,* translated by Theodore M. Greene and Hoyt H. Hudson, lxxix–cxlii. New York: Harper & Row, 1960.

————————. "The Importance of the Highest Good in Kant's Ethics." *Ethics* 73 (1963): 179–97.

Tufts, James Hayden. *The Sources and Development of Kant's Teleology.* Chicago: Chicago University Press, 1892.

Van der Linden, Harry. *Kantian Ethics and Socialism.* Indianapolis: Hackett, 1988.

Velkley, Richard L. *Freedom and the End of Reason: On the Moral Foundation of Kant's Critical Philosophy.* Chicago and London: University of Chicago Press, 1989.

Walsh, W. H. *Kant's Criticism of Metaphysics.* Chicago: University of Chicago Press, 1976.

——————. *Kant's Moral Theology.* Proceedings of the British Academy 49. London: Oxford University Press, 1963.

Warnock, G. J. "The Primacy of Practical Reason." *Proceedings of the British Academy* 52 (1966): 253–66.

Webb, Clement Charles Julian. *Kant's Philosophy of Religion.* Oxford: Clarendon, 1926.

Wood, A. W. *Kant's Rational Theology.* Ithaca: Cornell University Press, 1978.

——————. *Kant's Moral Religion.* Ithaca: Cornell University Press, 1970.

Yovel, Yirmiahu. *Kant and the Philosophy of History.* Princeton: Princeton University Press, 1980.

■ Works by Otto

Otto, Rudolf. *Life and Ministry of Jesus: According to the Historical and Critical Method* (1902). Based on a course of lectures. Trans. H. J. Whitby. Christianity of Today Series. Chicago: Open Court, 1908.

——————. *Naturalism and Religion* (1904). Trans. J. Arthur Thomson and Margaret R. Thomson. Ed. W. D. Morrison. New York: Putnam's, 1907.

——————. *Kantisch-Fries'sche Religionsphilosophie.* Tübingen: Mohr, 1904.

——————. *The Philosophy of Religion: Based on Kant and Fries.* Trans. E. B. Dicker. Author's notes on translation. London: Williams & Norgate, 1931.

——————. *Das Heilige* (1917; 25th ed., 1936). Munich: Beck, 1987.

——————. *The Idea of the Holy: An Inquiry into the Non-Rational Factor in the Idea of the Divine and its Relation to the*

Rational. Trans. and preface by John W. Harvey. London: Oxford University Press, 1958.

——————————. *Mysticism East and West: A Comparative Analysis of the Nature of Mysticism* (1926). Trans. Bertha L. Bracey and Richenda C. Payne. New York: Macmillan, 1970.

——————————. *India's Religion of Grace and Christianity Compared and Contrasted* (1930). Trans. Frank Hugh Foster. London: SCM Press, 1930.

——————————. *Kingdom of God and the Son of Man: A Study in the History of Religion* (1934). Trans. Floyd V. Filson and Bertram Lee Woolf. Lutterworth Library 9. London: Lutterworth, 1938.

——————————. *Religious Essays: A Supplement to "The Idea of the Holy."* Trans. Brian Lunn. The Oxford Bookshelf. Oxford University Press, 1937.

■ Works Discussed in Connection with Otto

Fries, Jakob Friedrich. *Wissen, Glauben und Ahndung.* Ed. Leonard Nelson. Göttingen: Vandenhoeck & Ruprecht, 1905.

——————————. *Knowledge, Belief, and Aesthetic Sense.* Ed. Frederick Gregory. Trans. Kent Richter. History of the Philosophy of Science. Cologne: Dinter, 1989.

——————————. *Dialogues on Morality and Religion. Selections from Julius and Evarogas* (1822). Ed. D. Z. Phillips. Trans. David Walford. Totowa: NJ: Barnes & Noble, 1982.

Nelson, Leonard. *Socratic Method and Critical Philosophy: Selected Essays.* Trans. Thomas K. Brown. New Haven: Yale University Press, 1949.

Schleiermacher, Friedrich. *On Religion: Speeches to its Cultured Despisers.* Trans. John Oman. With an introduction by Rudolf Otto. New York: Harper & Row, 1958.

■ Works on Otto

Almond, Philip C. *Rudolf Otto: An Introduction to his Philosophical Theology.* Studies in Religion at Chapel Hill. Chapel Hill and London: University of North Carolina Press, 1984.

Campbell, Charles Arthur. *On Selfhood and Godhood.* The Gifford Lectures 1953–1954 and 1954–1955. Muirhead Library of Philosophy. London: Allen & Unwin, 1957.

Davidson, Robert F. *Rudolf Otto's Interpretation of Religion.* Princeton: Princeton University Press, 1947.

Macquarrie, John. *Twentieth-century Religious Thought: The Frontiers of Philosophy and Theology, 1900–1980.* 2d ed. London: SCM Press, 1981.

Paton, Herbert James. *The Modern Predicament: A Study in the Philosophy of Religion.* New York: Collier, 1962.

▧ Works by Tillich

Tillich, Paul. "Über die Idee einer Theologie der Kulture" (1919). In *Gesammelte Werke*, vol. 9. Stuttgart: Evangelisches Verlagswerk, 1959.

——————. "On the Idea of a Theology of Culture." In idem, *What is Religion?* edited by James Luther Adams. New York: Harper & Row, 1973.

——————. "Die Überwindung des Religionsbegrieffs in der Religionsphilosophie" (1922). In *Gesammelte Werke*, vol. 1. Stuttgart: Evangelisches Verlagswerk, 1959.

——————. "The Conquest of the Concept of Religion in the Philosophy of Religion." In idem, *What is Religion?* edited by James Luther Adams. New York: Harper & Row, 1973.

——————. "Religionsphilosophie" (1925). In *Gesammelte Werke*, vol. 1. Stuttgart: Evangelisches Verlagswerk, 1959.

——————. "The Philosophy of Religion." In idem, *What is Religion?* edited by James Luther Adams. New York: Harper & Row, 1973.

——————. "Das System der Wissenschaft nach Gegenständen und Methoden" (1923). In *Gesammelte Werke*, vol. 1. Stuttgart: Evangelisches Verlagswerk, 1959.

——————. *The System of the Sciences: According to Objects and Methods.* Trans. Paul Wiebe. East Brunswick, NJ: Associated University Presses, 1981.

—————————. *The Religious Situation.* Trans. H. Richard Niebuhr. New York: Holt, 1932.

—————————. *The Interpretation of History: Collected Essays.* New York: Scribner, 1936.

—————————. "The Religious Situation in Germany Today." *Religion in Life* 3 (1934): 163–73.

—————————. "The Two Types of Philosophy of Religion." *Union Seminary Quarterly Review* 1 (1946): 3–13.

—————————. "The Problem of Theological Method." *Journal of Religion* 27 (1947): 16–26. Reprinted in *Paul Tillich: Theologian of the Boundaries*, edited by Mark Kline Taylor, 126–41. London and San Francisco: Collins, 1987.

—————————. *The Protestant Era.* Abridged ed. Ed. and trans. James Luther Adams. Phoenix Books. Chicago: University of Chicago Press, 1957.

—————————. *Systematic Theology* (1951–1963). 3 vols. Chicago: University of Chicago Press, 1967.

—————————. *The Courage to Be.* New Haven: Yale University Press, 1952.

—————————. *Biblical Religion and the Search for Ultimate Reality.* Chicago: University of Chicago Press, 1955.

—————————. *The New Being* (Sermons). New York: Scribner's, 1955.

—————————. "Philosophy and Theology." In idem, *The Protestant Era*, translated by James Luther Adams, 83–93. Chicago: University of Chicago Press, 1957.

—————————. *Dynamics of Faith.* New York: Harper & Row, 1958.

—————————. *Love, Power, and Justice: Ontological Analyses and Ethical Applications.* New York: Oxford University Press, 1960.

—————————. "The Philosophical Background of My Theology." *Kiritsutokyo Gaku* n.s. 2 (1960): 1–13.

—————————. "The Religious Symbol." Appendix. In *Religious Experience and Truth: A Symposium*, edited by Sidney Hook, 301–21. New York: New York University Press, 1961.

————. *The Eternal Now* (Sermons). New York: Scribner's, 1963.

————. *Morality and Beyond: Religious Perspectives.* New York: Harper & Row, 1963.

————. *Theology of Culture.* Ed. Robert C. Kimball. New York: Oxford University Press, 1964.

————. *Ultimate Concern: Tillich in Dialogue.* With D. Mackenzie Brown. New York: Harper & Row, 1965.

————. "The Right to Hope," A Sermon preached at Memorial Church, Harvard University, 1965. In *Paul Tillich: Theologian of the Boundaries*, edited by Mark Kline Taylor, 324–31. London and San Francisco: Collins, 1987.

————. *My Search for Absolutes.* Drawings by Saul Steinberg. Ed. Ruth Nanda Anshen. Credo Perspectives. New York: Simon & Schuster, 1967.

————. *A History of Christian Thought: From its Judaic and Hellenistic Origins to Existentialism.* Ed. Carl E. Braaten. New York: Simon & Schuster, 1968.

————. *Political Expectations* (Essays, 1971). Ed. James Luther Adams. Reprinted Lanham, MD: University Press of America, 1983.

————. *The Shaking of the Foundations* (Sermons). New York: Scribner's, 1976.

————. "Autobiographical Reflections." In *The Theology of Paul Tillich*, edited by Charles W. Kegley, 3–21. 2d ed. New York: Pilgrim, 1982.

————. "Personal Introduction to My Systematic Theology" (Unpublished essay). *Modern Theology* 1 (1985): 83–89.

▪ Works on Tillich

Adams, James Luther. *Paul Tillich's Philosophy of Culture, Science, and Religion.* Ed. George K. Beach. New York: Harper & Row, 1965.

————. "What Kind of Religion Has a Place in Higher Education?" *Journal of Bible and Religion* 13 (1945): 184–92.

Alston, William P. "Tillich's Conception of Religious Symbol." In *Religious Experience and Truth: A Symposium*, edited by Sidney Hook, 12–27. New York: New York University Press, 1961.

Clayton, John P. "Questioning, Answering, and Tillich's Concept of Correlation." In *Kairos and Logos: Studies in the Roots and Implications of Tillich's Theology*, edited by John J. Carey, 121–40. Macon, GA: Mercer University Press, 1984.

——————————. *The Concept of Correlation: Paul Tillich and the Possibility of a Mediating Theology*. Theologische Bibliothek Töpelmann. Berlin and New York: de Gruyter, 1980.

Hook, Sidney. "The Atheism of Paul Tillich." In *Religious Experience and Truth: A Symposium*, edited by Sidney Hook, 59–64. New York: New York University Press, 1961.

Kegley, Charles W., ed. *The Theology of Paul Tillich* (Addresses, Essays, Lectures). 2d ed. New York: Pilgrim Press, 1982.

Nuovo, Victor L. "On Revising Tillich: An Essay on the Principles of Theology." In *Kairos and Logos: Studies in the Roots and Implications of Tillich's Theology*, edited by John J. Carey, 37–61. Macon, GA: Mercer University Press, 1984.

Pauck, Wilhelm and Marion Pauck. *Paul Tillich: His Life and Thought*. New York: Harper & Row, 1989.

Pelikan, Jaroslav, ed. *Twentieth Century Theology in the Making*. London: Fontana, 1970.

Wiebe, Paul. "From System to Systematics: The Origin of Tillich's Theology." In *Kairos and Logos: Studies in the Roots and Implications of Tillich's Theology*, edited by John J. Carey, 109–19. Macon, GA: Mercer University Press, 1984.

INDEX

Reason, 31, 32, 76, (77), 257
intrinsic purpose, 114, 116
introspection, 152, 155, 156, 165,
168, 173, 174, 181, 184, 203,
204, 205, 210, 220; psychological
deduction, 184; relation to sympathy, 165
intuition, 36, 77, 95, 96, 109, 117,
124, 132, 156, 194, 216, 224,
231, 234, 280
is/ought dichotomy, (47), 125, 126
231, 277

James, William, 149, 183
Jesus, 153, 200, 153, 219
joy, 154, 196, 197, 202
Judaism, 205
judgment of taste, 69–97, 253; a
priori, 80; disinterested, 76, 88;
free play of cognitive powers, 84;
immediacy, 79, 95, 96; interest in
(analogous to moral), 91; merely
contemplative, 79; personal pleasure, 80; propaedeutic, 71; refer
to the supersensible, 95; singular,
79, 93; subjective, 71, 76, 93;
subjective purposiveness, 75, 93
justice, 22, 24, 118, 120

Kant, Immanuel, 151, 153–55, 157,
159, 163, 166, 178, 182, 186,
213, 216, 226, 293
Kierkegaard, Sören, 132, 157, 158,
307
kingdom of God, 49, 120, 121, 141–
43, 151, 263, 278, 282, 283
Kroner, Richard, 36, 37

language: mythical, 271, 299; negative, 187; religious, 47, 151, 158,
171, 211, 299, (307), 314; symbolic, xiv, 274, 299
liking, 78, 80, 81, 83, 89, 94, 200

Luther, Martin, 159, 186

Macquarrie, John, 161
McFarland, John D., 52, 53
meaning, 151, 159, 252, 253, 261,
272; awareness of an ideal, 213,
247, 248, 252, 255, 256; structure
of (Tillich), 247, 248; Tillich's
notion of, 247; ultimate meaning,
132, 216
mechanism, 5, 57, 74, 104–9
metaphor, 58, 59, 136, 223, 225,
230, 236, 296
metaphysical deduction, 155, 174,
179, 182, 183, 184, 210
metaphysics, 4, 207, 229, 234, 272,
273, 279; doctrine of world
views, 235, 275; of history, 243,
274–77; language of, 274;
pseudo-scientific, 273, 281, 282;
dependent on science or ethics,
223, 234, 274, 280
methodology, 229, 242, 249, 251,
276, 301, 316
miracle, 61, 68, 177
moral action, 37, 61, 62, 67, 132,
294; ability to identify, 67, 68,
95; causal explanation of, 54;
natural event, 13, 14, 52, 61, 66;
not futile, 129; occasions delight,
76; possibility of, 52, 53, 64;
problem of, 55, 58, 69
moral agency, 114–17
moral agent, 39, 57, 66, 67, 88, 89,
116, 118, 120, 123, 129, 137,
139, 140, 142, 142, 228, 287, 291
moral decision, 10, 18, 53, 54, 58,
61, 67, 88, 89, 117, 118, 136
moral education, 137, 138, 139, 140
moral example, 143
moral feeling, 16, 23, 72, 80, 89, 90,
188
moral history, 105, 120, 123, 130,

DATE DUE

			Printed in USA